Conspiracy of Dreamers: Capitalism at the Service of Humanity

Never stop dreaming!

by
M. Renée Orth
&
Paul J. Behrman

Copyright © 2012 by M. Renée Orth and Paul J. Behrman.

All rights reserved. No part of this publication may be reproduced, distributed, or transmitted in any form or by any means, including photocopying, recording, or other electronic or mechanical methods, without the prior written permission of the publisher, except in the case of brief quotations embodied in critical reviews and certain other uses permitted by copyright law. For permission requests, write to the publisher, addressed "Attention: Permissions Coordinator," at the address below.

>   Magnolia Lane Press
>   25632 Magnolia Ln.
>   Stevenson Ranch, CA 91381
>   ConspiracyofDreamers.com

Ordering Information:
Quantity sales. Special discounts are available on quantity purchases by corporations, associations, and others. For details, contact the publisher at the address above.

Printed in the United States of America
ISBN 978-0-9859869-1-9

Edition 1.1
Cover art by Silviu Nica

We dedicate this book to the memory of Claire Nuer whose commitment to co-creating a context for humanity continues to inspire us daily.

Contents

Preface	i
Introduction	1
Something's Happening Here	11
Two-Dimensional Space	17
Thinking about Thinking	19
A New Operating System	24
Word Problems	28
Speaking Metaphorically	31
A Road Map	37
1 - You Are Here	39
Paradox of the Destruction of the Fittest	39
Signs of Discontent	44
A Peace Wave?	48
2 – Capitalism as a Force of Nature	55
What is Capitalism?	58
A Sea of Starfish	61
Vestigial Structures	64
Pathological Mutation	67
Reptilian Capitalism	70
Diagnosing our Malaise	72
3 - Conspiracy of 1776	85
The Foundation of Liberty	86

Freedom *From*	88
Decoding a Cipher	92
The Art of Associating	93
Some Dreams are Nightmares	100
Liberty Endangered	103
Social Studies	109

4 – Surf or Sink — 113

Transcending the Illusion	113
Change Your Mind, Change Your World	116
The Mind Shift Meme	121
Lessons from our Cousins	125
Looking East	127
Drill Here	129

5 – Attaining Happiness — 133

A View from the Top	135
Scaling the Pyramid	138
To Have or To Be	140
Homo Economicus (or the having mode writ large)	146
Striving for Better, Not More	152

6 – The Philosopher's Stone — 157

Modern Alchemy	158
Systems Science – A Primer	161
Synergy	165
The Magic of Emergence	169

Phase Transition	173
Mobius Flip	174
An Unfolding Pattern	177
A Supersaturated Solution	180
7 - Metamorphosis	185
Life at the Edge of Chaos	187
Civilization as Emergence	190
Starfish and Spiders Revisited	192
Downward Causation	195
Precision Bias	199
Physics Envy	205
Silly Putty	208
Magic of Butterflies	211
8 – The Art of Steering	215
For Profiting Humanity Enterprises	216
Real Karma	228
Making Sense of Dollars	231
A True Cost Index	237
9 – Ripple Effects	259
An Eco-nomics Paradigm	259
Our Funneling Society	261
Taming the Leviathan	276
Automation Dystopia	277
Kindness Changes Us	280

Unleashing our Potential	283
10 – Twenty-First Century Dreamers	285
Root Expansion	286
Reaching for the Sun	291
Celebrating at the Top of the Pyramid	304
Hippie Redemption	309
11 – An Invitation to Dance	313
Epilogue	323
Acknowledgments	325
Endnotes	327

Preface

We have been on an extraordinary journey that began with a casual "what if" conversation over a glass of wine that led to the most creative period of our existence and has since hijacked our lives. We had been working together on an artificial intelligence project for two years and, in the process, learned many amazing things. Some of these lessons crystallized, almost by accident, into ideas that we believe can ignite the next stage in the evolution of capitalism. In this more evolved economy the highest aspirations of human beings – belonging, community, and contribution – are unleashed as forces in the free market, broadening and deepening the awesome power of capitalism and putting this power at the service of humanity.

At the core of this evolved version of capitalism are systems that use communication technology (smartphones, social networks, and the Internet, for example) to empower the buying public to make better choices when deciding how and where to spend their hard-earned money. By "better choices" we mean choices that are more aligned with the values of life, liberty and happiness. We believe in the possibility of prosperity, peace, and justice for all. Not in a someday-maybe kind of way, but in a here-and-in-our-lifetime kind of way – no revolution, legislation, or change in human nature required. But our optimism is tempered by pragmatism. We know the odds are not in our favor, but we also know that the more people who believe, the better our chances – which is why we wrote this book.

Ideas in this book challenge the conventional paradigms of economics and philanthropy, but they do so from a foundation of reason. Indeed, we have shared these ideas with many CEOs, partners of private equity institutions, and leaders of philanthropic institutions. None see a material flaw in the logic, and none disagree with the potential – but many of them nonetheless struggle with their gut feeling that our ideas can't be right: a sign that old habits of thinking are constraining the perception of real opportunity.

In this book, we pull from a broad swath of disciplines. We are not experts in economics, social theory, communication technology, evolutionary biology or many of the subjects we touch on in this book, but we consider this an asset: "In the beginner's mind there are many possibilities, in the expert's mind there are few," explained Shunryu Suzuki in *Zen Mind, Beginner's Mind*. If you want the future to look a lot like the past, then expertise is essential; if you want to create a future far better than the past, then expertise is overrated. What we bring to the table is a strong foundation in logic and reasoning, a thorough understanding of finance and business, creativity, curiosity, passion and optimism.

With an early stint as a McKinsey consultant and an MBA from Stanford, Paul began his career in private equity – becoming a Partner of two private equity companies and the founder and CEO of another. I, Renée, (foolishly, according to Paul) ignored my creative inclinations and followed a path of linear rationality to Berkeley Law School. Our minds work in different, but often complementary, ways. I have a passion for seeing connections and relationships, for spotting the bigger pattern suggested by the parts – I am clearly right brain dominant. Paul, on the other hand, is left brain dominant, he tends to see the parts, think linearly, and focus on the aspects of reality that can be quantified. Together our minds form a well-functioning whole – a dual-processor that delights in exploring new knowledge and new ways of thinking.

We know that time is precious, that asking you to read this book is the same as asking you to give a part of your life. We would not make such a request unless we believed that what we have to say has the potential to make a real and lasting difference. Gandhi taught that "A small body of determined spirits fired by an unquenchable faith in their mission can alter the course of history." We hope this book will inspire you to join a small, but growing, force of determined spirits on a mission to create a future of life, liberty and happiness for all.

M. Renée Orth
Stevenson Ranch, California
October 11, 2012

Introduction

One day, 3.7 billion years ago, an organism came into being, striving to survive amid the primordial stew of early Earth. This particular cell, and the DNA that dictated its physical form, was destined for greatness. Darwinian science calls it *LUA* for "last universal ancestor," and it formed the basis and the essence, for every living being on our planet. This microscopic dynamo was certainly not the first life on earth; rather, untold numbers of doomed variations gave it their best shot, and failed. To this very day, *LUA* reigns supreme in the biological tree of all planetary life.

It is beyond human comprehension whether God created *LUA*, or whether *LUA* resulted from a fortunate arrangement of inorganic material animated by natural forces, or both. We do know that through natural selection, reproduction and mutation, *LUA*'s pattern has expanded, divided and multiplied into the rich tapestry that is life on Earth.

Humanity's universal ancestors have been identified by science: "Eve" was born about 200,000 years ago on the African savanna. She is the matriarch of every one of us. "Adam" – our common patriarch – is much younger, having come into being about 70,000 years after Eve. Adam, Eve and their offspring struggled mightily to survive; many more lost the struggle than won. Each of us descended from the champions.

A dramatic shift in human survival strategy occurred about 10,000 years ago. Innovators harnessed nature's fertile potential by saving wild kernels of wheat and sowing them in convenient locations, thus sparking the Neolithic Revolution – and the beginning of civilization. The chain reaction set off by this momentous shift in human survival strategy continues to this day: agriculture allowed our ancestors to literally put down roots; form cities based on cooperation and coordination (forced labor notwithstanding), and focus their talents and energy on projects other than mere survival. Over time new advances arose, including specialization in a specific area of production, development of written language (originally a way to keep track of grain storage), and accumulation of vast amounts of knowledge. In short, advances in food production eventually allowed our ancestors to powerfully shape their material world to suit their own aims.

According to the Bible, this empowered and creative humanity came together to form a unified community that spoke a single language. They set out to build a tower to the heavens. On learning of their project, "the LORD said, Behold, the people *is* one, and they have all one language … and now nothing will be restrained from them, which they have imagined to do."[1] God thwarted their efforts, scattered them across the globe and fractured their language so they could not challenge his supremacy. Humanity now stands at the edge of another possible triumph of unity and cooperation. The project before us is the creation of a new earth, one that reflects the harmonious values that make our species unique – compassion, creativity, and love of truth and beauty. Our survival may depend on whether we seize this opportunity. As in the biblical story of the Tower of Babel, the key to this triumph is communication. The master cipher is at our fingertips in the form of the ones and zeros of binary code, the language of computers. A world of possibilities is emerging from this evolutionary leap in human communication. Will we seize this chance to transform our world for the better? Or will we continue to allow egoistic bickering and myopic thinking to blind us to the miraculous future that is within our grasp?

The window of opportunity is narrow. Humanity faces daunting challenges, but we also hold limitless untapped potential. If we are to succeed, we must soon realize our true potential as the reigning champions of the game of life. The time is upon us to choose our way forward. What will we imagine to do? Today, the biggest obstacle to creating a world of abundance, meaning, health and vitality is our collective failure to recognize that such a world is within our reach. This book is about the means of creating a future in which our loftiest values – love, creativity, empathy and justice – are manifested powerfully in the world. These means are found in a combination of communication technology and expanded human consciousness. Specifically, we can use technology to broaden and deepen a potent source of power: capitalism – the global economic system typified by free markets, freedom of contract, capital flow, and private property – can evolve to serve humanity in bringing forth a brighter future.

The current version of capitalism suffers serious failings. It is causing us to devour the natural environment, marginalize masses of humanity and erode our own spiritual and psychological health. The strong social quality of human nature is, in large part, responsible for our remarkable ability to survive. We flourish in communities and are fulfilled when we contribute to those around us. Unfortunately, capitalism and related changes have unintentionally undermined community and our ability to shape our world for the better, leaving many people alienated and disempowered. These are not fatal flaws; they are signs that it is time to push forward. Our system of capitalism is due for a major upgrade. Thankfully, capitalism has provided us with the means of executing this overhaul – technology.

Psychologist Abraham Maslow's famous *Hierarchy of Needs* proposes that, while material survival and safety (that is, food and shelter) are essential for fulfillment, they are only the beginning. Once a person satisfies these needs, she naturally turns to more ethereal pursuits such as community, creative expression, and spiritual transcendence. Capitalism, with its relentless pursuit of material growth, has served much of humanity exceptionally well in satisfying material needs (an admirable achievement indeed). However, its current form focuses on the material aspects of life, undermining our ability to scale Maslow's hierarchy. Evidence of capitalism's myopia is broad and deep: Western civilization is experiencing an epidemic of dissatisfaction; symptoms include loneliness, drug abuse, obesity, depression, escapism (through TV, video games, porn, etc.), anger and frustration.

Why are vast numbers of human beings experiencing deep psychological and spiritual suffering during the most materially affluent time and place in our species' history? Consumer culture is a prime culprit. From early childhood, we are taught that the secret to happiness is found in material wealth. We spend countless hours watching TV commercials, viewing billboards, and hearing radio advertisements that *inform us* of our needs and wants. We are trained to work hard to "get ahead," but never encouraged to ask, "ahead of what?" Social and psychological research proves that the materialism of consumer culture is toxic to true happiness. The actual source of the epidemic of dissatisfaction is a widespread failure to ascend to the higher levels of Maslow's *Hierarchy of Needs* – love, belonging, community, creative expression and spiritual transcendence – which are the most rewarding of human experiences.

There is an alternative to the myopic materialism of mainstream consumer culture – a path that leads toward the realization of human potential and authentic happiness. Those who strive to realize their full potential as helpful contributors to their communities, experience joy and increased self-worth. Happiness is not the destination; it is the splendor of the dandelions edging the path, the harmonious whistling of fellow travelers, and the invigorating breeze caressing your sunlit face as you stride ahead. This change in focus can counter the alienation and disempowerment that is draining many of their passion for life. If we are to meet the mounting challenges of global warming, exponential population growth, and nuclear proliferation, to name a few, we must make this cultural shift. Human potential is a natural resource that holds the possibility of transforming this planet for the better; we cannot afford to continue squandering it.

Humankind has developed a system of collaboration, cooperation and competition – capitalism – with a vast ability to develop and apply natural resources. It is unimaginably powerful because it reflects the combined motivation of billions of human beings – it is a force of nature. But capitalism, like any system, is only as good as its chosen goal, and only as intelligent as the quality of information to which it has access. If we are to develop the true potential of human beings and devote it to the task of creating a world of abundance, justice and peace, then we must reconfigure our most powerful tool. Capitalism's current goal of blind material growth must be replaced with a new and better ambition – realizing human potential.

Despite capitalism's power, it is often shortsighted. Humanity's highest ideals – love, truth, beauty and justice – are not well communicated in the nervous system of the economy, that is, by price and money. Thus, it is not surprising that outcomes, by and large, do not reflect our noblest goals. We look to government and nonprofits to bridge the gap between what capitalism provides and the society we'd like to live in. But these are no match for the overwhelming and expanding force of capitalism. If capitalism is to evolve, it must be pushed from within and from the ground up. In true evolutionary fashion, capitalism has provided the foundation for its next incarnation. Communication technology holds the key to upgrading capitalism so we can harness its power and use it to create a future of abundance in harmony with nature and with one another.

In light of the challenges facing humanity (and others that will inevitably arise) capitalism must evolve quickly to its next stage of development – time is of the essence. The next phase will include the following specific features:

❖ Transcendence of the for-profit versus non-profit duality. New charitable enterprises will arise with the goal of profiting humanity rather than a few owners, and these will do so through activities conventionally considered "commercial." Buyers will have expanded opportunities to contribute meaningfully to causes that matter to them simply by patronizing these "for profiting humanity" enterprises. These enterprises will apply the transformative force of free market capitalism to creating a better future for all.

❖ The power of crowdsourcing (proven by the success of Wikipedia) will be used to create a "True Cost Index." This index will enables users to discover the *true cost* of products and services – meas-

Introduction | 7

ured in terms of each user's expressed values (for example, environment, animal welfare, and social justice). With this information, buyers can make informed and intelligent choices that reflect love, truth, beauty and justice, and their choices will steer us toward a future that embodies these values.

❖ Software applications will connect informed and mindful buyers (using a True Cost Index), enterprises aimed at doing good, and wealthy donors willing to match the charitable contributions of others (important in overcoming the inherent inertia of habit). United, these groups can powerfully direct the flow of energy (money) to people and organizations working to shape the future in alignment with the highest and most humane values. As the financial arteries delivering funds to those bringing more love, truth, beauty and justice into the world expand and multiply, more people will dedicate their buying power to such efforts. As technology continues replacing human labor at an ever-quickening pace, growth in fields that enrich life quality (that is, people climbing Maslow's pyramid and helping others in their ascent) will provide fulfilling work that computers cannot perform.

Many examples of these changes in the structure of capitalism are already occurring – even from some not so likely market participants: Wal-Mart is developing a program that is, in many ways, a prototype of the True Cost Index.

An example of combining a conventional business enterprise with a related philanthropic cause illustrates the power of these ideas: consider the possibility of a group of wealthy environmentalists buying Orbitz.com. (At of the time of this writing, Orbitz is the smallest of several U.S. facing companies providing online travel reservations.) This new environmentally focused Orbitz contributes 100% of its free cash flow to offsetting the negative climate effects of air travel (that is, investing in projects that counter the harm caused by carbon emissions). This hybrid business-philanthropy model (what we call a "for profiting humanity enterprise") allows the traveling public to direct profits toward solving one of the most daunting problems facing the planet – global climate change. By enabling people to align their buying choices with their higher values – without financial sacrifice – an environmentally focused Orbitz turns a conventional commercial enterprise into a source of positive change. The result is a more intelligent and conscious form of capitalism.

These simple alterations can significantly improve human lives and the condition of the planet. Complex adaptive systems, such as capitalism, have leverage points – places where small changes powerfully affect the rest of the system. The reconfigurations described above apply pressure to sensitive leverage points and thus have the power to achieve extensive positive change. The world has seen the power of such leverage points to cause cascading failures, such as the 2008 financial crisis and its lingering after-effects. But leverage points can also be used to trigger cascading *successes*.

Creating a more evolved version of capitalism offers the possibility for people to fulfill their material needs in ways that align with the health of the environment. It may also spark virtuous cycles of empowerment, psychological health and spiritual well-being. By putting *contribution* at the core of the economic system, people will regularly experience the satisfaction of making a difference. Research has shown that giving people are happier, and happier people are more giving. This reinforcing beneficial cycle can spark a deepening of human consciousness, and a psychological and spiritual transformation – a powerful antidote to the epidemic of alienation and disempowerment affecting much of Western civilization.

This vision of a brighter future may seem to be a pipedream – just another idea fated to end up on the scrap heap of utopian history. But our optimism is based on science: intelligence arises from complex systems (such as civilization), and these systems arise from the coordination supported by efficient and expansive communication networks. Humanity is undergoing a metamorphosis of astounding implications. Literacy and access to information are spreading, binary code and the technology it enables are connecting people, and these developments are dramatically improving the collective intelligence of humankind. The raw materials now exist – the neurons and synapses of the collective human mind – and are multiplying as you read these words. It is time to put this potential to use: as the Abrahamic god foretold, once we, the people, are one, *nothing will be restrained from us which we imagine to do.*

Something's Happening Here

Humanity is witnessing an evolutionary unfolding of extraordinary proportions. People are coming together in ways that were impossible even a decade ago. An arising wave of unconventional organizations is empowering individuals, and opening up a new world of possibilities. Our future may very well depend on our ability to recognize and harness these possibilities for good – sooner rather than later.

The saga of the Iranian protests in 2009, though thwarted by the ruling theocracy, showed the potential of coordination empowered by communication technology. Pro-democracy protesters used the micro-blogging services of Twitter to communicate and direct the movement. Technologically savvy individuals from around the world, with little in common but their field of expertise and interest in promoting freedom, formed an improvised group to support the Iranian opposition – people they had never met in person, nor likely ever would. With the help of this consortium of volunteers, dissidents thwarted some of their government's censorship efforts, thus keeping alive their hope for freedom.[2]

The Arab Spring of 2011 revealed the power of organic, self-organized collective movements to reshape a society (though the final form that these societies will take remains to be seen). That these happenings occurred (and are occurring) in the Middle East, with scant democratic experience, highlights the impressive power of these emerging phenomena. Tunisian and Egyptian youth used the power of communication technology – the Internet and cell phones – to organize peaceful protests that toppled entrenched corrupt dictatorships. While many debate the importance of specific technological tools to these revolutions (for example, Facebook versus Twitter), there is little doubt that these events could not have succeeded without the coordination enabled by information technology. At the time, the decision by Egyptian President Mubarak to shut down the Internet, at a huge cost to an already struggling economy, was proof that he recognized the importance of technology to the revolution.

The Internet and the ubiquity of cell phone video cameras allowed the rest of the world to see events on the ground. Mubarak's usual roundup of journalists no longer shielded his actions from the eyes of the world. Sixty years ago, Mahatma Gandhi predicted that, "It may be long before the law of love will be recognized in international affairs. The machineries of government stand between and hide the hearts of one people from those of another." Despite Mubarak's status as a staunch and longtime U.S. ally, President Obama had no choice but to support the will of the Egyptian people because humanity could see with their own eyes the hearts of the Egyptian people. *Realpoli-*

tik met its match; Gandhi would likely be pleasantly surprised by the timeline.

Advances in communication technology have a history of inciting discontent and rebellion: the move of autocratic regimes to restrict access to the Internet is the modern equivalent of the British stamp duty of the 18th and 19th centuries. Through the stamp duty Britain imposed a very high tax on printed news sources, putting them out of reach of all but the wealthy with the aim of suppressing criticism of church and state, and thus squelching discontent.[3] Iranian mullahs understand what British aristocrats understood – information is power, it is the lifeblood of evolution (and sometimes revolution).

The outbreak of "people power" that sparked the Arab Spring appears to have spread: the *Occupy Wall Street* movement is taking hold across the globe as masses of people voice their frustration at our collective failure to create a world in alignment with the highest human values – compassion, love, justice and creativity. The Internet is allowing Occupiers worldwide to jointly deliver the same message: centralized power is being used to the detriment of humankind and the planet.

Centralized power is the core of another movement's message. The Tea Party has taken the U.S. political scene by storm with its demand for smaller government. Like the opposition movements in the Middle East, and the Occupiers, the Tea Party began as an organic self-organizing association. Inherently democratic Internet networking platforms facilitate the movement and fuel its momentum.

The Republican Party, a top-down hierarchical institution, has been unable to rein in the movement. The GOP is learning the same hard lessons as the mullahs in Iran and the dictators in Tunisia and Egypt – centralized power is getting more difficult to preserve. The power of the people is challenging the influence of the top-heavy institutions of the old paradigm.

While the solutions proposed by the Occupiers and the Tea Partiers are, for the most part, diametrically opposed, the problems identified by these groups are similar: both are responding to the fundamental threat of increasingly centralized power. The Occupy movement sees danger in the influence of corporations, while Tea Party worries more about the power of the U.S. federal government. The fears of both groups are justified, but they each fail to recognize that the decline in control of one of these leviathans will lead to an increase in the power of the other. Less regulation (the inevitable consequence of small government) will increase corporate power, while more regulation and taxation (even for the purpose of redistribution) will add to the power of government. Any successful effort to decentralize power that will not entail a disastrous decline in well-being (picture here the chaos following the French Revolution and Saddam Hussein's overthrow) will involve a bottom-up system reconfiguration. This grassroots reconfiguration can be most powerfully ignited by using free market forces. We have the ability to redistribute power from the leviathans of government and large corporations, to individuals and local organizations.

The emerging pattern of leaderless movements is not limited to the realm of politics. Like-minded individuals with a shared purpose are coming together to reshape the world in many areas. One inspiring example in North Carolina is the "Crop Mob," a group interested in community supported farming and *permaculture* (that is, the design of sustainable agricultural practices that align with nature, such as organic farming). They organize and communicate through social networking sites, and converge on a location to tackle a specific project, such as digging rice paddies. No money changes hands, but knowledge is shared and friendships are forged – community is built where none existed before. Without the efficient means of spontaneous communication provided by the Internet, the effort (time, energy, money for newsletters, phone calls) needed to organize and maintain such an improvised group would be a major obstacle. Now it can all be done simply and inexpensively despite Crop Mob's fluid and growing membership. Such productive communitarian events were once the privilege of close-knit small groups, like the Amish. Now, the opportunity to experience the richness and mutual support of a community of people with shared values and passions is available to all.

Revolutionaries, Tea Partiers, Occupiers and Crop Mobsters reflect a new trend in the organization of human systems – expansive, resilient and dynamic leaderless networks. Our future may depend on whether we harness the power of communication technology, and the collective effort it enables. In their book, *The Starfish and the Spider:*

The Unstoppable Power of Leaderless Organizations, authors Ori Brafman and Rod Beckstrom conclude that:

> In the digital world, decentralization will continue to change the face of industry and society. Fighting these forces of change is at best futile and at worst counterproductive. But these same forces can be harnessed for immense power ... when we begin to appreciate their full potential, what initially looked like entropy [that is, chaos or anarchy] turns out to be one of the most powerful forces the world has seen.

Brafman and Beckstrom use the metaphor of the starfish to describe decentralized bottom-up organizations and the spider to describe centralized top-down organizations:

> With a spider, what you see is pretty much what you get. A body's a body, a head's a head, a leg's a leg. But starfish are very different. The starfish doesn't have a head. Its central body isn't even in charge. In fact, the major organs are replicated through-out each and every arm. If you cut the starfish in half, you'll be in for a surprise: the animal won't die, and pretty soon you'll have two starfish to deal with ... They can achieve this magical regeneration because in reality, a starfish is a neural network – basically a network of cells. Instead of having a head, like a spider, the starfish functions as a decentralized network.

Starfish are the stars of this book. The magical power of decentralized networks holds the key to a potential leap in human evolution. We will explore what history and science have to teach us about the power of starfish, and dream up ways of using technology to harness this power and to put it to the task of creating a world worthy of our dreams and our potential.

Two-Dimensional Space

Before we dive into the world of starfish and dreams, there is groundwork, a foundation for what is to come, that must be laid. Many readers will find this groundwork too abstract and philosophical, yet it is important – any structure is only as stable and solid as its foundation. A superficial remodel wouldn't require such work, but a fundamental and lasting improvement involves deep digging.

Philosopher Robert Pirsig in his opus, *Zen and the Art of Motorcycle Maintenance*, astutely explained the importance of foundation retrofitting:

> But to tear down a factory or to revolt against a government or to avoid repair of a motorcycle because it is a system is to attack effects rather than causes; and as long as the attack is upon the effects only, no change is possible. The true system, the real system, is our present construction of systematic thought itself, rationality itself, and if a factory is torn down but the rationality which produced it is left standing, then that rationality will simply produce another factory.

Put differently, creating a world of justice, abundance and well-being begins with an examination of thinking – the subject of the rest of this introduction.

Written language is the medium we (the authors) use to communicate the thoughts presented in this book. While we are confident that this was the best choice given our abilities, it, like all media, shapes thinking. Language, particularly the written variety, is inherently linear – only one thing can be dealt with at a time. This works fine for fiction or memoirs, which unfold linearly, but for other subjects – like describing a holistic system with all its interconnectedness (the goal of this book) – linearity can be a frustrating constraint. This challenge is analogous to fitting a map of our spherical planet on a two-dimensional plane: the mapmaker must choose between accurately representing the shape of things, or their size. The choice is usually determined by the purpose of the map, for example, navigation or political geography, but compromise is always necessary.

We (the authors) also face competing goals: we want our ideas to be as accessible as possible, but we also seek to counterbalance the linear thinking that dominates Western minds, a tendency that obscures our underlying connectedness to one another and the environment. The world is in desperate need of less fragmentation and more wholeness. In dealing with this constraint, a writer must constantly choose between distorting her ideas to fit a linear framework, or subjecting her readers to some degree of messiness. We appreciate your willingness to wade through an occasional morass.

We draw on a wide range of disciplines – evolution, biology, psychology, politics, economics, social science, history and even a bit of physics. The whole we are trying to reveal is deep and wide. This crazy quilt of disparate ideas will ultimately form a coherent pattern – a rich and varied tapestry – but it will take time for the overall picture to emerge. Seemingly unrelated threads will be picked up and put down; each will be woven into an integrated whole that reveals a possible future of peace, abundance and joy. Two of these threads are introduced here.

Thinking about Thinking

The basic definition of *metacognition* is "thinking about thinking." To many this may seem esoteric and of little practical importance, but it deserves far more attention than it gets. The booming field of behavioral economics – the psychological study of human economic behavior – has uncovered serious flaws in our cognitive skills that impair perception and decision making.[4] By recognizing and learning from these defects we can better understand ourselves and others, and the world in which we live. With increased understanding may come improved competence in shaping the world to match our highest ideals.

If a scientist uses an incorrectly calibrated device, chances are the scientist's conclusions will be inaccurate. Decisions based on these conclusions could lead to less than ideal results: wasted resources at best, tragedy at worst. The same is true of the apparatus through which human beings perceive and evaluate the world – the human mind. As evolutionary psychologists have been pointing out for decades, the mind, like the rest of the human body, is a product of natural selection. Thus, human cognition is designed, not to accurately assess the world or to produce more happiness, but to perpetuate our genes. Our brains, especially the parts responsible for our uniquely human cognitive abilities, evolved in a specific environment: as hunters and gatherers on the African savanna. It is not surprising that many of the features of brain function that were helpful to hunters and gatherers are maladaptive in modern society.[5]

Human beings have not evolved much biologically in the past 10,000 years because genetic evolution requires a stable environment. Thanks to the rise of rapidly changing civilizations, humans today are remarkably similar to our ancestors. This is not to say humankind is not evolving, rather, human evolution is occurring at a different level – the level of culture. Culture is the means by which we express our intellect and creativity in cooperation with others. It gives us the ability to imagine something different from what is, to develop new ways of responding to and shaping our environment (including other human beings).

Culture, despite its unquestionable value, is a major source of error in human cognitive functioning. It provides prepackaged patterns used to understand the world. The human brain – particularly the left brain, which often dominates thinking – is an order-making machine; it interprets and classifies each experience, skillfully filing it away before it is even superficially considered.

This ordering function, acquired largely through cultural indoctrination, creates habitual thought patterns. Neurons will fire in the same way (people say, "that's how

I'm wired"), which prevents us from recognizing other possibilities. Consider the constellations identified by the ancient Greeks (and many other early civilizations). In randomly arranged heavenly bodies, they perceived elaborate tales and important messages about the future. These myths, that gave them a sense of understanding in an otherwise incomprehensible world, became their cultural *reality*.

Human beings today continue the same creative work as the ancient Greeks; we fill in the blanks and believe our story *is* reality. These lines are etched in the brain's neural pathways, making it difficult to see alternative patterns that may provide new and helpful ways of seeing the world. When presented with a pattern that does not match what we "know," it is often immediately rejected as "wrong" (that is, if the new pattern isn't ignored completely).

Imagine each of us is an actor in a movie, born into a role and a particular genre (Western, war, romantic comedy, drama). The possibilities we imagine for ourselves are limited to the stories consistent with the characters and setting of the genre. If you were born into a war movie, you will not conceive of a future in which you become a successful artist. Culture shapes perception in an analogous way.

By becoming aware of the movie we're born into – appreciating its benefits and recognizing its limits – it is possible to move beyond our default mode. With this awareness we can redefine ourselves and imagine new possibilities for the future. The language-centered analytic mode is static and retrospective. It's fine for making morning coffee (that is, repetitive or familiar tasks) but not necessarily the best for considering ways to address global warming, assessing the dangers of nuclear energy, or even predicting what will make us happy.

The past several decades have seen a wealth of new theories about human brain function, including how the two hemispheres of the brain work. According to current understanding, the right side is skilled at thinking creatively by seeing the world as an interconnected whole and feeling empathy and compassion. Children are naturally more right-brained until they learn to read and write; language is mainly a left-brain phenomenon. The left side is adept at creating order, applying linear rationality, seeing the details, and weaving stories about the way things are and labeling these stories "reality."[6] The reality creating role of language is reflected in the Bible's declaration, "In the beginning was the Word, and the Word was with God, and the Word was God." Language is a powerful tool.

The rationality of the left brain is capable of wondrous feats – consider the marvelous discoveries of modern science. However, this kind of thinking has a dark side. The rationality of the left brain is analytic; it looks at the pieces rather than the whole. "Analysis" comes from the Greek word *analusis* and means, "to break apart." "When analytic thought, the knife, is applied to experience, something is always killed in the process."[7]

In order to create a future that is better than the past, we must cultivate synthetic rationality. "Synthesis" comes from the Greek word *syntithenai* and means, "to combine or bring together." The process of developing synthetic rationality entails giving over more thinking to our right hemispheres.[8] If Robert Pirsig is correct and it is the structure of systematic thought, "rationality itself," that gives rise to civilization and its material manifestations (including our mounting problems), then synthetic rationality may be the key to creating a future in which love, truth, beauty and justice flourish.

Psychiatrist Carl Jung, a major proponent of synthetic rationality, identified the nature of the scientific method as a main source of the analytic tendency of modern Western thinking:

> This grasping of the whole is obviously the aim of science as well, but it is a goal that necessarily lies very far off because science, whenever possible, proceeds experimentally and in all cases statistically. Experiment, however, consists in asking a definite question which excludes as far as possible anything disturbing and irrelevant. It makes conditions, imposes them on Nature, and in this way forces her to give an answer to a question devised by man ... The workings of Nature in her unrestricted wholeness are completely excluded. If we want to know what these workings are, we need a method of inquiry which imposes the fewest possible conditions, or if possible no conditions at all, then leaves Nature to answer out of her fullness.[9]

This is not to say that the scientific method is not a valid means of inquiry – the technological advances it has enabled are beyond questioning. Rather, the collective failure to appreciate fully the drawbacks of the scientific method is, of itself, a violation of the fundamental aim of science – the search for knowledge.

Analytic reasoning should not be rejected; while the knife of analysis kills, it also creates. Analysis uses knives, synthesis uses glue; each is a useful tool in creating a more accurate map of reality and humanity's place in it, which is a critical first step in charting a course forward.

A New Operating System

As we continue to learn about the incredible apparatus with which we perceive reality, we also gain the ability to consciously choose the beliefs that are most true, useful and supportive to our well-being. In the past, human beings were programmed with a default operating system shaped by both nature and nurture. This default programming constrained choices, though for most, these constraints were imperceptible: as imperceptible as water is to fish. The ability to become aware of our default settings, and the freedom to choose a different way, are a uniquely human gift.

In developing our "reprogramming" ability, we have been aided by the emergence of liberal democratic states that value individual freedom (itself a result of people challenging the status quo). Ever increasing numbers of us are consciously choosing to live differently, to be the authors of our own destinies. Many have written about this evolutionary shift in the fields of psychology, spirituality, and healing.[10] This book extends the conversation to the realm of economics.

The Zen Buddhist idea of "beginner's mind" is the practice of approaching both novel and well-known subjects with openness, eagerness, and an absence of preconceptions. Shunryu Suzuki's book *Zen Mind, Beginner's Mind*, explains that "In the beginner's mind there are many possibilities, in the expert's mind there are few." The great industrialist Henry Ford echoed Suzuki when he proclaimed that he was "looking for a lot of men who have an infinite capacity to not know what can't be done." Beginner's mind is an alternative operating system that is flexible and adaptable. It is designed to see possibilities rather than limits. Given the challenges facing humanity, more possibility is a good thing.

The quantum physicist Max Planck said, "A scientific truth does not triumph by convincing its opponents and making them see the light, but rather because its opponents eventually die and a new generation grows up that is familiar with it." Planck's observation reflects the tendency of experts (and everyone is an expert in something) to hold tightly to mental patterns (that is, the stories the left brain has labeled "reality"). In the past, slow changes to thought and perception were not a serious threat to humanity. This is no longer the case. The accelerating pace of technological progress requires that we quickly develop the ability to adjust our thinking and assess the risks and benefits of new discoveries – our increasingly dynamic world requires increasingly dynamic human beings.[11] If we fail to develop this ability, we are likely to continue to damage the planet and squander our potential.[12] Simply put, humanity can no longer afford to hold on to its beliefs at the expense of progress – value rigidity is now a major threat to our survival.

Science is bringing the Zen practice of beginner's mind into the light of modern empiricism. Researchers found that undergraduates who wrote about how they would experience a day off as a 7-year-old performed better on a creative thinking test than students who wrote about how they would experience a day off as their adult selves.[13] (How much of the creativity-numbing effect of adulthood is actually the product of an education system that routinely devalues visual arts and music in favor of preparing for standardized tests?)

While reading this book, you are invited to experiment with beginner's mind. In the course of discussing our ideas with people of various backgrounds, we (the authors) have been continuously struck by the tendency to pigeonhole these ideas into existing mental models of the world: conservative or liberal, right-wing or left-wing, capitalist or socialist, crazy or brilliant. To see a pattern that transcends the limits of these old thought lines, one must be willing to let go (at least momentarily) of the old pattern. Much like the famous gestalt drawing shown here, one cannot see the young lady until one lets go of the image of the old woman.

This leads to another preliminary matter: a suggestion for how to read this book. Using the analytic tool of language, two general ways of reading can be distinguished – as a spectator or as a participant. Western culture tends to foster the spectator approach to life; we mimic television's talking heads. Pointing out the flaws in others is easier than tackling problems. (This phenomenon may be true in the rest of the world as well, but we don't presume to know.) This tendency likely has deep roots in the psychological make-up of human beings: human systems can only work with the given spectrum of human nature – shaping it for better or worse, but never creating something that was not already there in some form. Egos feed off the weaknesses of others, which explains the popularity of tabloid magazines and reality television shows that offer every reader or viewer at least one chance to feel superior.

What does it mean to be a participant in a book? It does *not* mean suspending one's critical faculties. Instead it requires *awareness* of one's critical faculties and questioning whether disagreements with the writer's logic or underlying values come from habitual thinking or from fundamental disputes. Reader participation also involves following the threads and dealing with the messiness caused by efforts to fit nonlinear ideas into a linear format. Keep in mind that we do not claim to be "anything other than just one person [well, two to be precise] talking from one place in time and space and circumstances."[14] We are not proposing absolutes or rules, but offering a version of reality that we hope may be useful here and now. Meet us halfway with a beginner's mind and together we might get somewhere, and have some fun along the way.

Word Problems

Reality lives in language. "We don't talk about what we see; we see only what we can talk about."[15] Languages, in the words of Aldous Huxley, are "implicit philosophies" that shape reality and imagination (that is, the possibilities we can conceive in our minds).[16] This quality of language is not so obvious, or very interesting for that matter, when talking about material things: chairs, tables, or birds for example. However, there are infinite ways to classify and arrange the more ethereal ideas of the mind – relationships, truth, beauty, justice, etc. The particular way one's language divides up the world is so much a part of thinking that it is easy to succumb to the illusion that this particular vision of the world is *the* reality. Consider Pirsig's perspective:

> [T]here is a knife moving here. A very deadly one; an intellectual scalpel so swift and so sharp you sometimes don't see it moving. You get the illusion that all those parts are just there and are being named as they exist. But they can be named quite differently and organized quite differently depending on how the knife moves …
>
> It is important to see this knife for what it is and not to be fooled into thinking that motorcycles or anything else are the way they are just because the

knife happened to cut it up that way. It is important to concentrate on the knife itself.[17]

Goethe also saw the potential dangers of language to understanding: "How difficult it is...to refrain from replacing the thing with its sign, to keep the object alive before us instead of killing it with the word."[18] By concentrating on the knife, that is, by being aware of language, the object can be kept alive before us. Studying the living object enables deeper and truer understanding.

The object being kept alive in these pages is humanity; we are a living entity made up of 7 billion individual cells, that is, human beings. Throughout this book, the personal pronouns "we" and "us" are often used to reference humanity (a breach of conventional academic writing style). Separating you (the reader) and us (the authors) from one another and the whole of humankind, which results when humanity is continually referred to as an abstract object – an "it" – obscures the truth of our connectedness. The stylistic conventions of Western academia encourage writers and readers to look on humanity as an "it." This is an example of "the knife" at work: analytic language creating a division between the thinker (the subject) and humankind (the object). This implicit philosophy gives rise to a reality in which human beings are at the mercy of war, genocide, and financial booms and busts as much as we are at the mercy of the tides, earthquakes and gravity. There is a different reality available, and it begins with the recognition that *we are humanity*.

We do not freely wield "the knife" because we do not create our language. Even when a person chooses to learn a foreign language it's a prepackaged deal handed down by past generations. It is humanity's collective history controlling the range of possibilities that we can talk about, see, and thus create for our future. Imagine, for example, a world built of Legos: could a person, who only ever knew a world of colored plastic fitted blocks, conceive of the smoothness, fluidity and luminosity of Michelangelo's *David*? Perhaps it's possible, but it would be exceedingly rare – and the artist would almost surely be insane by the standards of her society.

There is no satisfactory solution to this language difficulty. But awareness brings attention to its constraints, and makes us more likely to push up against, and beyond, these limits – to eagerly shape new Legos.

Language tends to divide the interwoven whole of human existence into separate subsystems. For example, "social" describes our personal connections, "economic" our financial interactions, and "political" our governance system. While these are helpful classifications, their use obscures the truth that these are areas of an intricately interwoven whole that *we are* and that *we create*. English lacks a satisfactory word for the underlying whole. "Society" implies a national scope (a distinction less relevant by the day). "Civilization" seems remote and relatively static – beyond our ability to influence, something studied in history class. In this book we refer to the "human system," "human society" and the "human organism" to signal the interwoven whole of human interactions.

Speaking Metaphorically

"Communication technology" is not limited to smart phones, computers and the like, but refers to the broader stream of evolution of which these gadgets are the most recent innovation. The pioneers of this technology, our ancient ancestors, explored the range of sound they could produce with their throats, tongues, and mouths. Written language, numbers, money, and the printing press are a few of the innovations that enabled external communication (between people) and internal communication (abstract thinking).

Language is chiefly a tool of analysis rather than synthesis. Since much of what is shared in this book relates to the emergence of patterns in the human social organism – the whole rather than the parts – the analytic tendency of language is an obstacle. We (the authors) compensate for this by using metaphors liberally – we humans are weavers, threads, surfers, cells, light waves and dancers. Neuroscience has found that the right hemisphere of the human brain, the side of synthesis, is in charge of using and understanding metaphors. Metaphors are a bridge between the precision of analysis and the accuracy of synthesis. Metaphors are an essential

{ "If you want to change the world, you have to change the metaphor."
 - Joseph Campbell }

part of human learning – we expand our knowledge and understanding by comparing new information and experiences to those we have already encountered. Human beings learn through analogy.

Metaphors are not just tools of language, they are tools of thinking.[19] As with literal language, it is important to cultivate awareness of the constraints metaphors can impose on one's conception of the world and what is possible. Scientists are proving that metaphors powerfully shape the way we see the world. Stanford psychologists conducted an ingenious series of experiments aimed at measuring the effects of metaphors.[20] They had people read one of two paragraphs describing an increase in crime in a city and then asked the readers to suggest ways of addressing the crime problem. In one version of the passage, crime was described as a "wild beast preying on the city" and "lurking in neighborhoods." Seventy-four percent of the readers of this version suggested measures involving enforcement or punishment (building more jails, for example). Only 25% proposed social reforms (improving education, for example).

A second group read paragraphs that were exactly the same *except* crime was described as a "virus infecting the city" and "plaguing neighborhoods." After reading this version, only 56% suggested more enforcement (18% less than the first group). Forty-four percent suggested social reforms (19% more than the first group). The metaphors affected how the participants perceived the problem and possible solutions more than political party affiliation or gender!

In a follow-up study the experimenters replaced the vivid metaphorical language with a single reference to crime as either a "virus" or a "beast." The results were almost identical with the first study: *a single word shaped the participants' thinking in profound ways*. When readers were asked to identify the words that influenced their thinking, most cited the crime statistics (which were identical in every version). Very few mentioned the metaphorical reference. In sum, *metaphors have a profound – but largely unconscious – effect on our thinking*. Might we be able to use this power to open doors that we did not even know existed?

"Capitalism is a machine" is a common metaphor particularly relevant to the project of pushing the evolution of the current economic pattern. Review these real world illustrations of this structuring metaphor in the media:

> Increasing taxes can help *fuel* capitalism.
> The entrepreneurial spirit has been the vital *engine* of prosperity.
> The *wheels* of commerce.
> The economy is *picking up speed*.
> Housing prices fall as economy *stalls*.
> Small business helps *drive* the economy.
> Service growth *gears* down, *stokes* double-dip fears.
> Economic recovery hits *brakes*.

The capitalism is a machine metaphor is pervasive for good reason. It is not only powerfully descriptive, but it also provides a sense of control and thus a degree of comfort. Human beings make machines, and machines serve their makers. Machines can be diagramed, analyzed and understood completely. Also, capitalism has grown in step with humanity's mastery of machines, so the metaphor also has a material historical grounding. However, the capitalism as machine metaphor warps our perception of reality and shapes the world in some less than ideal ways.

Machines have no soul, no compassion, no intellect. Machines are designed to accomplish one goal – they cannot spontaneously adapt or reevaluate priorities beyond their programming. Machines are static and, at least theoretically, there is an ideal design that its engineers are trying to create. Most importantly, *machines are dead.* By speaking and, more importantly, thinking about capitalism as a machine we are creating a world in which our most powerful collective system is dead, soulless, and dumb – picture a zombie from a low-budget B movie. Sadly, our machine lacks a well-considered destination or product. Much like cancer, its primary imperative is growth at whatever cost, even at the cost of its own destruction – of *our* own destruction.

We are all casualties, to varying degrees, of the machine metaphor. Machines demand well-matched wheels and gears, and properly shaped cogs. There is little tolerance for deviation from the precise specifications needed for the machine to run. Imagination, creativity, curiosity and diversity – many of the very traits that have enabled humanity to thrive – are devalued. Persuasive evidence of this devaluation is seen in the U.S. public education system's emphasis on standardized tests and budget cuts to art and music programs. American society is shaping wheels, gears and cogs and using static calipers to assess the fitness of these parts for their future positions inside the machine. This process smothers the natural light-filled curiosity and creativity of our children.

As psychologist Erich Fromm explained, capitalism results in a hierarchy of values, "Capital commands labor; amassed things, that which is dead, are of superior value to labor, to human powers, to that which is alive."[21] Moreover, the amassed material wealth of the past, commands the people who are alive here and now, inhibiting our ability to adapt quickly to new realities – inhibiting our survival. This is true of the unconscious machinelike capitalism of the past and present, but it does not need to be its future. Capitalism still thrives *only* because the machine metaphor, and the reality it has shaped, has not been powerful enough to defeat the human spirit.

An alternative metaphor offers a powerful and expansive vision for humanity: capitalism as a Broadway musical extravaganza. It is bursting with life, enthusiasm, beauty and talent – it thrives only when humanity thrives. It can be quite profitable, but money is incidental to the fulfillment of real human needs – material comforts, connection, inspiration, entertainment, hope, catharsis, etc. We are all, simultaneously, cast and crew (producers), audience (consumers) and investors (owners). Success depends on nurturing and showcasing the talents of each of us in our diverse roles. The props and costumes (that is, material stuff), while often essential, are secondary to people; these will not save an otherwise lackluster production from box office failure. In this metaphor, capitalism is evolving, soulful and, most importantly, *alive*. The goal, rather than blind growth, is the collaborative expression of what it means to be a human being and the joyful celebration of the experience of life in its infinitely varied forms.

The question posed to each of us will be "what is your talent, and what can *we* do to help you shine?" Each of us has an inner voice of authentic truth yearning to be expressed. Imagine a world where our human system is consciously and deliberately focused on bringing forth the potential within each person.

Today, masses of people feel little connection to those around them, get meager satisfaction from the activities that consume most of their waking lives, and spend the short amount of leisure time they have numbing themselves to the purposelessness of their existence. Now imagine a future where people embrace their role in the community of humanity, eagerly contribute time and talent to making a real difference in the lives of others, and gain a deep sense of joy and satisfaction from their participation in something greater than themselves. The power unleashed by this shift in the human system of

> "The difference between what we do and what we are capable of doing would suffice to solve most of the world's problem."
>
> - Gandhi

capitalism is the key to unlocking a door to a new world, where grace is available to all in exchange for a helping hand ... where anything is possible.

A Road Map

The route before you is roundabout. Philosopher Robert Pirsig explained the merit of such an approach:

> You look at where you're going and where you are and it never makes sense, but then you look back at where you've been and a pattern seems to emerge. And if you project forward from that pattern, then sometimes you can come up with something.[22]

Chapter 1 offers a candid assessment of humanity's current circumstances because the first step in getting to where you want to go is figuring out where you are. Chapters 2 and 3 look back at where we've been. In Chapter 2 evolutionary theory uncovers the source of the immense power of capitalism and illuminates some of its limits. Then, in Chapter 3, we look to the wisdom and successes of the dreamers of 1776 for guidance. From this grounding in history we hone in on our specific coordinates and calibrate our compass. Chapters 4 and 5 turn to the essence of what it means to be a human being. From this existential grounding, we clarify the makings of a "good society." Chapters 6 and 7 look to the sciences of sociology, anthropology, psychology, physics and systems to explain the workings of complex adaptive systems, such as life, the human organism, and capitalism. From here we see possible leverage points in human systems, especially capitalism, that can empower us to create a better future. Chapters 8, 9 and 10 apply this wisdom and knowledge to imagining a new and more intelligent form of capitalism. This reconfigured economic system unleashes a world of possibility by linking communication technology with the highest human values – love, truth, beauty and justice. Chapter 11 offers a vision of a world transformed by the power of the most valuable untapped renewable resource on this planet – human potential. This is a resource that can be tapped with no drilling, no new technology, no legislation, and no environmental risk assessment. In this future, our most powerful system, capitalism, is put at the service of humanity.

1 - You Are Here

In the U.S. media today, extreme rhetoric is clearly contributing to paralysis and division, and shrinking areas of common ground. Right-wing media pundits foretell the end of freedom and democracy while the left-wing warns of cataclysmic climate change and the corporate take-over of our government. This chapter lays out an objective perspective on the current state of affairs and concludes that there are reasons to celebrate and as well as causes for alarm. By highlighting our shared opportunities and challenges, we may gain a broader and more accurate perspective from which to consider future possibilities.

Paradox of the Destruction of the Fittest

Human population has exploded in the past two hundred years, with advances in agriculture, medicine and hygiene lowering infant mortality and extending life expectancy. At a purely biological level, we are like a pond scum that overgrows its environment, and thus begins to destroy the very conditions that enabled its growth. In a twisted irony, our great adaptive ability to shape the material world to meet our needs has sown the seeds of our potential destruction. Global warming, nuclear holocaust, and countless other man-made cataclysms threaten survival – a situation we call the Paradox of the Destruction of the Fittest. Mother earth's natural rhythm includes ebbs and flows, and sometimes booms and busts.[1] The following is a survey of some of the most likely sources of future busts.

It is in our nature to acclimate quickly to new conditions. Most of us were born and raised in the nuclear age. This familiarity obscures the gravity of nuclear power's threat to our continued existence. If you drop a frog in boiling water it will immediately jump out and escape more or less unscathed. But if you drop a frog in tepid water and gradually increase the temperature it will continue to bathe passively until fully cooked. We are in danger of becoming boiled frogs.

History warns of the dangers of complacency. Hitler's success was in no small part attributable to his mastery of the "slow boil" technique. Starting with gradual limits on Jewish civil liberties and incremental land grabs across Europe, before the rest of the continent knew what had happened tragedy and oppression reached inconceivable proportions.

The secrets of atomic energy, unwittingly released as Einstein unveiled the still astounding truth that matter and energy are two sides of the same coin, is a genie that cannot be put back in its bottle. Proliferation seems beyond control. North Korea's fascist leadership has enough plutonium for 12 warheads,[2] enough to keep any person of sound mind awake at night. Iran is likely on its way to developing its own nuclear ability and recently unveiled its unmanned drone christened the "Ambassador of Death." These would-be wielders of the most dangerous weapons in existence believe immodestly dressed females cause earthquakes, and Allah rewards martyrs with 72 wives in heaven (or virgins, or celestial beings, depending on one's interpretation). Just as discomforting, Pakistan is one coup (or election) away from putting an arsenal of 70 to 90 nukes in the hands of Islamic extremists.

Besides the grave risks of intentional nuclear attacks, the nuclear materials we have spread across the globe will continue to pose a serious threat to life for millennia. Plutonium remains poisonous for at least 500,000 years – far longer than *Homo sapiens* have existed – and tons of it is routinely transported along U.S. highways, railroads, and in the skies.[3] If history is any indication, human civilizations will continue to rise and fall, while man-made radioactive waste outlasts them all: the ruins of the Roman Empire were attributed, hundreds of years after their construction, to giants. Our memories and our institutions are fleeting, and, not surprisingly, we forget how fleeting they are.

Illustrating both our complacency and our short memories, in 2006 workers discovered a nuclear bunker filled with food and medical supplies in the base of the Brooklyn Bridge. Less than sixty years after its construction, no record of the bunker existed. Most communities have abandoned the notion of building underground-fortified protection from a nuclear attack, not because the risk has been reduced, but because we have adjusted to the idea of the threat.

Japan is still dealing with the aftermath of the meltdown of the Fukushima nuclear reactor following the devastating March 11, 2012 earthquake and tsunami. The government's complex software modeling program (designed to predict the course of radiation drift) proved grossly inadequate, leaving "experts" scratching their heads as radioactive hot spots emerged in seemingly random locations.[4] Faith in our ability to deal effectively with the effects of our scientific discoveries is wildly overinflated. We tend to think the future will look like the past (a flaw in our default operating system), but the truth is we are playing an inherently unpredictable game, and we are adding to its volatility.

Global climate change presents another challenge that is stretching the bounds of the human imagination. Regardless of whether you believe human activity is chiefly responsible for the change, it is now beyond doubt that it is happening and the chances of halting it are slim.[5] If humanity is to adapt to its new climatic reality and avoid the possibility of extreme instability and devastating human casualties, then we must evolve ahead of nature's imposed timeline.

Climate change threatens to aggravate a challenge we've managed, for the most part, to keep at bay – feeding our growing population. Dire predictions about our inability to feed ourselves go back over two centuries. In the early nineteenth century, Thomas Malthus warned of the dangers of exponential population growth in light of arithmetic food supply expansion. Others, such as Paul and Anne Ehrlich, authors of the 1968 book, *The Population Bomb*, resumed Malthus' warnings (and continue the message today[6]). So far they have been wrong, due in large part to extraordinary technological advances.[7] But, global warming combined with continued population growth loom large on the horizon – Malthus and the Ehrlichs may have, after all, just been premature. Surely there is a limit to the carrying capacity of our planet; if we do not address the shared responsibility of limiting our numbers, we may eventually learn the hard way what that limit is. Indeed, rising food prices hint at the very real possibility of a serious crisis in the near future, launching a wave of political and social instability. (Rising food prices contributed to the political unrest in Tunisia and Egypt.)

These are just a sampling of the potentially cataclysmic disasters we may face, manifestations of the Paradox of the Destruction of the Fittest. There are plenty of other dire possibilities – peak oil, GMOs, biological weapons and super-bacteria, to name just a few.

History has lessons for dreamers who underestimate the potential obstacles in the way of universal peace and prosperity – optimism must be tempered with vigilance. The Austrian writer Stefan Zweig wrote of the exuberant optimism he experienced firsthand in the years before the eruption of WWI:

> A different rhythm prevailed in the world. None could foretell all that might happen in a single year! One discovery, one invention, followed another, and instantly was directed to the universal good; for the first time the nations sensed in common that which concerned the commonweal…because of our pride in the successive triumphs of our technics, our science, a European community spirit, a European national consciousness was coming into be-

ing...But whoever experienced that epoch of world confidence knows that all since has been retrogression and gloom ... And the worst was that just the sentiment which we most highly valued - our common optimism - betrayed us.[8]

The course of progress is not a straight line, and it is not guaranteed. While there is much to celebrate, we must not become complacent. The stakes are high, perhaps (given the power of our technology) higher than they've ever been in our short stint on this planet.

Signs of Discontent

While the risk of extreme cataclysm is disconcerting, there are other signs – more subtle yet incontrovertible – that we might want to consider a different approach to our future. Many of us (Americans in particular) are becoming more and more isolated from one another. We are spending more and more time working in jobs that do not reflect our goals or hopes for the future. We are eating ourselves into disease, mesmerized by television and electronic distractions, popping antidepressants like candy, and imprisoning ever more of our fellow human beings. We may be pursuing happiness, but evidence suggests that few are achieving it.

For increasing numbers of Americans, the American Dream is coming to resemble a mirage: the top 1% of US taxpayers received 12.3% of all pretax income in 1987. Twenty years later the share going to the top 1% nearly doubled, reaching 23.5%. Over the same period, the share of income garnered by the bottom 50% of taxpayers fell from 15.6% to 12.2%.[9] As of April 2011, 1 in 7 Americans receives food stamps.[10]

The American social fabric is thinning; people are communicating less with one another. According to a comparison of two surveys, taken in 1985 and 2004, discussion networks are shrinking. The number of respondents who stated there is no person with whom they discuss important matters increased from 10% to almost 25%. The mean network size decreased by about a third (one confidant), from 2.94 in 1985 to 2.08 in 2004.[11] Considering empirical evidence linking loneliness to compromised immune function, this is not just an emotionally tragic state of affairs, but a serious health risk.

Additional evidence points to a wave of isolation. The most basic of social units – the family – is undergoing rapid disintegration. The Unites States' 50% divorce rate tops the world. Most know, either directly or through loved ones, the emotional turmoil and financial ruin that often accompanies the unraveling of a marriage. These personal tragedies are straining our social fabric (a fact that deserves more attention and study). Couples that manage to stay together do so in an environment that fosters an underlying sense of wariness and unhappiness rather than true partnership and trust. From this perspective we understand divorce to be a contagious epidemic threatening the well-being of individuals and communities. This fundamental (almost invisible) shift in the social landscape has serious effects that go beyond the personal lives of those involved. Human potential is more likely to be realized when fostered from childhood in a stable family environment (though it need not be the traditional nuclear variety).[12]

Another sign of increasing isolation is the dramatic rise in the percentage of the U.S. population living alone. In 1950, the percentage of single-person U.S. households was just over 9%. By 2010, that percentage rose to 27%. Interestingly, the epicenter of single living is Manhattan, the most densely populated city in the U.S., where over half of all households consist of one person. We (the authors) have lived alone, and we understand the attraction, especially when the choice is a roommate rather than a loved one. However, solitary living is generally not conducive to creating a sense of community, fostering human connections and nurturing a feeling of security.

Other distress signals abound in these United States: job satisfaction in the U.S. has been on a steady decline, with only 45% of people reporting satisfaction from their work, down from 61% in 1987.[13] It's estimated that up to 70% of adults are overweight (and about half of these are obese). Ten percent of Americans take prescription antidepressants. At current rates, the average American will spend over 9 years watching television in a lifetime. The U.S. has the highest documented imprisonment rate in the world. In short, if improving our quality of life is an important goal, then it appears America has significant room for progress.

These signs of deep dissatisfaction exist in the most materially wealthy society in the history of civilization. We suspect these two facts (discontentment amid material plenty) are related: somewhere along the journey, the means were confused with the ends, or, as Tom Robbins so eloquently wrote:

> The introduction of money, with its seductive, if largely ambiguous promises, added a fresh measure of zip to the sport of life, but *the zip turned to zap when the players, stupefied by the ever-shifting intangibles, began to confuse the markers with the game.*
>
> So, even for those of us who can't personally witness Salome's dance, the fifth veil surely will fall. It will fall at the moment of our death. As we lie there, helpless, beyond distraction, electricity stealing out of our brains like a con man stealing out of a sucker's neighborhood, it will occur to many of us that everything we ever did, we did for money. And at that instant, right before the stars blink off, we will, according to what else we may have learned in life, burn with an unendurable regret – or have us a good silent laugh at our own expense.[14]

Empirical research has shown again and again that once a person's basic material needs are met, more money does not translate into greater happiness. We squander our waking lives chasing after more stuff we by and large do not need. It is stuff that is produced at the expense of our true happiness and the well-being of future generations. As Thoreau expressed it, "The price of anything is the amount of life you exchange for it." Judging from the current state of America's collective psyche, many are trading their lives for lifeless material things under the delusion that these things will bring them happiness.

The point is *not* that things are horrible and only getting worse. It's important to recognize that, in the past century, our species has experienced quantum leaps in our overall standard of living (though the distribution of these improvements has, thus far, been uneven in the extreme). But our material gains have not brought progress in the art of living well, and continued advances are unlikely given the challenges on the horizon.

We can choose to see these challenges as insurmountable or as signs that we're doomed to misery, or we can choose to see them as indicators of where we have wandered off-track and thus as valuable signposts. To that end, let's look at some hopeful signs that we may not be as far from the path as we might fear.

A Peace Wave?

We've all heard of crime waves sweeping a city, often during a summer heat wave, but have you heard of a "peace wave"? Harvard professor Steven Pinker makes a compelling case that humanity is in the midst of a major transformation into kinder beings. Pinker cites a wide array of data that empirically shows the truth of his thesis: "Violence has been in decline over long stretches of history, and today we are probably living in the most peaceful moment of our species' time on earth."[15] Indeed, homicide, both in and out of war, saw a dramatic decline in the twentieth century. Pinker summarizes this good news as follows:

Cruelty as entertainment, human sacrifice to indulge superstition, slavery as a labor-saving device, conquest as the mission statement of government, genocide as a means of acquiring real estate, torture and mutilation as routine punishment, the death penalty for misdemeanors and differences of opinion, assassination as the mechanism of political succession, rape as the spoils of war, pogroms as outlets for frustration, homicide as the major form of conflict resolution – all were unexceptionable features of life for most of human history. But, today, they are rare to nonexistent in the West, far less common elsewhere than they used to be, concealed when they do occur, and widely condemned when they are brought to light.

Pinker struggles to explain the cause of this trend of kindness. He dismisses the possibility of an evolutionary explanation, concluding that, "Even if the meek could inherit the earth, natural selection could not favor the genes for meekness quickly enough." Culture is the primary means by which human beings are evolving now, and culture has a powerful influence on personality. Pinker is correct that *genes* for meekness could not have been favored in the brief time since the dawning of our pacifist phase. But *cultures* that value human life and the rule of law have been favored by natural selection in this brief time frame. The default operating system "installed" in individuals who develop in these pacifist cultures inclines them toward respect for others (that is, meekness).

To see clearly our current position in the timeline of evolution – where we've come from and where we might be headed – it's important to first consider one of the more thorny debates in science: nature versus nurture. If humans are hardwired by DNA, then the prospects for transforming human civilization in a short period will depend on genetic engineering rather than cultural evolution. Empirical studies have determined with a convincing degree of reliability that intelligence and personality are determined by both nature and nurture in close to a 50/50 ratio.[16] What constitutes "nurture" remains a mystery (for example, parenting appears to play a small role as long as extreme abuse isn't involved). For now we must be content to define nurture in the negative: it's something (or things) that is not in our genes.

What is important for the present discussion is that, while we are tied to our genes, our tether is long enough to give us room to maneuver – we are not mere puppets. Through a better understanding of human nature, we can learn to use our room to maneuver to its fullest, allowing us to be, as much as possible, authors of our own destinies. We can apply our intelligence to finding ways to work with, rather than against, the innate part of us, which is not within our direct control, thus expanding the range of our autonomy. The evolutionary history of *Homo sapiens* sheds light on the relatively fixed aspects of human nature – the anchor that controls the range of our potential.

Before mapping the human genome, scientists decoded the genome of the microscopic, spineless, primitive *Caenorhabditis* worm. Roughly 18,000 genes provide the blueprint for 969 cells that comprise *Caenorhabditis*. Based on this benchmark, geneticists guessed that the human genome would likely include over 100,000 genes – given our complex biology of over 50 trillion cells. The current count puts the number of human genes in the neighborhood of 22,000. Not many more than the simple *Caenorhabditis*, and fewer than a grape plant, which has over 30,000 genes.[17] Clearly, there is a lot more to life than simply carrying out the programs written in one's genetic code. It appears that much of the magic of life is in the *relationships* between our genes, the physical structures our genes map (what biologists call "phenotypes") and our environment. Epigenetics is the study of these relationships.

Our emerging ability to consciously program our operating system – to intentionally rewire the patterns of our thought processes – is transforming our species within a time frame that would be impossible through mere genetic selection. Human beings are exceptional because of our freedom to choose and to shape our material world to suit our needs, and we are learning to focus this ability on ourselves. We are using our intellect to self-evolve. Pinker identifies the watershed time and place in the kindness transformation of our species. The Age of Reason in Britain and Holland, which led to the Age of Enlightenment, encouraged the questioning of traditional customs, institutions, and ethics. During this time, a critical mass of human beings awoke to the realization that their default operating system was full of bugs that were causing suboptimum functioning – a major modification was in order.[18]

Astoundingly rapid changes in our beliefs about race and gender equality, religious tolerance and sexual orientation provide evidence of the continued vitality of the Age of Enlightenment. People are consciously choosing to draw new maps and chart new courses. They are expanding the greatest natural resource on this planet – human potential. It is no coincidence that the advances of the last two centuries followed the arrival of the Age of Enlightenment: serfs and slaves generally do not invent, innovate, create, or write – these are the province of free men and women.

That we went from the race riots of the 1960s to the Obama presidency in a generation is Exhibit A in the case for the breakneck pace of human self-evolution. Women could be legally excluded from jury pools in the U.S. until 1975. Today, 3 of the 9 justices on U.S. Supreme Court are women. Peaceful protesters overthrowing entrenched dictators in Tunisia and Egypt – a part of the world not known for honoring human rights – is still more evidence of the groundswell of positive change sweeping humanity forward.

While the process of pacification brought on by a newfound reverence for human life and liberty may be reaching a tipping point, it has been in long in the making. The great teachers of the ages – Lao Tzu, Buddha, and Jesus, to name a few – foretold this sea change. Nearly every major spiritual teaching includes the core belief that we are all brothers and sisters, family in the cosmic sense, and that narrow-minded selfishness is simply a failure to grasp the inviolability of our interconnectedness: love your neighbor as yourself. The rapid decline in violence arises from our growing recognition that there are a whole lot more of "us" and a lot fewer "them," and the "thems" that remain are really not so different.[19] We are consciously reordering our relationships and reshaping what it means to be human. We are self-evolving.

Science is confirming the truth of our sense of unity. Geneticists have shown that race is purely a human-made notion that exists in language (that is, our created "reality"), but not in the objective world of DNA. Can our newly discovered sense of unity triumph over the extremism gaining momentum in many parts of the world, including the United States? Will humanity be brought to the brink of extinction? While there is cause for optimism, the answers to these questions are far from certain – the choices we make today will determine our future. Whether we make these choices consciously, or allow them to be made for us by the push of ideology and the pull of dogma will, ultimately, decide the fate of our species.

With this picture of where we are, we can see that while we face some serious challenges, we also have amazing potential: the best chance of solving the former is by realizing the latter. Possibly the most powerful leverage we have for tapping our unrealized potential lies in our economic system which, as we are about to see, contains the collective power of humanity backed by the force of billions of years of evolution.

2 – Capitalism as a Force of Nature

Our species, like all life on this planet, is evolving. Thus, it is not surprising that one of our most useful adaptations is also evolving. Capitalism embraces some of the most useful strategies emerging from the creativity and striving of human beings – free markets, private property, specialization of labor, and freedom of contract, to name a few. Capitalism has driven much of the unprecedented innovations of the past two hundred years. However, today it controls us, we do not control it. Before we explore its deep evolutionary roots, and the limits of its current incarnation, we will view it through the eyes of the Scottish Enlightenment thinker, Adam Smith.

Adam Smith was among the first to document the power of individual liberty to advance the material wealth of an entire society. Smith believed in the potential of human productivity and ingenuity to create "universal opulence." As a professor of moral philosophy at the University of Glasgow, Smith authored the now historic text, *An Inquiry into the Nature and Causes of the Wealth of Nations*. He published his book in March of 1776 – an auspicious year for liberty. Smith posed a theory of economic progress based on his observation that free enterprise and a minimally intrusive state lead to material progress.

Smith witnessed the self-regulated efficiency of a marketplace driven by the freely chosen decisions of individual economic actors. Such a system increases wealth for all because, to advance one's individual economic interests, one must produce goods or services of value to others. Cooperation involves aligning one's actions with the needs and preferences of others. Competition gives rise to innovations that bring new, better or less expensive goods and services. Capitalism strikes a dynamic balance between these two important, but potentially competing, drivers of progress. Smith explained that governments disrupt this efficient system when they compel individuals to deviate from their natural inclinations. Such coercion was rampant in Smith's time when mercantilism, a system of high tariffs designed to limit imports, and colonization, aimed at increasing exports, was the standard economic model.

Important, but rarely discussed, is Smith's expansive view of human nature. He did not, as many think, favor a system in which greed and base self-interest reign supreme. His words on the capacity of human beings for benevolence and altruism must inform an understanding of his economic theory:

> And hence it is, that to feel much for others and little for ourselves, that to restrain our selfish, and to indulge our benevolent affections, constitutes the perfection of human nature; and can alone produce among mankind that harmony of sentiments and passions in which consists their whole grace and propriety. As to love our neighbour as we love ourselves it the great law of Christianity, so it is the great precept of nature to love ourselves only as we love our neighbour.[1]

Smith's opening passage in his opus on morality, *A Theory of Moral Sentiments*, includes this profound assessment of the human capacity for empathy:

> How selfish soever man may be supposed, there are evidently some principles in his nature, which interest him in the fortune of others, and render their happiness necessary to him, though he derives nothing from it except the pleasure of seeing it. Of this kind is pity or compassion, the emotion which we feel for the misery of others, when either see it, or are made to conceive it in a very lively manner. That we often derive sorrow from the sorrow of others is a matter of fact too obvious to require any instances to prove it; for this sentiment, like all the other original passions of human nature, is by no means confined to the virtuous and humane, though they perhaps may feel it with the most exquisite sensibility. The greatest ruffian, the most hardened violator of the laws of society, is not altogether without it.

Smith was clearly among the virtuous and humane who feel the suffering of others. It was discovered after his death that he had given much of his material wealth in anonymous acts of charity. Smith saw something beautiful in the new economic pattern he witnessed unfolding, but his expansive and optimistic view of human nature was central to his understanding. The "greed is good" credo of the modern capitalist would almost certainly inspire severe dismay in Smith, and would likely have made him less optimistic.

History has confirmed the accuracy of Smith's vision of the potential of free markets to create "universal opulence." Empirical studies have proved that free enterprise has a significant positive effect on standards of living. With few exceptions (mostly due to mental illness or addiction), even the poorest citizens in developed countries enjoy conveniences and comforts that were unimaginable to even the wealthiest of Smith's time. Potable water (hot or cold) from the tap, flushing toilets, electric lights, television, and telephones are taken for granted by millions. While capitalism has brought universal opulence to many, it is not a panacea. Its failure to protect the environment, honor the values of justice and fairness, and maximize the realization of human potential is becoming increasingly clear. The question facing humanity today is, "How best can we bridge the gap between what capitalism has created and what human beings need to thrive physically, psychologically and spiritually?" The nature of capitalism must be understood before we can seek answers to this question.

What is Capitalism?

Adam Smith explained the "invisible hand" of the free market long before the term "capitalism" existed. Karl Marx remarked that capitalism works "behind the backs" of both the capitalists and the workers. Capitalism is simply the cumulative result of what humans do when, as described by Smith, they are in a "system of natural liberty." In fact, capitalism sprouts even in harsh environments of unnatural oppression. The fascist and communist government of North Korea recently stepped up its efforts to crush all manifestations of capitalism by forcibly closing local markets that had sprung up spontaneously across the country. To know what fuels capitalism we must begin with a fundamental understanding of the forces that motivate human beings. From there we may be able to turn around, wrest control of the steering wheel from the invisible hand which currently has us poised to plummet over a cliff, and put capitalism at the service of its creator – humanity. We now have the potential to change course and unleash the latent power ensconced in the capitalist machine by freeing the cogs and wheels – the people. We can give ourselves a chance to fulfill our true potential as the living, breathing, dancing, singing performers in the musical of life. We can infuse our economic system with the wisdom and compassion that is the true source of human greatness – and provide the best hope of addressing the looming challenges facing humanity and the planet.

Evolutionary biology and the science of emergent systems (a field of study that covers many disciplines and is the focus of Chapter 7) offer a logical approach to understanding capitalism. Natural selection (itself obedient to the law of physics and chemistry) is a fundamental driver of evolution. It is a manifestation of the drive of all life to replicate. This simple drive, when placed in a competitive environment, gives rise to the dizzying array of ever changing life forms that populate this planet. Human striving arises (at least in part) from the drive to reproduce in a competitive environment. Nature is creative, and we are nature's creative creation!

Here the path of proto-economist Adam Smith intersects with another renowned and forward-looking thinker, the psychologist Abraham Maslow. In Maslow's theory people are motivated by a hierarchy of needs. The most urgent are the physical needs of food and shelter, and then come the more intangible needs of love, belonging, esteem, self-actualization, and enlightenment.[2] In conventional economic terms, these are the demands we seek to supply. Capitalism is an efficient means of providing the material goods that fulfill the physical and safety demands of our species. These needs are most directly dictated by the laws of physics and chemistry (nutrition, hydration, shelter).

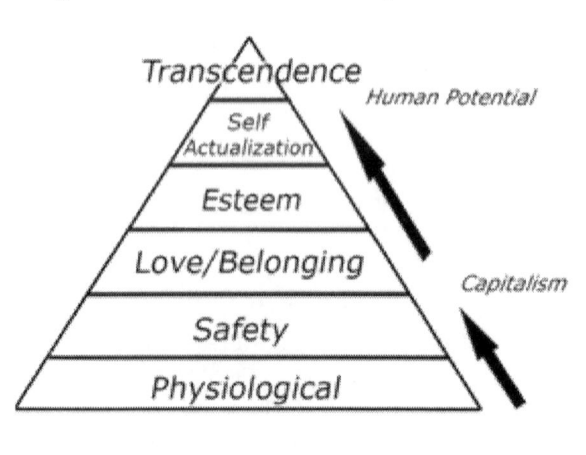

Capitalism, at its most basic, is a system in which people coordinate, cooperate, and compete to meet their needs. Some institutions, traditions and norms promote more complex and fluid coordination, and thus, a more efficient provision of goods and services. Examples include a reliable judicial system that predictably enforces clear laws, a government that provides infrastructure and preserves order, a stable monetary system, private property, freedom of contract, and the corporate form.

Capitalism, in its current incarnation, is not nearly as useful in the quest to satisfy Maslow's higher level needs. The drives to create, to commune, and to reach out for newer, richer and more meaningful experience are neglected if not actively thwarted. The limits of present-day capitalism, and the consumer culture it has spawned, is a major obstacle to overcoming the modern epidemic of isolation and discontent, and humanity's seeming inability to solve its most vexing problems. By identifying the limits of capitalism and exploring ways to advance its evolution we can shape a future in which humanity's latent creative power is unleashed and applied to solving our most pressing challenges.

A Sea of Starfish

Viewing capitalism through the lens of evolution makes clear a source of our inability to bridge the gap between what capitalism delivers and that to which human beings ultimately aspire. Capitalism is a self-organizing system – a starfish in Brafman and Beckstrom's starfish and spider metaphor. Such systems work from the bottom up, are organic, democratic, flexible, adaptive and agile. Rather than being means of distributing power, they are a means of organizing complexity with no centralized direction. Starfish systems tend to foster the growth and development of their individual constituents, which is the source of their strength. These are tendencies, not rules, and starfish can give rise to systemic challenges of their own. The horrific efficiency of the 1994 Rwandan genocide proves that the power of starfish can be used, much like the Force of Star Wars lore, by the dark side of human nature. Eight hundred thousand Tutsis and moderate Hutus were killed in the span of 100 days in a spontaneous and decentralized massacre. Hitler, whose centralized institutional genocide moved much more slowly, would be impressed.

Bureaucracies, like formalized government, are structures of conscious human design – the spiders of Brafman and Beckstrom's metaphor. These institutions impose the decisions of a small subgroup of society (legislators, executives, bureaucrats, bishops, mullahs) on the whole. But they are often not competent arbiters of society's shifting needs and priorities. Spider institutions are centralized, top-down, dictatorial, rigid and static. They prefer predictability and control to creativity and individual autonomy. Like the first "hierarchy" (literally "sacred rule"), that of the Catholic Church, spider institutions are mainly a means of controlling an existing distribution of power. This is not to say these institutions don't value creativity, but that creativity is a means to the end of enhancing the power of those at the top. The Church built cathedrals in large part to inspire awe, and thus ensure obeisance; governments erect monuments to signal their strength and authority; corporations hire graphic designers to attract buyers and build brand identity. Great art may result, but it is incidental to the main objective of preserving power.

The differences between capitalism and government bureaucracy parallel important differences between a human brain and a computer. Jeff Hawkins and Sandra Blakeslee, in their book *On Intelligence*, explain the inability of artificial intelligence (thus far) to come anywhere near human intelligence. The human brain is a self-organizing system – self-learning, flexible and decentralized. Conventional computers are the product of human design – programmed, rigid and centralized.[3] Bureaucracy is more like the artificial intelligence of the recent past (that is, not so bright). Capitalism is more likely to reflect *real* intelligence. Unfortunately, today's capitalism often reflects the intelligence of reptiles – cold and calculating – rather than human intelligence of compassion and joyful creativity.

The power of self-organizing systems is rooted in their ability to nurture and benefit from the wisdom, knowledge, creativity and skill of their parts. Top-down authoritarian institutions tend to create minions whose main contribution is their ability to carry out orders from on high. Self-organizing systems leave each level free to figure out how to carry out its contribution to the system. Thus, individual creativity and innovation are fostered to the benefit of the whole. Spider institutions suppress this autonomy because it threatens the status quo.

Of course, starfish and spiders are ways of describing two ends of a spectrum. Reality is much more complex – the varieties of starfish-spider hybrids far outnumber the purebreds. In politics, religion and economics the past several centuries reveal a trend away from spider forms, and toward starfish forms. Witness the shift from aristocracies and dictatorships to democracy; from the Holy Roman

Empire to the Protestant Reformation; from feudalism and communism to free markets. Civilization is moving toward a starfish dominant paradigm, and this movement is bringing staggering progress on many fronts.

Vestigial Structures

The failure of state-sponsored communism in Russia and its satellites, likely the most ambitious effort in recorded history to control a society through human designed institutions, clearly showed the limits of bureaucracy. Our own efforts to guide economic forces with the controls of government have met with similar, though less dramatic, disappointment. Controlling the natural force of capitalism with government bureaucracy is the equivalent of battling a Class 5 hurricane with a supersized electric fan. The failure of this approach is writ large across our country and our planet – abject poverty and environmental degradation amid an abundance of material wealth.

The defining characteristic of communism – "from each according to his ability, to each according to his need" – is at work in the U.S. government. Civil servants managing multibillion dollar operations typically earn less than $200,000 per year. Yet average pay for nonexecutive positions is often on par with, or slightly higher than, similar positions in the private sector. [4] A handful of bureaucrats and politicians decide what constitutes appropriate compensation. Thus, the judgment of a few replaces the collective wisdom of the market. Undoubtedly some senior government managers forgo financial wealth out of a wish to contribute to society, but often we're getting what we pay for, ineptitude and incompetence.

Public education is failing to equip children for jobs in science and technology. Teacher compensation is a major cause. Pay is based on a teacher's education level and seniority (bureaucratically determined standards), rather than the market value of her expertise.[5] Thus, science and math specialists who have lucrative job opportunities in the tech industry are paid the same as English teachers who have far fewer and less well-paid alternatives. Not surprisingly, many potential science and math teachers choose not to go into teaching. This leaves many children to learn from less than stellar teachers (and some generous souls who sacrifice their financial well-being to be educators). Free market forces, like competitive market pricing, that propel us forward in other areas are deliberately kept out of the educational system. Children, and our future, suffer.

The Bernie Madhoff ponzi scheme fiasco dramatically showed government bureaucracy's limited ability to police capitalism effectively. Incentives are a major reason SEC enforcement agents overlooked many red flags. Government jobs with mediocre pay are considered stepping-stones to the much better pay of the private sector where the value of government contacts can be monetized. The "police" slated with the duty of overseeing Madhoff's dealings were angling for jobs as his underlings. The blatant conflicts of interest inherent in this system fundamentally undermine its integrity. This is what happens in systems that misalign incentives and try to circumvent market forces.[6]

A further problem with human designed institutions of government is their geographic limits. Capitalism has no borders. International institutions have limited power to deal with the harm caused by multinational business. Compare the brawn of global corporations to the relative impotence of the United Nations. This imbalance leaves the largest and most potentially destructive actors in the economy without a countervailing force. The consequences are business practices that wreak havoc on human beings and the planet with little concern for anything other than the bottom line.

The ever-strengthening influence of commerce and industry in politics is increasingly undermining the ability of governments to play the role of umpire in the game of capitalism. In the U.S., energy companies formulate policy, corporate lobbyists draft congressional legislation, and both political parties are beholden to the business interests that fund their campaigns. (The Supreme Court's 2010 *Citizens United* decision, which granted corporations the right to free speech, unraveled a century of reforms aimed at curbing corporate campaign contributions.) In many parts of Europe, bondholders, not voters, are dictating public policy.

We can view our consciously designed institutions as a form of scaffolding, a necessary forerunner to more complex, stable (though dynamic) and robust starfish-like solutions. As a new human system takes shape, the need for the scaffolding fades – without the need for a drastic deconstruction. Inefficient government bureaucracy will naturally atrophy if we can create enough efficient starfish organizations to replace it. Eventually, many areas of government may become the equivalent of a vestigial structure (a remnant of a past stage of evolution).

The solution to large, top-heavy, centralized bureaucracy is not a wrecking ball, but a better alternative. Decades ago, big government emerged because we had important needs – education, elder care, food and shelter for poor families – that were unmet by both society and the free market. These needs persist. Dismantling the scaffolding before alternative systems gain footing will leave gaping holes in our social fabric, creating instability and threatening progress.

Pathological Mutation

Capitalism has helped our species become champions of the game of survival of the fittest, but we now face systemic dysfunctions that threaten our continued success and obstruct the path to deep and lasting happiness. Cancer spreads as a malformed version of cells multiply at a rate that overwhelms healthy cellular reproduction. Similarly, the current version of capitalism threatens to destroy the very life form that gave rise to it.

Evolutionary biology explains the Paradox of the Destruction of the Fittest. It shows how the adaptive strategy of capitalism can shift from improving to destroying survival. A strategy is only helpful or harmful relative to a specific environment. As an environment changes (including changes brought about by the adaptive strategy in question), so does the usefulness of the strategy. For example, white fur works well for polar bears only as long as they inhabit snow-covered terrain – our terrain is changing.

Human history provides many examples of this process. As certain tribes discovered agriculture, put down roots, and amassed material wealth in a central location – that is, they changed their survival strategy – they became convenient targets for those who remained nomadic. This divergence likely led to the first large-scale warfare.[7] These competing strategies dueled for supremacy over thousands of years. Finally, the agricultural strategy and its offshoots – cities, specialization of labor, mechanization, in short, civilization as we know it – prevailed. Genghis Khan, the leader of the nomadic tribes of Mongolia, applied his hunting and horsemanship skills to conquer most of Asia and the Middle East. His grandson, Kublai Khan, led an agrarian civilization. Raiding and looting may be a way to gain power, but it is not a sustainable strategy for preserving it.[8] Similarly, raiding and looting Earth's natural resources is the way human beings have multiplied, but it is not a workable strategy for continued survival.

The strategies of communism and capitalism are competing for supremacy. Though capitalism appears to have its rival on the ropes, the contest is not over. China's hybrid approach (a top-down political system with pockets of economic autonomy) is looking like a strong contender. Capitalism is also facing internal challenges: the turmoil caused by reckless financial moves and systemic imbalances are forcing Western economies to the brink of ruin. When, in 2009, the Pentagon held economic war games, China came out on top in every scenario.

Biologists use the term "evolutionarily stable strategies" (ESS) to describe ways of operating (farming, for example) that place adopters at an advantage over users of other ways (hunting, for example). ("Stable" is a relative term, often two or more ESSs alternate as the dominant strategy.) Importantly, an ESS within a species is not necessarily the best strategy for its long-term overall survival. For example, had the nomads proved victorious and wiped out the agricultural way of life, human beings might be much closer to extinction today (especially if we ignore the danger of technologically triggered catastrophes). The marauder strategy is only as successful as the supply of wealthy farmers is plentiful. Thus, the total success of the raiding strategy would entail the destruction of an essential part of its environment (that is, farmers), leading to its doom.

Evolutionary biology provides a clue to a possible solution to the Paradox of the Destruction of the Fittest. Capitalism is an ESS, but it is altering its environment in a way that is damaging to long-term survival. Other life forms cannot assess the long-term effects of their strategies – they are at the mercy of the dynamics of evolution. Human beings, on the other hand, can foresee challenges, imagine alternatives and invent new, more adaptive, strategies.

Our future may depend on whether we use these abilities to their full potential.

Reptilian Capitalism

Despite the advances brought by capitalism, masses of humanity and the health of our planet are in a dismal state. The devastating results of much human activity are at odds with what we personally know about human beings. We love our families and will go to great lengths to help our friends. Indeed, true evil is a rare thing. The vast majority of us have a fundamental wish to help others, and make a positive impact on the world around us. The roots of compassion and altruism run deep in the wiring of our brains, but this truth is often not reflected in what we see in the world at large.

When faced with the tragedies and injustices in the world, our natural reaction is to see ourselves as uncommonly caring. We assume that huge numbers of callous people are responsible for all the unnecessary suffering (bankers and corporate execs are high on this list at present). While there are wide variations in altruism and compassion among people, an innate hard-heartedness of human beings is not the main culprit. Rather, the blame falls on the limits of capitalism, the currently dominant survival strategy. These limits stultify our morality, disconnect us from our power, and insulate us from the consequences of our actions. Capitalism has us behave in ways that often move us farther from where the vast majority of us want to be – on a path of discovery and striving among peaceful, compassionate and joyful fellow travelers.

The capacity for altruism and compassion arose with the neocortex (the six-layered covering on mammalian brains that supports higher level processing). Our reptilian ancestors, and their cold-blooded offspring, lack a neocortex. This is why our reptile cousins exhibit behaviors we consider objectionable (eating their young, for example). Now that human evolution is happening chiefly at the cultural and technological levels, it is urgent that we more fully include altruism and compassion in culture and technology.

An understanding of the evolutionary roots of capitalism sheds light on why its outcomes are often inconsistent with our personal values. The biological imperative of all life is reproduction (and reproduction requires survival). Thus, the first order of business for any survival strategy is to address immediate physical needs – food, shelter and security. These needs – the same ones that motivate our distant reptilian cousins – are the primary drivers of the current incarnation of capitalism. Thus, it is no wonder that capitalism often results in outcomes that appear thoughtless, cruel, and shortsighted. The last 300 million years of evolution are not integrated into the awesome power of our economy.[9] (This may be the reason David Icke and his followers believe there is a conspiracy of reptilian humanoids controlling our world.)

This failing of capitalism is a stage in our evolution, although not necessarily a fatal flaw. We now have the ability to move beyond this phase. We can use our intelligence to rearrange our economic system and develop a new strategy that reflects our higher level drives. Specifically, we can expand and deepen the force of free markets so it better reflects the most humane aspects of our nature, rather than chiefly our reptilian side. This more evolved form of capitalism may deliver results that are consistent with what we truly want. A healthy planet, an end to unnecessary suffering, strong community, an appreciation for individual liberty and worth, and a purpose beyond survival and the accumulation of material wealth are within reach.

If we do not act, we risk triggering a "cascading failure" – a potentially cataclysmic chain reaction that could leave human civilization in tatters. The emerging science of systems (the subject of Chapters 6 and 7) shows that big events – earthquakes, market crashes, extinctions – are not rare in networks with structures common in human systems. Unfortunately, we have witnessed dramatic hints of this dangerous potential in our global economy since 2007. On the bright side, "cascading successes" are also possible.

Diagnosing our Malaise

No strategy for improving the future can succeed that is not at least minimally aligned with human nature. The eventual failure of state sponsored communism clearly shows what happens when a strategy is out of sync with who and what we are. China's has (thus far) avoided the fate of the U.S.S.R. by tapping the power of entrepreneurial ambition through policies that grant a degree of economic freedom to an elite few. The creative power of the evolutionary process builds on previous successes. In developing new strategies we must work from the raw material – human nature – that evolution has provided.

State-sponsored communism ignored (among other things) the need for a minimum degree of freedom to strive for a personally defined ideal life. Similarly, the current version of capitalism neglects vital aspects of human nature. This misalignment is responsible for much of our isolation, alienation, and harmful behavior.

Capitalism, and the industrialization it has spawned, has unintentionally nullified some of the most important adaptive advantages of the last 300 million years. The need for love, belonging, community and contribution enabled our ancestors to thrive and evolve beyond their reptilian predecessors. Evolutionary biologists explain the adaptive advantages of cooperation: a hunter in a small community kills a large animal that yields more meat than his (or her) family can eat before it spoils. The best place to store the excess is in the bellies of fellow hunters, and their families, in the hope that they will reciprocate when he (or she) isn't so lucky. [10] As community deteriorates so, too, does the benefit of cooperation.

Urbanization, mobility, and population growth have accompanied capitalism's progress. These changes put our need for community into conflict with the satisfaction of material needs. Simply put, capitalism has eroded the conditions that make cooperation useful, leaving an essential part of our nature largely unfulfilled. We are left trying to fill this void with the material riches and distractions capitalism provides. The costs of this trade-off are felt in our hearts and reflected in the state of our planet. We can and must evolve our systems to realign the advantages of cooperation with the satisfaction of our material needs. Any survival strategy that makes us choose between happiness and meaning on one hand, and economic security on the other, is unworthy of our potential.

We (the authors) recently visited an Embera village in the rain forest of Panama. The Embera are an indigenous tribe who live much like their ancestors did, other than the outboard motors used to power their hand-carved canoes and a smattering of modern clothing. Small communities of extended families subsist mainly on fishing, harvesting corn and the fruits and root vegetables of the forest. The tribes near Panama City rely, in part, on tourism (sales of hand-crafted baskets) to fund what little they need from the outside world. But there are many villages in the remote Darién Province, far from the reaches of modernity.

Our guide was an American ex-patriot, Anne, who fell in love with an Embera tribesman while working on the filming of a movie at one of the villages. The couple split their time between Panama City, the U.S. and his village. By modern standards, the Embera are some of the most impoverished people in the world – no electricity, no running water, and limited access to health care. Despite this material poverty, Anne and her husband claim to be happiest during the time they live with the tribe. They are also convinced that the average Embera is far happier than the average American, something that struck us as fascinating. We thought about how this community likely shifted from a collective mode of production and distribution to a more modern economic system. Before selling the first basket or buying the first outboard motor, the Embera likely had few material wants they could not personally satisfy. Before learning about the "stuff" of the developed world, in some ways, this "poor" group of people could have almost any material thing they wanted – not all that different from a billionaire.

Like most of us, the Embera are born into a family and community that meet their physical and safety needs. But in their communal village neighbors freely share goods and services, and ensure all are cared for. Their path to higher level needs of love, belonging, self-esteem, and self-expression is, in many ways, significantly shorter and less arduous than for inhabitants of the developed world. (However, the routes leading to the top are less diverse for the Embera, constraining the ultimate experience of life for some.) The Embera love to speak with Anne about the "outside world." One fact they find unfathomable is that many Americans live great distances from family and friends. The Embera people derive their fulfillment mainly from community; community which is increasingly missing from the lives of many in the developed world. We suspect American culture's obsession with celebrities and television are, at least in part, a result of an unfulfilled need for human connection. Viewers imagine that television and film personalities are their friends – an ultimately dissatisfying illusion.

It is easy to understand the indirect and harmful effects of capitalism on community. Quite simply, the advantages of community are negatively correlated with its size. In a small community, such as an Embera village, satisfaction of an individual's altruistic drive is in complete alignment with survival. A giving person witnesses firsthand the benefit of her contribution and is confident that if, in the future, she is in need, someone in the community will be there to help. A small community can serve (among other things) as the social safety net provided (to some degree anyway) by government in most modern Western countries.

When a community becomes large, dispersed, and mobile the cooperative drive no longer serves the aim of survival. The example of the successful hunter sharing his meat explains this fact: if he does not know his fellow hunters well, he has little assurance that they will reciprocate in the future. The cost-benefit analysis changes: the hunter may be better off drying the extra meat, even if it involves significantly more work and a risk that much of it may spoil. What was once a winning survival strategy becomes, due to changed circumstances, a losing strategy.

Robert Pirsig's philosophy classic, Zen and the Art of Motorcycle Maintenance, touched on the link between urbanization and television culture on the one hand, and loss of community and connectedness on the other:

We see much more of this loneliness now. It's paradoxical that where people are the most closely crowded, in the big coastal cities in the East and West, the loneliness is the greatest. Back where people were so spread out in western Oregon and Idaho and Montana and the Dakotas you'd think the loneliness would have been greater, but we didn't see it so much.

The explanation, I suppose, is that the physical distance between people has nothing to do with loneliness. It's psychic distance, and in Montana and Idaho the physical distances are big but the psychic distances between people are small, and here it's reversed.

It's the primary America we're in. It hit the night before last in Prineville Junction and it's been with us ever since. There's this primary America of freeways and jet flights and TV and movie spectaculars. And people caught up in this primary America seem to go through huge portions of their lives without much consciousness of what's immediately around them. The media have convinced them that what's right around them is unimportant. And that's why they're lonely. You see it in their faces. First the little flicker of searching, and then when they look at you, you're just a kind of an object. You don't count. You're not what they're looking for. You're not on TV.

But in the secondary America we've been through, of back roads, and … Appaloosa horses, and sweeping mountain ranges, and meditative thoughts, and kids with pinecones and bumblebees and open sky above us mile after mile after mile, all through that, what was real, what was around us dominated. And so there wasn't much feeling of loneliness. That's the way it must have been a hundred or two hundred years ago. Hardly any people and hardly any loneliness. I'm undoubtedly overgeneralizing, but if the proper qualifications were introduced it would be true.

People probably weren't so lonely a hundred or two hundred years ago, but many were hungry and vulnerable to hardships most of us rarely think about today. It wasn't necessarily better then, but our gains have come at a cost. As we saw in Chapter 1, our isolation is mounting as our social fabric frays and thins.

Western society is rife with systems designed to foster aggressive competition. In education, grading on a curve is one striking example of how we instill in our children the warped view that another's success is necessarily one's own failure,[11] thus encouraging envy and creating psychic distance between people. Through this veil we see everything as zero-sum, a world in which losers and winners are always an unavoidable fact of life. We create a world where this is true, but it need not be so. Indeed, much of what makes life worth living is multiplied rather than diminished by sharing – knowledge, love, music, beauty, humor.

Our economic and political systems are full of structures that separate people from the consequences of their actions. This "disintegration" of cause and effect reveals itself in outcomes that defy common sense. We get bridges to nowhere, wars without end, pollution of vital natural resources, "food" bereft of nutritional value, and loans to people with no realistic means of repayment.

Morality, rooted in compassion and empathy, exists solely at the level of the individual.[12] Systems reflect these human qualities only to the degree to which they can effectively preserve and foster the moral responsibility of individuals. When systems (be they governments, religions, corporations, markets, or mobs) dominate the will of individuals, morality is destroyed. Thus, in spider-like institutions that dictate from on high, decisions tend to reflect the selfish values of our reptilian ancestors, un-tempered by the more evolved and humane values of compassion and care. History offers plenty of extreme examples of the personal nature of morality, when people followed orders despite their atrocious consequences: Nazi Germany, the U.S.S.R. under Stalin, the Cultural Revolution under Mao. Less dramatic but still tragic examples surround us, so pervasive we have to struggle to see them.

Norbert Wiener, a mathematician on the cutting edge of the mid-20th century "machine revolution," powerfully described the dangers of relying on centralized and dehumanized institutions to guide our course:

> When human atoms are knit into an organization in which they are used, not in their full right as responsible human beings, but as cogs and levers and rods, it matters little that their raw material is flesh and blood. *What is used as an element in a machine, is in fact an element in the machine.* Whether we entrust

our decision to machines of metal, or to those machines of flesh and blood which are bureaus and vast laboratories and armies and corporations, we shall never receive the right answers to our questions unless we ask the right questions.[13]

The questions asked today of humanity's most powerful machines of flesh and blood concern material growth: do we have more than we did last year? How much more? How much more relative to others? Given the modern malaise of isolation and disempowerment, not to mention the distressing state of the natural environment, it appears that these may not be the right questions.

Joseph Campbell clearly saw the potentially destructive force of machinelike human systems when he asked, "Is the system going to flatten you out and deny you your humanity, or are you going to be able to make use of the system to the attainment of human purposes?" Morality – our capacity for compassion and empathy – is at the core of our humanness. It does not exist in "the system" except to the degree that we, as individuals, withstand its dehumanizing top-down pressure. The future depends on our response to Campbell's challenge. It appears we have two primary alternatives. We can figure out how to raise superhuman people able to resist the oppressive force of the system (not a sustainable long-term solution). Or we can remake the system so it is aligned with, not against, our humanity. We can redesign it to nurture rather than repress our most humane qualities, and aim at fostering the realization of our full potential as responsible human beings. Said differently, we should follow Norbert Wiener's advice and ask the right questions otherwise we will continue creating a world that falls far short of our potential and our dreams.

The corporate form and its more recent offshoots are a formalized means of separating cause and effect, of severing the link between morality and our most powerful institutions. Anonymous stockholders collect profits with no danger of being held accountable, either legally or socially, for any harm done in the process. As essayist Ambrose Bierce put it, "Corporation: An ingenious device for obtaining profit without individual responsibility." This feature of modern capitalism, while enabling a free flow of capital, is a primary source of much of the human-made tragedy unleashed on the world. Fixing this flaw without drying up the capital market is critical to the continuing evolution of human systems. (Capital fluidity is essential to efficient and robust coordination and cooperation that provides us with the goods and services we need to flourish.)

Many who have recognized the destructive effects of our economic system call for a reversion to preindustrial ways. "Bartering" is a word often used among proponents of this approach, as if money really is the root of all evil. Assuming such a solution is theoretically possible, the resulting (and dramatic) decrease in our standard of living would undoubtedly shock pro-bartering anti-technologists. There is a reason why our ancestors invented money: it makes our lives better in innumerable ways.

(This is not to say, however, that bartering can't play an important role in local economies.)

Within the U.S., the anti-globalization movement and growling isolationist sentiments are similarly devolutionary. As we will explore in Chapter 7, evolution's direction is not reversible. We must move forward by integrating and tuning our collaborative self-organizing human system. The new system will nurture the full depth and breadth of human potential in harmony with the ecosystem of which we are an integral part.

Psychology offers insight into the source of the epidemic of disempowerment and alienation. "Cognitive dissonance" arises when a person holds contradictory beliefs. Because we are rational, when faced with such conflict, we must alter our beliefs to avoid contradiction. For example, a person believes that, 1) she is good, 2) she can positively impact her world, and 3) unnecessary human suffering should be minimized. When faced with the tragedy that surrounds her, she has to make a choice. She can choose to follow the path of Mother Teresa (give up everything and dedicate her life to others), adjust her beliefs to avoid dissonance, or some combination of the two. (Recent revelations of Mother Teresa's 40-year crisis of faith during which she felt "darkness," "loneliness," and "torture" suggest that personal solutions to this conflict are likely to be unsatisfactory.)

One response to this dissonance involves compromise: to preserve the belief that she is good, she must amend the belief that she can positively impact the world around her, or that unnecessary suffering should be avoided. This compromise typically takes the form of some combination of disempowerment (she can't impact the world around her) and alienation (others do not experience suffering the same way, empathy is suppressed). From here, we see how the conflict between our survival needs and our altruistic drives that results from lost community contributes to the epidemic of alienation and disempowerment. This epidemic likely has a thing or two to do with our addictions to drugs (both illicit and prescribed), television, video games, junk food, shopping, and pornography (we're not fessing up to our favorites). Dwelling in feelings of futility and isolation is too painful; we eagerly take whatever escape is available.

By now you're probably ready to cry in your beer and potato chips as you reach for the remote to turn on *American Idol*, but don't lose hope yet. As you will see in the following chapters, we have the knowledge and technology we need to heal the source of this psychic wound, and in the process lift humanity to new heights. Light waves, in their normal state, are incoherent (valleys and troughs of the waves are out of sync). When coaxed into coherence (meaning valleys and troughs are aligned) light waves transform into a laser beam (thanks to which you can use the remote to switch off the TV). Like light, our species has latent potential we can use to create a world we would be proud to leave to our children. The key to unlocking this potential is the same – aligning ourselves, individually and collectively, with our best nature and with one another.

As we will see in the next chapter, this idea is not revolutionary, but it was in 1776.

3 - Conspiracy of 1776

In Chapters 1 and 2 we located our position on the evolutionary map; examined the deep currents that brought humanity to this time and place, and developed some ideas about the sources of many of our problems. This leaves two important questions: Where do we want to go from here? And how do we get there? At first blush, these questions seem to have no hope of finding a consensus answer. Nonetheless, we are heading somewhere – as individuals, societies and as a species – so careful consideration of the destination, the route, and the means of transport will benefit us all.

Pondering these crucial questions leads to another: Why are these questions so rarely asked (or answered) today? One reason may be due to an over-reliance on the scientific method, which in the words of Robert Pirsig "has always been at the very best 20-20 hindsight. It's good for seeing where you've been. It's good for testing the truth of what you think you know, but it can't tell you where you ought to go."[1] The question of "the good" is not often asked by scientific minds. Norbert Wiener identified this lack of focus on the "ought to" questions as a particularly modern American problem: "There is one quality more important than 'know-how' and we cannot accuse the United States of any undue amount of it. This is 'know-what' by which we determine not only how to accomplish our purposes, but what our purposes are to be."[2] As will be seen, this has not always been true of America.

We are now at a pivotal moment in our evolutionary history where we have the wherewithal to consciously choose our purposes and our future. We are not at the mercy of our default operating systems or the spider institutions erected by past generations. So we ought to get about the business of deciding where it is we'd like to go. We don't all need to end up in the same place – indeed, diversity is essential to evolution.

Thankfully, much of the groundwork has been laid. The remarkable insight and intelligence of our forebears illuminate a way forward. The founders of the United States, in the *Declaration of Independence*, outlined the direction they believed we ought to head – toward a society that protects and values the unalienable rights of life, liberty and the pursuit of happiness. In fact, Enlightenment thinkers saw liberty as a means to an end, rather than as an end in itself: freedom is important because it enables individuals to independently choose their ideal of happiness and decide for themselves how to achieve it.

The Foundation of Liberty

Thomas Jefferson was responsible for including the ethereal idea of happiness in the *Declaration of Independence*. By examining evidence of Jefferson's thinking on happiness we can get a richer understanding of its meaning in the context of the Revolution. The political philosopher John Locke was the most likely inspiration for Jefferson's invocation of a right to pursue happiness.[3] Importantly, Locke warned not to confuse *imaginary* happiness for *solid, true and real* happiness:

> *The necessity of pursuing happiness [is] the foundation of liberty.* As therefore the highest perfection of intellectual nature lies in a careful and constant *pursuit of true and solid happiness;* so the care of ourselves, that we mistake not imaginary for real happiness, is the necessary foundation of our liberty. The stronger ties we have to an unalterable pursuit of happiness in general, which is our greatest good, and which, as such, our desires always follow, the more are we free from any necessary determination of our will to any particular action.[4]

Both Locke and Jefferson embraced the Epicurean ideal of happiness, which Jefferson set forth in clear terms:

> Happiness the aim of life.
> Virtue the foundation of happiness.
> Utility the test of virtue…
> Virtue consists in 1. Prudence. 2. Temperance. 3. Fortitude. 4. Justice.
> To which are opposed, 1. Folly. 2. Desire. 3. Fear. 4. Deceit.[5]

The founders' view of happiness offers insight into the modern malaise of alienation and disempowerment. Contemporary culture encourages habits that take us farther from the virtues that nurture happiness – watching television, playing video games, eating unhealthily, and shopping as recreation. As the Taoist master Lao Tze advised, "watch your habits, they become your character; watch your character, it becomes your destiny." Our habits are steering us toward an unhappy destiny. We are squandering our liberty.

The perspectives of Jefferson and Locke provide a guide for changing our course, to creating a happier destiny. First, real happiness should not to be confused with sensual pleasure (though temperate indulgence in passion and pleasure is not necessarily contrary to real happiness). Happy Meals and happy hours are detours. Second, automatic or thoughtless reaction to life's challenges, temptations and opportunities is unlikely to foster true happiness. This brings us back to the default operating system concept from the Introduction. When choices are dictated by the unexamined beliefs and attitudes determined by biological and social circumstances, freedom is illusory and happiness is distant. In the following chapter we will explore the possibility of consciously rewriting our personal operating system – the first step towards true freedom and real happiness.

Freedom *From*

The great statesmen and philosophers who framed the goals of the budding United States consciously created a new system of government, free from faulty, limiting, old-world beliefs (save racism and sexism). But they were grounded by a practical appreciation of the failings of human nature. The founders set a course that much of the world (and ever more of the world in recent times) has followed.

The American dreamers of 1776 sought to create a constrained system of government that would be relatively incapable of impinging on the rights of citizens. Jefferson explained the strategy: "The two enemies of the people are criminals and government, so let us tie the second down with the chains of the Constitution so the second will not become the legalized version of the first." The objective was to ensure freedom *from* government. Their project was necessarily a political one – it was about creating a system of government that would honor the rights of human beings to direct the course of their own lives. Over two hundred years after their heroic efforts, most of the developed world now lives their dream. Freedom of speech and religion, racial and gender equality under the law, access to an unbiased judicial system and a sphere of integrity over one's body and belongings are among our solidly entrenched Western values. If the revolutions taking hold in the Middle East are a sign, these *Western* democratic values are fast becoming *global* values.

Citizens of the United States enjoy an expansive space within which to create their lives and attain happiness. But many Americans remain narrowly focused on a political system that is structural-

> "We don't need a revolution in the United States. We already had one, thank you. What we need now is an American Evolution, where We the People evolve into the citizens the country's founders dreamed of."
> - Swami Beyondananda

Conspiracy of 1776 | 89

ly incapable of competently delivering essential ingredients for living a good life – affordable health care, quality public education, profitable work and a reliable safety net. Indeed, this is precisely what the founders intended – a government too divided to pose a serious threat to individual liberty. We are looking in the wrong place for our salvation – we are using a hammer to fasten a screw; our frustration is real, but our ineffectiveness is not the fault of the hammer.

Disillusionment with government and politicians is not mainly the result of any inherent failings of republican democracy or office holders. Rather, it is a symptom of the success of our system. Our material wealth has raised expectations. We are no longer satisfied with the basic needs of mere physical survival, which not long ago were the chief concern of the average citizen. The standard equipment for most citizens of the developed world are luxuries our grandparents could not have fathomed in their youth. Reliable and fuel efficient cars, smart phones, satellite television displayed on large, high-definition color screens, and lightning fast Internet access with the knowledge of the world at one's fingertips. That obesity is a pressing health issue in the developed world, especially among the poor, is striking evidence of how far we have come in providing the material essentials of life.

It is no wonder that a centuries old form of government, intentionally designed to be slow moving and of limited scope, is incapable of delivering what we now want. But beware: giving government authority to deliver what we now want would entail a concentration of power that would threaten our freedom (and cause Jefferson to roll over in his grave). The creation of a good *society* is by its nature a *social* project; we must focus attention on our social systems if we are to succeed.

Put differently, the founders built a strong foundation. It's up to us to erect a marvelous structure upon it, while taking care to not damage the foundation in the process. The founders' tools (politics) were suitable for their task, but the skills and tools we need are of a different kind. We must leverage the wealth of knowledge and abilities of humanity, not just a narrow subset of politicians and bureaucrats.

Our political and psychological discontent is rooted in the fact that the human social organism is in a transition phase. We are languishing at the end of a heroic and triumphant epic – the story of how we freed ourselves from authoritarian rule and the bonds of brute survival – and the time has come to begin writing the next saga. Thanks to the success of past dreamers, most of us need not be as brave in pursuing our own dreams – we will not be burned as heretics, or hung as traitors.

> "Now that you're free, America, what is it that you want? That is the question one asks every morning, every night, every July 4."
>
> - Roger Rosenblatt

Decoding a Cipher

Conspiracy theorists have made much of the symbols and text on the one-dollar bill; seeing clues to evil plots for world domination. Personally, we're not sure why malevolent conspirators would advertise their plans in such a public manner. Instead, we infer much less sinister meaning from the curious symbols and phrases on the Great Seal of the United States (completed in 1782), which has decorated America's most common paper currency since 1935. Thomas Jefferson, John Adams and Benjamin Franklin were among those who contributed to its design, thus it is a window into the minds of the dreamers on whose shoulders we now stand.

The pyramid, on the obverse of the Seal, is a potent symbol of humanity's relentless drive to create and to stretch the limits of our ingenuity. Its construction is unfinished – a sign of our fore-dreamers' understanding that human civilization's evolution will never be complete (though it will, like all things, come to an end). It is our turn to contribute to the unfolding tale of human striving.

Under the pyramid is inscribed the Latin phrase, "Novus ordo seclorum" which means "new order for the ages." An inaccurate translation is "new world order," which fuels the warnings of plans for world domination by an elite cabal, often associated with the Free Masons, the Illuminati, or the Bilderberg Group. A more reasonable interpretation seems likely. The values reflected in the founding of the United States, were radical for their time (and remain so in many parts of the world) and represented a new way of ordering human relationships with individual freedom and happiness at its core. Jefferson described the essence of this new order: "May [our Declaration of Independence] be to the world, what I believe it will be (to some parts sooner, to others later, but finally to all), the signal of arousing men to burst the chains under which monkish ignorance and superstition had persuaded them to bind themselves, and to assume the blessings and security of self-government... All eyes are opened, or opening, to the rights of man." Jefferson's proclamation also hints at the symbolic meaning of the all-seeing eye atop the pyramid: it is witnessing the unfolding of human freedom and with it, human happiness and potential.

The foresight of Jefferson's prediction is becoming clearer by the day. Those of us fortunate enough to live where democracy is firmly entrenched can help ensure its continued evolution: we can show the rest of the world the marvels democracy unlocks when aligned with our creativity and compassion. We can put our miraculous potential to the task of extending freedom to all, and in so doing, protect our own freedom and deepen our own happiness.

The Art of Associating

Now that many of us have achieved freedom *from* coercive control (whether by political, religious, family or other institutions), we must practice exercising our freedom *to*. How we choose to exercise (or not exercise) our liberty will profoundly shape the future. As the liberal student of American democracy in the 1830s, Alexis de Tocqueville taught, "The health of a democratic society may be measured by the quality of functions performed by private citizens." De Tocqueville found the United States to be a healthy democratic society:

> Americans of all ages, all conditions, and all dispositions constantly form associations. They have not only commercial and manufacturing companies, in which all take part, but associations of a thousand other kinds, religious, moral, serious, futile, general or restricted, enormous or diminutive. The Americans make associations to give entertainments, to found seminaries, to build inns, to construct churches, to diffuse books, to send missionaries to the antipodes; in this manner they found hospitals, prisons, and schools. ... Wherever at the head of some new undertaking you see the government in France, or a man of rank in England, in the United States you will be sure to find an association.
>
> *Nothing, in my opinion, is more deserving of our attention than the intellectual and moral associations of America ... In democratic countries the science of association is the mother of science; the progress of all the rest depends upon the progress it has made.*
>
> *Among the laws that rule human societies there is one which seems to be more precise and clear than all others. If men are to remain civilized or to become so, the art of associating together must grow and improve in the same ratio in which the equality of conditions is increased.*[6]

Unfortunately, the health of American democracy, when measured in terms of the art of associating, appears to be declining. For example, statistics on traditional organizations (Lions, Rotary, Kiwanis Clubs) that address community challenges reveal a dramatic downward trend.[7] Optimistically, it is possible these surveys fail to measure less conventional means of organization (Crop Mob, for example). But the decline in social engagement goes well beyond the bounds of formal (or informal) groups. Baby boomers are less likely to entertain friends, organize bridge or poker games, let alone *know* their neighbors, in comparison to their parents. Baby boomers' children (Gen Xers) are even less likely to engage in such informal social activities. Americans seem to have lost their community spirit.

Social scientists debate the cause of this trend. Robert D. Putnam's best seller, *Bowling Alone*, surveys the potential culprits in the decline of American social capital. He concludes that suburban sprawl and increased work hours are responsible for about 20% of the downward trend. Putnam points to television as a prime suspect in the disintegration of American social capital. Americans are spending ever more of their lives mesmerized by a glowing box of light that tends to dim, rather than enlighten, the experience of the world and one another.[8] Of course, not all television viewing is equal – it is a powerful communication medium that can inform and energize collective action, or misinform and numb viewers into complacency. However, regardless of the programming content, a person is not actively engaged in the art of associating while staring at the flat screen. The interactive nature of the Internet may pull us out of the spectator mode of television viewing toward the participant mode of discussion forums, social networks and multiplayer role-playing games. Time will tell if we choose to realize this potential.

Part of the observed decline may be just relative: a spike in civic and social engagement among the "war generation" (those born in the 1920s and 30s) is making us look worse than we really are.

The collective efforts of a nation fighting for justice and survival galvanized this generation during their most impressionable years, laying a foundation for a lifetime of community organization and engagement. Thus, it might not be that baby boomers and Gen Xers are uniquely disengaged, but that their parents and grandparents (respectively) were uniquely engaged. Television and the generational imprint of war are the answers provided by the analytic tool of the scientific method, and they are certainly informative, but they do not tell the whole picture.

A pattern began to form hundreds of years ago, when people started to break the bonds of servitude to authoritarian institutions in significant ways: the Protestant Reformation and the signing of the Magna Carta were watershed moments in the rise of the individual. However, in the process of claiming our individual power, we stretch and sometimes break the bonds in our social fabric that formerly provided the physical and psychological security needed to function well in this world.[9] Today, we are no longer bound to follow the dictates of church leaders or kings, but no longer are the church or royalty obligated to provide for our basic needs; nor are we bound to one another in our obedience and servitude. We loosened many restrictive threads of our social fabric, yet are still trying to reweave it in a way that aligns liberty and the pursuit of happiness with the need for security and community.

Thankfully, we have not disintegrated into chaos and have managed, in fits and starts, to recreate security and community. Early efforts, which continue to this day, involved recreating old hierarchical structures, but holding the power to appoint the occupier of the top spot (republican democracy, for example). While this is a step in the right direction, it is not the best we can do. Advances in the art of associating may be signs of the beginnings of a later stage – the starfish stage – of this evolutionary unfolding. The recent disintegration of the American social fabric may be a devolution or it may represent a stage of collective rethinking. The baby boomers found their parents' rigidity and respect for authority unappealing. In reacting against it, they embraced personal freedom and diversity, and in the process unraveled part of the social tapestry. Today we have the benefit of circumspection and can begin to weave a new pattern that includes the best of both worlds. We can draw on the vital and strong threads of collective action and community while including the elastic and luminous threads of diversity and acceptance.

An alternative and less optimistic view of our fraying social fabric is seen in the parallels between the decaying Roman Empire and our own social unraveling. "Panem et circenses" or "bread and circuses" describes the willingness of the Roman populace to trade their power as citizens for the superficial pleasures (Locke's "imaginary happiness") of cheap food and entertainment. The modern malaise surveyed in Chapter 1 (evidenced by the rise in obesity and television viewing) points to the possibility that history is repeating itself. Americans are trading their liberty and power for trivialities. But this theory leads us to ask, why now? Why are so many people willing to make this tragic deal today?

This devolution is undoubtedly the result of a confluence of interrelated forces. As explored in Chapter 2, unintended effects of modern capitalism disconnect citizens from one another (alienation) and from their ability to contribute meaningfully to their communities (disempowerment). The Vietnam War, Watergate, and, more recently, nonexistent weapons of mass destruction in Iraq contributed to a loss of faith in the political system and rise in cynicism. In the past forty years, the American political process has become far less participatory and more of a spectator sport – Americans give money to candidates, but no longer volunteer their talents to political campaigns.[10] Though cynicism may have first spread among the electorate, it has now also infected leaders. Rather than calling forth the best in our natures, many politicians (with notable exceptions) and the power brokers who appoint them pander to baser inclinations (racism, nationalism and greed) and manipulate with bread and circuses.

A fact likely contributing to Americans' disengagement is that the goals that inspired earlier generations have been reached. We lack a focus for our own collective striving that would inspire a strong sense of civic duty. Events and movements of momentous import galvanized our predecessors. Revolting against tyranny, fighting for freedom, triumphing against evil, realizing a manifest destiny, surviving the Great Depression, achieving women's suffrage, securing civil rights, and protesting the Vietnam war – these events called forth the heroes and heroines in our grandparents as they strode the path paved by their forebears. Put differently, the siren song of bread and circuses is harder to resist when there is not even a faint whisper of a rousing victory march on the horizon.

From this viewpoint we can see rough outlines of possible solutions (which will be fleshed out in later chapters). First, we need to inspire civic engagement – by offering people opportunities to take part in something bigger than themselves and their nuclear family that do not require wholesale changes in their lifestyle. Reweaving our social fabric will be a gradual process, an evolution rather than a revolution. Second, we need a galvanizing vision of the future, something to work toward together. In the past, war served this purpose to great effect, but we must find a way of inspiring coordination and cooperation without the need for a Hitler. As William James wisely advised over a century ago, we need a "moral equivalent of war" if we are to preserve or improve our ability to form powerful collectives with the discipline needed to positively reshape our world.

Psychologist Erich Fromm (a contemporary of Abraham Maslow) eloquently described a way forward: "There is only one possible, productive solution for the relationship of individualized man with the world: his active solidarity with all men and his spontaneous activity, love and work, which unite him again with the world, not by primary ties [that is, institutions] but as a free and independent individual."[11] (Fromm points to a quality of good societies that we will return to later – transcendence of the self versus other duality.) Technology is directly connecting more and more individuals, circumventing centralized institutions that, until recently, were necessary for large-scale collective action. With this change comes the possibility of bringing Fromm's vision into being in a powerful and widespread way.

Some Dreams are Nightmares

As we consider means of reweaving our frayed social fabric, we must be aware that our current splintered condition harbors a potential dark side. People suffering from insecurity and fear are vulnerable to following irrational paths that lead away from life, liberty and the attainment of true happiness. No student of history can doubt that horrific things are possible when a critical mass of human beings, starved for connection, meaning and security, surrender their will to a charismatic leader. We've learned that community can be built through a common ideology that demonizes others. Adolph Hitler's horrific triumph was in part the result of the alienation and powerlessness felt by the lower middle class in post WWI Germany.[12] His awareness of this exploitable weakness is reflected in a passage from *Mein Kampf*:

> The mass meeting is necessary if only for the reason that in it the individual, who is becoming an adherent of a new movement feels lonely and is easily seized with the fear of being alone, receives for the first time the pictures of a greater community, something that has a strengthening and encouraging effect on most people .... If he steps for the first time out of his small workshop or out of the big enterprise, in which he feels very small, into the mass meeting and is now surrounded by thousands and thousands of people with the same conviction ... he himself succumbs to the magic influence of what we call mass suggestion.

The comfort of belonging, strengthened by the egoistic satisfaction of feeling superior to others, was a major psychological source of Nazism's power. The same is true for extremist ideologies of today – fundamentalist religious movements (of which Islam is but one, though among the most frightening), right-wing militia groups, and neo-Nazis to name a few. Community, when divorced from freedom and compassion, is a dangerous force.

Since we are unlikely to cure human beings of their tendency to hand over their power to charismatic leaders any time soon (though small changes on this front can have huge effects), we must find a practical solution. This feature of human nature must be harnessed, as it has in the past, for positive change. A powerful vision of a future based on liberty and compassion, and a way to get there, can create healthy community and inspire concerted social action.

Other risks to liberty abound. The increasingly global challenges facing our species demand global answers. If the international entities granted the authority to address these issues are also given some or all of the powers of the expansive welfare state, such as control over healthcare, education, and pensions, the resulting concentration of power will be positively Orwellian. Such changes will very likely be gradual and subtle – and thereby exceedingly dangerous. Thus, the urgency for a dynamic and robust society to counterbalance (and eventually shrink) the scope and power of centralized government will only increase.

The dangers posed by a strong centralized government with access to surveillance technology, and with no respect for the principle of individual liberty, need not be left to the imagination. Dubai, with its façade of luxury masking rampant greed and human rights abuses, is proof of the dangers of absolute power joining forces with omnipresent surveillance.[13] The willingness of U.S. citizens to surrender their privacy in the face of post 9/11 terrorist threats offers good reason to fear the rise of "Big Brother" even in nations with relatively deep respect for individual liberty.[14]

The rise of China, with its deep-seated collectivist values[15] that discount the importance of liberty, also poses a challenge to classical liberal values. Many predict a cold war of ideology in the coming decades, as Western liberalism competes with China's authoritarian quasi-communism for the hearts and minds of humanity. The winner will be the one demonstrating a superior ability to provide for the material, psychological and spiritual well-being of its constituents. Or the one that manages to crush the will of the people through force. China regularly and publicly invests in the infrastructures of developing nations, signaling its awareness of the competition of ideals. It is time for lovers of freedom to step up to the plate. If the Western democratic ideals are to triumph, we must show – through convincing real-world proof, not pompous rhetoric or military might – that our way is the best way. To this end, it is urgent that we again become masters of the art of associating, and imbue technology and capitalism with a human soul.

The potential of technology to positively transform civilization and enable humanity to continue on the path toward peace and freedom is not our destiny. It is a possibility that faces strong countervailing forces. We must be diligent.

Liberty Endangered

There is a serious threat already taking hold of U.S. democracy. The promises of life, liberty and the pursuit of happiness are increasingly hollowed by special interests' influence in the political system. Congressional aides write legislation to regulate industry, then "graduate" to high paying lobbying positions for those same industries. The Supreme Court granted corporations the right to spend unlimited amounts of money to influence elections. The voice of the people is a faint whisper amid the cacophony of deal making and influence peddling.

Political scientists (applying public choice theory) explain the system dynamics that lead to this type of corruption. Benefits are concentrated while costs are diffuse. Thus, beneficiaries can exert more influence on policy makers than the masses of relatively disinterested citizens who are busy living their lives. The effects of this dysfunction are reaching a critical level. Unsustainable programs (Medicare, for example), public worker pensions, and military spending are threatening long-term economic stability.

The unrelenting drive for material gain that fuels most economic efforts is gaining a disturbingly strong hold on our political system. Milton Friedman, an ardent proponent of free market capitalism, warned of the danger of joining economic interests to political clout which makes concentration of power "almost inevitable."[16] Friedman saw the danger posed by government intervention in the economic realm, but similar dangers exist where, as is increasingly the case, the economic realm is intervening in government.

Society's myopic focus on monetary gain to the detriment of other considerations leads to behavior that does not reflect our higher values. Long-term effects are ignored in favor of immediate return. For example, mortgage-backed securities masked fundamentally defective subprime debt, resulting in a time bomb that crippled the economy. When business plays a central role in crafting legislation, drafting regulations and electing our leaders, too much influence emanates from the economic motives of a few, to the detriment of the rest.

Concentrated power is toxic to liberty: power corrupts, and absolute power corrupts absolutely. It is often those with the best intentions that lay the groundwork for the centralization of power. Milton Friedman warned, "the great tragedy of the drive to centralization, as of the drive to extend the scope of government in general, is that it is mostly led by men of good will who will be the first to rue its consequences."[17] The most immediate reactions to public problems often involve the creation or expansion of bureaucracy. The long-term cost of increasingly centralized power seems a vague and far-off problem relative to the issue at hand. But short-term fixes often come at the potentially disastrous price of not only liberty, but also the progress liberty enables. Worse still, these fixes often end up aggravating the original problem.

> "As the years pass, the power of government becomes more and more pervasive. It is a power to suffocate both people and causes. Those in power, whatever their politics, want only to perpetuate it."
>
> — Justice Douglas

While it is easy for those on the political left to see the dangers posed by business interests' influence over government, there is also reason for concern regarding labor unions' sway in politics. California offers a stark illustration of the insidious influence of public sector labor unions. Over the past three decades the state prison guard union has become one of the most powerful lobbying groups.

Under its influence, California has increased the number of prisons from 12 in 1980 to 33 in 2000. From 1980 to 2010 California's prison population rose from 22,600 to 167,000 – an increase of over 800% – helping to make the U.S. the top incarcerator in the world.[18] This political clout has directly and severely constrained the freedom of tens of thousands of human beings – a more stark illustration of the threat of centralized power to liberty is difficult to imagine.

In 2006, Roderick Hickman resigned from his post as Secretary for the California Department of Corrections and Rehabilitation, because the overwhelming power of the union made it impossible to do his job. According to Hickman, the union controlled policy decisions, including undermining efforts to divert offenders from prison and reduce the prison population.[19] This reality should open the eyes of those who decry the *Citizens United* decision while condemning politicians who take a hard line on public unions.

The danger that public sector unions pose to democracy is real. They can and do warp government for their own purposes. In fact, these workers were barred from unionizing until the middle of the 20th century. A no less died-in-the-wool, pro-government figure than FDR warned of the risk posed by public worker unionization: "Meticulous attention should be paid to the special relations and obligations of public servants to the public itself and to the Government.... The process of collective bargaining, as usually understood, cannot be transplanted into the public service."[20] Unfortunately, FDR's sage advice has gone unheeded.

Public sector unions are corrupting democracy. As proclaimed by one of its leaders, "We have the ability, in a sense, to elect our own boss."[21] The more powerful unions become, the more they are able to hijack the political process. In the end, government workers and their union reps decide public policy, rather than voters and their elected representatives. A symbiotic relationship develops: the unions contribute money and votes, and politicians reciprocate with increased benefits. A favored perk is the "defined benefit" pension, which can double as politicians' discretionary cookie jars (aka, "slush funds") that enable them to spend money now without raising taxes to fund the expense. The tab is left for future politicians – and citizens – to deal with. This corrupt two-headed beast is a parasite, diverting essential resources from the rest of society and seriously compromising our collective well-being.

Further, since government enjoys monopoly power in most of the services it provides, and is not going out of business any time soon, workers need not worry about compromising the financial viability of their employer. Similarly, the importance of their jobs (the very reason the government provides their services) – firefighting, law enforcement, transportation, education – gives these workers leverage to demand unreasonable benefits. Negotiated contracts can extend far into the future, leaving new leadership bound to the decisions of their predecessors (even through bankruptcy), thus thwarting the democratic process. The havoc caused by these systemic breakdowns is coming to light – massive unfunded pension obligations are threatening the future of many states, including California. The fate of Greece, teetering on the brink of default due to its gluttonous public sector, offers a stark warning.

The connection between capitalism and democracy runs deep and is unbreakable; if you are beholden to a higher power for your survival, then freedom is an illusion. When power is concentrated, individual freedom is threatened. It matters little whether the power is in the hands of a dictator, a large bureaucratic government, or a monopolistic corporation.

Before WWII, the BBC – which held a government radio monopoly – banned Winston Churchill from the airwaves because anti-Hitler views conflicted with the opinions of those in power at the time.[22] Today Rupert Murdoch's hold on US and British media outlets poses a similar threat by enabling him to manipulate public opinion in conformity with his personal political agenda.[23]

In the U.S., the debate between big and small government typically breaks down according to party lines, with Democrats in favor of and Republicans against government-run social programs. The irony is that, since WWII, Republican presidents have increased government spending (as a percentage of GDP) more than Democratic presidents. It appears the true disagreement is not the size of government, but which part of the government should be bigger – social programs or the military. Each, if too large, is a threat to freedom. Conservatives are quite cognizant of the dangers of government at the moment (with Obama in office); liberals need only recall George W. Bush's presidency to sense the threat of a too powerful central government. Frustration at this state of affairs has fueled the rise of the Tea Party, which so far is more adept at pointing out problems than proposing realistic sustainable solutions.

Politicians on both sides of the partisan divide are incapable of or unwilling to constrain the scope of government. This should not be surprising, considering the sacrifices necessary to run for political office (time, huge sums of money), and the colossal effort needed to dismantle a dysfunctional behemoth. Very few of those who are truly antiestablishment are willing to pay the high price of becoming part of the establishment. The few who do are vulnerable to the seductive siren song of political power – we are adaptable creatures. Thus, the job of shrinking government must fall chiefly to those outside the political system.

Social Studies

The passion for shrinking the size of government must be matched with solutions that fill the important role now played (with varying degrees of competence) by government. Preserving the ideals of life, liberty and the pursuit of happiness requires a foundation – a threshold level of order, safety, and public goods (education and infrastructure, for example). Today this foundation is predominantly provided by government. An alternative source of these essentials is society itself – the voluntary coordination and cooperation that leaves power in the hands of the people.

The inability of Iraq and Afghanistan to build strong and stable democratic governments shows the connection between government and society as a source of order and security. Neither has a foundation of a stable society, what sociologists call "social capital," or respect for the individual on which to build democratic institutions. Religious and tribal identities are like quicksand, making democracy fragile and unstable. Russia is another example of a nation seemingly incapable of establishing a sustainable genuine democracy. Its failure is due, in part, to the continued influence of Soviet anti-modernism (rampant corruption and a rigid bureaucratic hierarchy). Social capital cannot flourish in this harsh environment. If America were to shrink the size of government without an accompanying expansion and deepening of society, it would risk harming the order, security, and public goods necessary to preserve freedom and enable the attainment of real happiness. Put simply, we should be careful not to throw the baby out with the bath water. If we do not responsibly exercise our freedom *to*, we run a serious risk of losing our freedom *from*.

We should think of our goal as the creation of a safe and nurturing environment in which people can flourish within the opening cleared by the dreamers of past generations. We are gardeners – preparing the soil, providing sufficient irrigation, securing our progress against scavengers, trading seeds, sharing knowledge and raising barns.

Through collective action in a community of caring people we are better able to realize our unique individual potential. We have a choice. We can continue delegating much of this important work to a bureaucratic government, or we can do it ourselves through a robust, vibrant and free society.

The idea that a more robust society is the solution to big centralized government is not new or fringe: John Kennedy famously intoned, "Ask not what your country can do for you; ask what you can do for your country." JFK's call is being echoed today across the Atlantic. In the United Kingdom, "Big Society" is a plan backed by the coalition of Conservatives and Liberal Democrats whose aim is to shift governmental power to local people and communities. In touting the merits of his plan, Prime Minister David Cameron sings the praises of the starfish:

> We know instinctively that the state is often too inhuman, monolithic and clumsy to tackle our deepest social problems. We know that the best ideas come from the ground up, not the top down. We know that when you give people and communities more power over their lives, more power to come together and work together to make life better – great things happen.[24]

While Cameron's effort to tap the latent power of the starfish model is commendable, transforming spiders into starfish is fraught with difficulties (like dealing with those whose livelihood and identity depend on preserving the status quo). Creating an environment in which existing starfish can thrive and multiply seems a much more natural and efficient approach.

The creative leaps taken by the conspiracy of dreamers, Class of 1776, should not be seen as an isolated episode. Rather, their achievements were a watershed moment in the unfolding of the full breadth and depth of human potential. Along this journey, most of our ancestors had precious few choices about the course of their lives. Instead, they toiled as slaves, labored as serfs, fought wars to protect the interests of the powerful, and were burned at the stake for their religious beliefs. The first step in unlocking their fetters was securing their freedom *from* state coercion, from the authoritarian institutions that controlled and used them for ends not of their own choosing. While there remains progress to be made on these fronts (even in the Western world), the next turning point is upon us. It is time to exercise our freedom *to* and use it to create a better future for all of humanity. In adventuring through this uncharted territory we may arrive at the true, real and solid happiness that our forebears set out for long ago.[25]

4 – Surf or Sink

The human being is part of the whole, called by us the "universe," a part limited in time and space. He experiences himself, his thoughts and feelings, as something separate from the rest – a kind of optical delusion of consciousness.

This delusion is a kind of prison for us, restricting us to our personal desires. Our task must be to free ourselves from this prison by widening our circle of compassion to embrace all living creatures and the whole of nature in its beauty.

– Albert Einstein

Transcending the Illusion

I (Renée) can recall vividly the first time I awakened to an awareness of the illusory quality of our separateness. Paul and I were scuba diving in the Sea of Cortez, where we suddenly found ourselves in a school of mackerel – the tiny dashes of silver moved as one, reflecting the sunlight above. A pair of sea lions darted into the glimmering river of mercurial fish, parting the current as if by a repulsive magnetic force. We were resting on the seabed, looking up at the entwined sea lions encircled by a halo of glowing liquid mackerel. Light and shadow danced in synchronous movement. It was an experience words can only point to from a distance – it was beyond the reach of language. Perhaps the water changed my perception, but it seemed that we were all part of the same living, breathing, dancing organism. I've carried this feeling with me ever since, sometimes more, sometimes less: the line we draw between you and me, us and them, is more a habit of thinking than a quality of reality. In Einstein's words, this moment of grace and atonement ("at-one-ment") freed me from the prison of separateness.

Since this awakening I have encountered many thinkers, from diverse areas of knowledge, who have expressed the idea of a unity of being. Among them are the Advaita Vedanta philosophers who, for thousands of years, have been teaching that all of reality is grounded in a non-dual unified energy. (The ground of being, *Brahman*, in Hindu and Advaita teachings, likely comes from the same roots as *Abraham* in the Judeo-Christian tradition – unity is everywhere.) The physicist David Bohm and neuroscientist Karl Pribram developed the theory of a holographic universe. They suggest (generally speaking) that all of physical reality is composed of repeating patterns within repeating patterns that emanate from an integrated whole. Bohm called this whole the "implicate order." Ancient wisdom and the edges of modern science point toward the underlying unity of all existence.

I discovered that my experience of atonement is part of a stream of human thought spanning thousands of years, traversing the globe, and crossing an array of disciplines. Einstein, Buddha, Christ, Lao Tzu and innumerable others whose names are lost to history were among the illustrious dreamers who repeated the truth, "We are one." Their message is getting louder by the day.

This is not to say that our individuality ought to be discounted. Indeed, our vibrant existence owes much to the dynamic interplay between collective and individual aspects of being. But blindness to our underlying unity is an obstacle to realizing our true potential as unique beings. Real happiness, the kind Jefferson had in mind, is most probable when, as Einstein said, we escape the prison of our separateness and move beyond our personal desires.

The looking glass of evolution brings into view the empirical truth of essential oneness. Once the Earth stabilized sufficiently, some patterns of atoms developed an ability to create copies of themselves. Eventually some of these fecund molecules joined together to form the beginnings of a cellular structure; something akin to the lipid bilayers that make up the walls of our cells. Then, single celled organisms came into being and ruled the Earth for billions of years. Amid this increasingly competitive primordial stew some cells began to explore the possibility of collaborating and, through trial and error, learned the value of collective effort. We are the descendants of those cells. Today evolution is repeating itself (like a hologram) as humanity continues to explore ever-evolving patterns of collaboration. Most of us are active participants in the complex interconnected form of collaboration known as global capitalism, which continuously reshapes our material world. This is where the rubber is hitting the road on the evolutionary highway.

Scientists in the field of social neurology are documenting the ways our brains are hard-wired to sync with one another. If you doubt how critical this synchronizing ability is to our survival, consider the challenges facing those with autism, that is, those whose synchronizing ability is severely impaired. Babies provided solely with the material necessities of survival, but not human contact, are severely stunted. Lonely people are more vulnerable to illness.[1] Solitary confinement is the harshest punishment our prisons offer short of execution. We are social creatures, hardwired to connect and to live in communities. Indeed, our sociability is a key feature distinguishing us from our primate cousins. Each of us is a part, a cell, in the larger organism of humanity, which is itself part of the organism of Earth. Failure to grasp fully the implications of this biological reality imperils our continued evolution, and possibly our survival. This planet is full of organisms that stalled on the evolutionary highway, whose ancestors resembled them in nearly every material respect. One purpose of this book is to act as a road sign on this highway: "Right lane must exit, merge left to continue evolving."

Change Your Mind, Change Your World

We live in a world of self-fulfilling prophecies: our stories about how the world works have a powerful influence on how the world works. This is not new age self-help mumbo jumbo (though some extreme versions do push the envelope of rationality). Clearly, the force of gravity and the impermeability of solid objects are not created by our beliefs – there are huge areas of our physical existence that no amount of attitude adjustment can alter. However, major parts of reality are socially constructed. There are facts that are true only because a critical mass of human beings have bought into their truth. Barack Obama is the President of the United States, red traffic lights mean stop, diamonds are valuable, U.S. Treasury Bonds are safe investments. All of these are true only because enough people agree (or agreed) that they are true.[2] If an epidemic of amnesia struck the entire human race these "facts" would evaporate, while gravity would continue keeping us rooted to the Earth. Our beliefs create these socially constructed parts of our reality. Thus, we have the ability to transform reality by simply changing enough minds.

Politicians and corporations know the importance of convincing others of *their version* of the truth, usually for the material benefit of a few at the expense of many. To shape the future for the benefit of all humanity, we must first awaken to the power of belief and to our ability to choose consciously. So, what is the source of *your beliefs*? Have you consciously chosen your beliefs about the world, or were they instilled by your parents, peers, television, religion, and culture? This indoctrination works if you're content with the status quo, but not if you want to create a better world.

The power of belief extends to our own physiology. The form a human body takes is based on the recipe contained in its genes. As any cook knows, a recipe is only one part (though important) of the meal-making process. The quality of the ingredients (you are what you eat), the environmental conditions (the humidity of the oven, for example), and the skill of the chef all combine to create the end product. Similarly, the physical form we take is not completely dictated by our DNA.

Beliefs have a strong influence on how the body perceives, and responds to the outside world. If, for example, you're terrified of snakes, you're more likely to mistake a coiled rope on the ground for a snake. When you see the rope your mind will scream, "Snake!" and your body will follow its genetically coded strategy for avoiding danger (a burst of adrenaline followed by a rapid flight). Your belief about the danger of snakes thus caused your physiological response.[3]

If this kind of error (that is, seeing danger where none exists) occurred regularly it would have a damaging impact on your health. In fact, research shows that if these errors occur during pregnancy, the fetus faces a higher likelihood of suffering mental disorders (a result of epigenetic changes to stress hormone processes). These afflictions include anxiety and paranoia, and thus the child will be more likely to mistake ropes for snakes or, more generally, to see the world as a scary place.[4] A society filled with scared, anxious and stressed people is likely to result in conditions that warrant fear and anxiety. For example, there would be many nervous people with itchy fingers toting guns with hair-triggers. We mistakenly think we look at our world through a window, when we're actually gazing into a mirror. As the Talmud teaches, "We do not see the world as it is. We see the world as we are."

Although the specific means by which beliefs shape our physiology are fairly new discoveries, the power of the mind to condition our biology is old news. Knowledge of the placebo effect – the positive response of a patient to an inert medication – dates to at least the ancient Greeks. Interestingly, the placebo effect may be increasing in strength in the U.S. This change has prompted drug companies (normally cutthroat competitors) to join forces to uncover the roots of the strengthening placebo effect "problem." This is a problem for them because FDA approval of a new drug requires proof that it is more effective than a placebo. Thus, the increasing strength of the placebo response is raising the bar for drug manufacturers to bring new products to market. One theory explaining the increased placebo effect is that the mass marketing of drugs is conditioning Americans to believe in their effectiveness. This belief is, in turn, shaping our physiological reality, giving our minds more power to heal our bodies.[5]

A telling example of the truth that our beliefs shape our perceptions and our perceptions determine our reality is provided by two of the most famous economists of all-time – Adam Smith, and Karl Marx. As we have seen, Adam Smith, an optimist, saw the potential greatness of human beings working in harmony. His reality was shaped by his view that human nature included a major dose of benevolence. Smith's view of human nature was undoubtedly based in part on his own nature – he was uncommonly charitable. His was a world of abundance, of the real potential for universal opulence. Smith was a dreamer, and many of us are now living his beautiful dream.

Marx, on the other hand, saw history through the lens of conflict and struggle. In his view, wealth was capped by the capacity of labor (since he believed only labor produces value). Thus, distribution rather than growth was the heart of the matter – universal opulence was not a possibility in his world. Marx witnessed three of his children die of malnutrition while he, despite holding a doctorate, did not find employment. Apparently the dictate "from each according to his abilities, to each according to his needs" was an abstract concept for Marx rather than words to live by. A common word in the titles of his works is "critique" (or some variation of it).

In contrast to Smith's benevolence, Marx's life is the story of a cynical man locked in the prison of his personal ambitions. His world of scarcity could only be improved through violent revolution. Marx saw a nightmare, and his nightmare became reality for millions trapped within the confines of the Iron Curtain, and is still the reality for millions who live in North Korea. (Although, in Marx's defense, perhaps in recognition of the fearsome conception of reality spawned by his work, he ultimately denied being a "Marxist.")

Our concept of the world – the stories we tell ourselves about what matters and what is possible – shapes our reality. If, like Marx, we think of the world as a scary place where people are doomed to misery and lack, then we will create scarcity. Our precious lives will be wasted piling sandbags, suspiciously eyeing one another, preparing for the coming tsunami (of our own making). If, like Smith, we conceive of the world as a magical place in which we all have the potential to experience grace and joy, then we will share abundance and hope. We will spend our precious lives shaping surfboards, discovering balance and alignment, harnessing the thrilling power of the ocean to move us forward in rational exuberance. Marx was miserably stacking sandbags; Smith was joyfully riding the waves. Whose example will we follow?

The Mind Shift Meme

Regardless of your particular location on the political spectrum, you likely have convenient scapegoats when things go wrong (which is pretty much a daily occurrence). From the left, your favorite go-to punching bags may be "Corporate America" and Fox News. On the right your targets may be the "Liberal Media" and the Communist conspiracy taking hold in Washington. Both sides are united in condemning politicians and espousing the need to bring values back to Washington. It's doubtful either side's solutions would get to the heart of the problems we face.

One of the most distinguished dreamers of the twentieth century, Albert Einstein, explained, "Problems cannot be solved by the same level of thinking that created them." We have a choice, we can continue to be spectators, jeering and cheering from the sidelines, or we can rise to a new level of thinking and become participants. The same old tune of "less taxes" versus "more government" is simply not going to get us where we want to be. (Our leaders' recent compromise, lower taxes and more spending, is clearly not a viable long-term solution.) As long as we remain spectators, our elected leaders will mirror the values we express in our actions: complacency, self-interest, and a failure of imagination. If we are to transform our world into the place we would choose for ourselves and our children, we should consider the wisdom of the elders of the Hopi tribe and be "the ones we have been waiting for."

Well-meaning people speak passionately of the "fight," "crusade," "war" and "struggle" in their pleas to energize change. Implied in these messages is the notion that conflict is necessary to bring about a better world. Conflict is the source of much of what we are trying to change, conflict with nature and between races, classes, tribes, ethnicities. Our inability or unwillingness to let go of the old ways of thinking is the greatest obstacle to positive change. This is also *great news*, as it is within our power to change our ways of thinking.

A very cynical family member recently stated that we have no chance of changing the world because we don't have an army; our "enemies" have all the power, military and otherwise, while we have none. We explained our perspective to him: over here (gesturing to the salt and pepper shakers on the table) the power-having groups (the so-called enemies) are battling at the OK Corral and making a fine mess of things. Even if we gathered our best posse to join the fight, we would accomplish nothing worthwhile. We would become a part of the very dysfunction we seek to correct.

We envisage getting a critical mass of dreamers to build a new community, a safe distance from Tombstone.

In this community, all who are sick of violence, conflict and vitriol can contribute to the creation of a better future. Humanity will always have its share of rotten apples. (Psychologists estimate that about 4% of our species fits the definition of "sociopath".) But without a fertile place to grow, the damage they can do will be limited. In sum, the same old political tug-of-war will not solve anything. Real change will come from charting a new course, informed by the lessons of the past and illuminated by a positive vision of the future.

If we can let go of the superficial satisfaction of defeating our enemies, and instead focus on what we want to create in the world, we have an open road ahead of us. Now, our cynical relative might think, "what is this hippy-dippy pipe dream utopian load of #%*?!" Well, it's the same d@m% pipe dream of nearly every person in human history who made a lasting positive difference in the world.

Richard Dawkins, the provocative evolutionary biologist, first coined the term, "meme." A meme is like a gene, but at the level of culture. It's an idea or norm that spreads throughout our human systems. Memes are the means of our collective evolution. They can be incredibly powerful agents of change. Witness the transformative power of the memes of the Age of Enlightenment – individual worth, liberty and democracy.

Ideas and beliefs are like a virus. Their contagion is a function of virulence or stickiness, and the structure of the system through which they spread. Ideas can be malignant (extremist religions), benign (fashion trends) or beneficial (recycling). The network of humanity is undergoing a transformation that allows memes to spread with ease. Ideas can now move across the network with velocity. They can evolve much faster than the material stuff of our systems. They have the potential to change the systems through which they travel.

Many people are changing their patterns of thought from conflict to compassion, from scarcity to plenty, from passive cynicism to proactive optimism. We call this the "Mind Shift Meme." This beneficial meme is spreading rapidly. The expanding popularity of yoga, for example, and the spreading interest in the spiritual teachings of the Dalai Lama, Eckhart Tolle and Deepak Chopra, point to the momentum of the Mind Shift Meme. This meme is not new: it is the core teachings of some of the greatest dreamers in human history – Jesus, Buddha, and Lao Tzu among them.

The Mind Shift Meme is empowering. Participating in the creation of something great is far more satisfying (and fun) than watching the destruction of something beautiful. The change needed to create a better world is in complete alignment with personal satisfaction – it is a path to attaining real happiness. Making the Mind Shift becomes far easier as those around you are shifting too – we are incredibly sensitive to the mental states of people around us.[6] This potent meme has the power to alter fundamentally the workings of the human system. It is not just an idea, it is an alternative operating system that boosts the effectiveness of our hardware (our minds). Our individual growth combines to rewire the collective human network, making it more intelligent and resilient. The Mind Shift Meme, aided by dramatic advances in communication technology, makes possible a world that is beyond what most would dare to dream.

Lessons from our Cousins

Our primate cousins, baboons, offer an inspiring example of the power of social transformation. Primatologist, Robert M. Sapolsky, studied the "Forest Troop" of baboons in Kenya for years. The troop was typical of baboons – aggressive males atop a rigid hierarchy used violence to preserve their positions of power. Then tuberculosis killed half the males. The disease didn't strike randomly, it hit only those who frequented a nearby garbage heap within another troop's territory. This dump, being a source of prime grub, was the site of much fighting, so only the most aggressive males ventured to compete. Thus, tuberculosis wiped out the most aggressive males in the Forest Troop. (It decimated the troop whose territory included the heap.)

Sapolsky described the dramatic social transformation that emerged following the TB outbreak:

> There remained a hierarchy among the Forest Troop males, but it was far looser than before: compared with other, more typical savanna baboon groups, high-ranking males rarely harassed subordinates and occasionally even relinquished contested resources to them. Aggression was less frequent,

particularly against third parties. And rates of affiliative behaviors, such as males and females grooming each other or sitting together, soared. There were even instances, now and then, of adult males grooming each other -- a behavior nearly as unprecedented as baboons sprouting wings.[7]

Most surprisingly, the pacifist culture of this troop persists decades later. Male baboons leave their birth-troop at puberty to join a foreign group, so for a behavior (or lack thereof) to continue, it must be passed to the newly arrived transplants. Normally, these males are initially shunned and must endure outcast status for quite some time before earning a place in their new troop. In contrast, young males joining the Forest Troop are given a warm welcome by the females and this seems to set a cooperative and congenial tone for the future. The transplants adopt the gracious ways of their adopted tribe.

While exposing aggressive people to a deadly illness might be an effective means of social engineering, it's not likely to garner widespread support. But there is still a lesson to learn from the Forest Troop: we are not at the mercy of a violent and aggressive human nature written in our DNA. We have at least as much flexibility in our nature as baboons. If an accidental outbreak of TB could bring lasting positive change to the Forest Troop, then we humans should certainly be able to use our outsized brains to create a more peaceful and healthy society. Changing a few social norms, and choosing leaders (political, corporate, and community) who embody values that encourage cooperation (respect for others and an inclusive attitude, for example) are practical and effective ways to bring lasting improvements to a society.

Looking East

The Mind Shift Meme applies the principles of Jujitsu ("the art of being yielding") to our relationship with ourselves and others. We can use the force within the system we're trying to transform to reshape the system, thus improving its performance. We can adjust the way our human networks work by slightly altering structures and dynamics, and building on our strengths, rather than by directly resisting what is. These slight changes can reverberate through our systems, triggering cascading successes that will efficiently transform our world from the ground up.

Let's apply some simple common sense. If we are trying to achieve an outcome different from the past, it makes sense to find the root causes rather than simply treating effects. The superficial effect-treating approach is never-ending and therefore inefficient – it also becomes more difficult to keep up if we don't also address the root cause. We can keep bailing water, or we can plug the holes in the ship. As we will explore in later chapters, in complex dynamic systems (our planet, for example) we often unwittingly cause more problems than we solve when we take a superficial problem-focused approach to change.

The world is infinitely complex, so identifying root causes is more art than science. In fact, the very notion of cause and effect, which arises from a linear and analytic view of the world, can hinder our understanding of the systems with which we are dealing. Complex systems (such as human civilization) include feedback loops. These loops are not linear and cannot be broken down into isolated, independent elements. Everything is entangled in a dynamic web of connections. A more holistic and synthetic conception of the world will give us a map that more accurately represents the territory, thus improving the chances of a successful journey.

Systems science encompasses many fields of study (biology, physics, and economics to name a few). This area of inquiry has built a bridge between the empirical world of modern mainstream science into the artist's world of relative truths, qualitative values, and unpredictability. As we cross this bridge we see that many relationships in our economic system may be beyond our capacity to understand completely. However, if we practice beginner's mind, we may detect underlying patterns in systems (both human and nonhuman) and recognize variations of those patterns in civilization today. Indeed, one aim of this book is to highlight evolutionary patterns, such as the need to shift focus from the political to the social realm, the ascendance of starfish organizations, and the expansion of human consciousness.

Through this new lens we also see clearly that many of the biggest challenges we are dealing with today are largely a result of our failure to understand that we are parts of a whole. This whole is a mind-bogglingly complex web of interdependent subsystems (and sub-subsystems, and supra-systems). Because of our interconnectedness our actions have significant unintended effects. In fact, the "law of unintended consequences" is one of the few absolutes to which we would consider subscribing. (Just ask the drug companies whose huge spending on advertising may be increasing the placebo effect and unintentionally hindering approval of new drugs – unintended consequences are everywhere.)

Viewing the world through the prism of complex systems gives us power to rise above old myopic thinking. With this newfound vision we can unleash the latent potential of humanity and create a world of peace, justice and prosperity. By letting go of the need to distill all of existence into concrete mathematical formulas, we get in return a world of infinite possibility.

Drill Here

Many dire predictions throughout modern times proved inaccurate or premature: the population bubble foretold by Malthus in the late 1700s, the "peak oil" equivalent of the 1880s which warned of a severe coal shortage, and the "Population Bomb" warnings of the 1970s. These predictions failed to account for humanity's ability to adapt and develop new technologies. Because of our singular creative power, we have thrived to the point of becoming a serious threat to the continued survival of our biosphere (the whole of which we are a part). We need a new strategy.

Advances in agricultural technology have allowed our species to keep pace with population growth. Our creativity and mastery of the scientific method have postponed the Malthusian tragedy of mass starvation. However, much of this short-term progress has come at the expense of long-term sustainability. Chemicals are poisoning the planet and exhausting the topsoil, antibiotic use in livestock is causing dangerous bacteria to evolve at breakneck speeds, and petroleum stores (billions of years of stored energy) are dwindling rapidly. We must apply our creative energy to developing better solutions. Permaculture – the science and art of working with nature to produce food sustainably and efficiently – is an example of a systemic solution. In tandem with the leveling off of population growth that accompanies increased standards of living, and a widening recognition of women's rights, permaculture likely holds the best hope for a systemic and sustainable answer to the challenge of feeding humanity without continuing to steal from our children.

Permaculture is an illuminating example of the treasure of knowledge that awaits us, once we learn to work with, rather than try to dominate, nature. While it's a fairly novel approach in modern Western culture, it has ancient roots. *Terra preta* – a nutrient dense soil with high levels of micro organic activity – proves that pre-Columbian South Americans used permaculture techniques to create efficient high-yield forest gardens. *Terra preta* has the miraculous ability to self-generate that is, once established it continues to grow on its own. Modern science has yet to unlock the mystery of its self-generating capacity. *Terra preta* offers a compelling illustration of the vast untapped potential lying dormant on this planet. (In fact, some believe the carbon sequestering capacity of *terra preta* (that is, its ability to take carbon out of the air and hold it in the soil) may be an answer to climate change.)

An example from the practice of permaculture illuminates the potential unleashed by aligning with nature: the forest garden. Begin with a healthy environment (fertile soil and adequate irrigation) and protection from foraging animals. Then plant a wide variety of locally suitable edible vegetation – trees, bushes, shrubs, groundcover, vines. Diversity is absolutely essential. The gardener nurtures, but does not force, nature's hand. Some plants will find their ideal conditions – the best combination of light, soil, moisture, and proximity to beneficial plants. Others will die off, having lost out to varieties better suited to the local conditions. A dynamic and diverse ecosystem arises which *allows* nature to provide its bounty of nutrients and energy with a minimum of human intervention. Forest gardeners give up the symmetrical rows and micromanagement of conventional gardening in favor of nature's inherent wisdom and power.

Bill Mollison, a co-founder of modern permaculture, shares our optimistic view of the potential of working with, rather than against nature: "Though the problems of the world are increasingly complex, the solutions remain embarrassingly simple." We have the ability to thrive in sync with nature; in fact, it is the only way we truly can. There is no triumph over nature that is not, ultimately, self-defeating.

Henry Ford understood the power of belief as he famously advised, "If you think you can do it, or you think you can't do it, you are right." If we believe that human beings can be reduced to and understood by the programs written in DNA – organic robots programmed with the delusion of free will – then we are merely passive observers at the mercy of circumstance. Sadly, much of Western science is based on the assumption that all existence can be distilled to a handful of physical laws. This belief is creating a world that confirms its correctness. It is a self-fulfilling prophecy that is at the heart of an epidemic of alienation and disempowerment: in Henry Ford's terms, we think we can't, and we are proving ourselves right.

This sad state of affairs holds within it the key to our salvation – we have the power to transform our world here and now. When a critical mass of us becomes conscious of our limiting beliefs, and chooses to shift our thinking and embrace our true potential as manifestations of the creative power of the universe, the possibilities unlocked will be beyond our wildest dreams. We are already well on our way.

5 – Attaining Happiness

The word "happiness" comes from the Icelandic word for luck, "happ." Clearly we are not content to leave our happiness to the whims of chance – we prefer to take the "happ" out of happiness. As Freud noted, "the intention that man should be 'happy' is not included in the plan of 'Creation.'"[1] Biological evolution has no apparent need for happiness beyond the minimal threshold needed to avoid suicide and libido-hampering depression. Short-term hedonic sensual pleasures are a means by which our genes persuade us to do what is necessary for their survival and reproduction, sex and eating first among them. Thankfully we can use our intellect to transcend our genes and reach true happiness.

If happiness arises from physiological responses to stimuli, then the key to achieving happiness is controlling the conditions that trigger the chemicals produced by our bodies that induce "happy" feelings. In fact, a neurosurgeon can install an electrode in your brain that will enable you to experience sensations of ecstasy at the push of a button. The following describes the result of such a procedure in a patient being treated for chronic pain:

> At its most frequent, the patient self-stimulated throughout the day, neglecting her personal hygiene and family commitments. A chronic ulceration developed at the tip of the finger used to adjust the amplitude dial and she frequently tampered with the device in an effort to increase the

stimulation amplitude. At times she implored her family to limit her access to the stimulator, each time demanding its return after a short hiatus.[2]

Despite her unlimited access to extreme pleasure, we doubt many would describe this woman's experience as joyful or healthy. Physical pleasure is not happiness.

On the other hand, we can think of happiness as something that arises at the level of consciousness – a *state of being*, rather than an emotion. In a happy state we exercise free will and strive for new experience, rather than merely react to stimuli. From this perspective, the key to experiencing more happiness is developing the capacity to choose one's state of being. Happiness is, in large part, an inside job. This helps explain why physical pleasure, such as that induced by carefully placed electrodes or taking opiates (or, more commonly, Happy Meals and happy hours), is often destructive to real happiness. Sensual pleasure overwhelms our ability to exercise free choice, placing us at the mercy of our biology.

Eckhart Tolle's spiritual teachings have helped millions deepen their happiness and life satisfaction. Tolle describes three states of being available to those who have adequately developed their ability to choose: acceptance, joy and enthusiasm. Acceptance may be the best option when faced with uncomfortable circumstances that would induce misery in less conscious people. Joy is experienced when the present moment is embraced. Enthusiasm, which literally means "possessed by god," is the highest state of being. A person is most likely to experience enthusiasm when at one with the present moment and thus with the underlying oneness of existence. (Renée's diving experience is an example of enthusiasm.)

Tolle's framework offers a useful way of viewing the real happiness described by Jefferson and Locke. The aim of a good society is to create conditions that foster people's ability to choose their state of being (by adopting the Mind Shift Meme, for example), and to maximize time spent in joy and enthusiasm. Thus, enabling happiness has both internal and external elements.

Given the critical role of language in shaping our perception of the world and its possibilities, "happiness," with its lucky etymology and widespread use to refer to superficial hedonic satisfaction, is probably not the best choice of words. Locke's warning of the dire consequences of confusing imaginary for real happiness points to the danger of using such a nebulous term to describe such an important idea. That happiness, so central to our lives, is such an ambiguous term may be one reason so few seem to be attaining it. "Conjoyment," a combination of contentment and joy, has been suggested as an addition to the English vocabulary.[3] We will use conjoyment to mean the *real* happiness of Locke and Jefferson (though we won't give up on happiness completely).

A View from the Top

Abraham Maslow was among a handful of pioneering psychologists of the early 20th century who focused on what is now known as "positive psychology." Rather than focusing on treating neurosis, its aim is achieving individual psychological well-being. This shift in focus was enabled by the material plenty ushered in by capitalism that released many from the heavy demands of mere biological survival. We continue on this path by developing a *positive psychology of society* that is, looking at how our collective systems can evolve to enable a fuller expression of human potential.

Maslow delved deeply into the nature of human fulfillment. Two of his teachers, Ruth Benedict (whose work we will highlight in the next chapter) and Max Wertheimer, inspired him. He sensed they were fundamentally different from others he had encountered. They were, in his words, "remarkable human beings." Maslow studied these two and soon realized that their patterns could be generalized. This insight eventually led him to develop his now famous framework for understanding human psychological well-being, the *Hierarchy of Needs*. In his *Hierarchy*, Maslow ranked human motivations in the following order: physiological, safety, love and belonging, esteem, self-actualization, and transcendence.[4] In other words, people tend to advance from a focus on material wealth (supporting physical survival), to psychological health, and then to spiritual wellness. (Though the rigidity of the hierarchy is dubious, it is directionally correct.)

Maslow explained that self-actualized people "listen to their own voices; they take responsibility; they are honest; and they work hard. *They find out who they are and what they are.*"[5] Locke and Jefferson would recognize their ideal citizen in this description; a person who embraces the responsibility that comes with freedom and consciously chooses his path to real happiness. Self-actualized people are content neither as cogs in a machine nor as blind acceptors the status quo – they are dreamers.

In the terms used by economists, Maslow's categories of needs are the *demands* each human being tries to satisfy. Capitalism is an efficient adaptation for providing the material goods that fulfill physical needs. Only after large numbers of people were secure in their primary needs did it make sense to focus on the higher level needs. Robert Pirsig told of this shift from material, to psychological and spiritual concerns nearly 40 years ago in his opus, *Zen and the Art of Motorcycle Maintenance*:

> What's wrong with technology is that it's not connected in any real way with matters of the spirit and of the heart. And so it does blind, ugly things quite by accident and gets hated for that. People haven't paid much attention to this before because the big concern has been with food, clothing and shelter for everyone and technology has provided these.
>
> But now where these are assured, the ugliness is being noticed more and more and people are asking if we must always suffer spiritually and esthetically in order to satisfy material needs.

Psychologist Viktor Frankl, echoed Pirsig's sentiments when he wrote of the *search for meaning* as the essential human striving:

> For too long we have been dreaming a dream from which we are now waking up: the dream that

if we just improve the socioeconomic situation of people, everything will be okay, people will become happy. The truth is that as the *struggle for survival* has subsided, the question has emerged: *survival for what?* Ever more people today have the means to live, but no meaning to live for.[6]

Nearly four decades later we are still asking the question, "survival for what?" While some find satisfaction in yoga, meditation, philanthropy, nature and artistic expression, many are still searching for answers in material possessions. Dissatisfaction with the "solutions" offered by mainstream culture – consumer goods, the cult of celebrity, junk food, video games and television – is a likely cause of our society's malaise. Without something beyond our individual selves or nuclear families to strive for, we are consumed by personal desires, and shut off from our connection to one another and the whole of existence.

Scaling the Pyramid

Maslow thought of human needs as forming a pyramid, with physiological and safety needs at the base, love, belonging and esteem in the middle, and self-actualization at the peak. He later explored the idea of "transcendence." He defined it as "the very highest and most inclusive or holistic levels of human consciousness, behaving and relating, as ends rather than means, to oneself, to significant others, to human beings in general, to other species, to nature, and to the cosmos."[7] Eventually, Maslow, too, glimpsed the illusory quality of our separateness. At the farther reaches of our nature, we have the potential to live in harmony with ourselves and our world. It is possible to integrate the seemingly contradictory demands of self and other, material and spiritual, doing and being, competition and cooperation. Together we can chart a course, and build pathways to this relatively uncharted, but infinitely rich, territory of human nature.

Joseph Campbell described a fundamental feature of pyramids in a way that affirms Maslow's idea of transcendence: "When you're down on the lower levels of the pyramid you will be on either one side or the other. But when you get to the top, the points all come together, and there the eye of God opens." At the apex, in the moment of transcendence, and regardless of the path taken, we experience our underlying unity.

The eye has an important quality relevant to its symbolic meaning. As explained by Viktor Frankl, another founder of positive psychology, a well-functioning eye does not perceive itself.[8] Indeed, if an eye sees itself, it is failing (as with cataracts or glaucoma). The same is true at the top of the pyramid of human potential. It is "by rising above and growing beyond ourselves, [that] we exercise the most creative of all human potentials."[9] Maslow's self-actualization is a side effect of self-transcendence: "it is ruinous and self-defeating to make it the target of intention. And what is true of self-actualization also holds true for identity and happiness. It is the very 'pursuit of happiness' that obviates happiness. The more we make it the target, the more widely we miss it."[10]

The pyramid metaphor symbolizes the striving that is the hallmark of life itself. Our task is to create a system that empowers individuals to strive for their best life. Striving may look different to each of us; success will be in the process rather than in the outcome. You know you are on the right path when you will feel the light within radiating and illuminating the truth of your being.

The Gospel of Thomas, an ancient Gnostic text discovered in 1945 in a cave in Egypt, includes a seemingly paradoxical teaching: "If you bring forth what is within you, what you bring forth will save you. If you do not bring forth what is within you, what you do not bring forth will destroy you." The insight of positive psychology resolves the paradox. Our purpose is to express our fullest potential, in striving we transcend both our circumstances and ourselves, in stagnation we turn inward and wither.

To Have or To Be
Since Jefferson's fateful decision to inject happiness into political discourse, and the pioneering forays of positive psychologists, many social scientists have been searching for the secrets to real happiness. Key findings point to the need to refocus our efforts, let go of fleeting superficial happiness and reach instead for deep lasting conjoyment. Specifically, the possessions we think will make us happy bring only fleeting pleasure. Lottery winners experience a brief high, followed by a return to their previous level of life satisfaction.[11] People who assign a high priority to material wealth tend to be less happy than those who do not.

In the words of one happiness expert, "Materialism is toxic for happiness."[12]

Sadly, increasing numbers of Americans are focused on the mighty dollar and the stuff it buys. Each year, UCLA conducts a national survey of college freshman about values. In the late 1960s and early 1970s, 45-50 percent of respondents rated staying current on politics and helping clean up the environment as very important personal goals.[13] Forty percent gave "being very well off financially" that same rating. In 1998 (as the last of the Gen Xers entered college), concern with politics and the environment declined to 26 percent and 19 percent, respectively. Over the same period the percent of those questioned who said it was "essential" or "very important" to be financially well off rose to 75%.[14] In a nutshell, we are motivated increasingly by materialist values that are damaging our psychological well-being (and the health of the planet).

The culture of consumerism has tapped into the bottom rungs of human motivation and has amplified them, creating a grossly distorted vision of reality that puts *having* things ahead of *living* life. This view of life undermines our true potential and hinders conjoyment. Millions of people toil in unfulfilling jobs so they can make interest-only payments on credit cards used to buy things that provided fleeting pleasure. Indeed, because of recent changes in bankruptcy laws, many debtors in the US now face a lifetime of servitude with no possibility of release.

The UCLA survey results show that happiness (at least in mainstream U.S. culture) is grounded increasingly in what psychologist Erich Fromm called "the having mode." People in the having mode view life through the lens of possessing things, people and experiences. This perspective is deeply rooted in our thinking and pervades the English language: we "have" fun, we "have" a good marriage, and we "have" a good life. It's a symptom of the analytic materialist view of reality. This way of thinking deepens our sense of separation from one another and nature, and distances us from real happiness.

The having mode underlies the Paradox of the Destruction of the Fittest. Our obsession with things, and the accompanying neglect of our spiritual and psychological wealth, sows the seeds of our destruction. We forgot somewhere along the way that the accumulation of wealth is a means to an end, rather than an end in itself.

There are places where people catch monkeys by drilling a small hole in a coconut, just large enough for a monkey to fit its hand. The monkey catchers put some enticing food in the coconut and attach it to an immovable object. When the monkey reaches in to grasp the food, making a fist, its hand will not fit back through the hole, so he's stuck and easy prey for the hunters who are waiting in the wings. [15] The monkey forgets, at least momentarily, that the food is a means to an end, the end being its survival. Its confusion leads it to make a very poor choice. The monkey's survival strategy is too rigid, making the monkey vulnerable to changing realities. The most serious challenges to our survival are of the monkey trap variety, which is good news, since the main thing we have to change is our minds.

An alternative to the having mode is the "being mode" which entails viewing life through the lens of experience. In this mode, happiness, love and success are not possessions, they are dynamic and ever-changing experiences. Fromm's "having versus being" conception of the world is not new. Buddha, Jesus and Lao Tzu warned of the dangers of materialism: "Lay not up for yourselves treasures upon earth, where moth and rust doth corrupt, and where thieves break through and steal ... For where your treasure is, there your heart will be also."[16]

The world around us is a direct reflection of what is within us. Research shows that community, love, connection, free expression of talents, forgiveness and acceptance are essential for real happiness to thrive.[17] The Mind Shift Meme lays the ground for creating these conditions. When we give up conflict and judgment in favor of compassion and acceptance, and move away from passive cynicism toward proactive optimism, we become more loving, accepting and generous people. From this foundation, we create strong and vibrant communities of people inspired to realize their potential and contribute to the well-being of others. Our collective failure to embrace

> Creation is a better means of self-expression than possession; it is through creating, not possessing, that life is revealed.
> - Vida Dutton

Attaining Happiness | 143

the principles of our most celebrated spiritual teachers, and the advice of a growing number of psychologists, is understandable given our experience. By becoming aware of the roots of our attachment to the having mode, we can take an important step toward letting go and moving beyond its limits.

Moving from the having mode to the being mode amounts to a declaration of independence from the dead things for which we have been trading our lives. This should not be mistaken for asceticism; it is not about living a less pleasurable life. Rather, it's about exercising the freedom to choose our priorities consciously and wisely, rather than allowing others – our culture, institutions and peers – to choose for us.

In classical psychoanalytic theory, as a child goes through successive stages of development. Events can disrupt a child's progress through these stages, resulting in a "fixation" that may show up as an unhealthy attachment to a person or object. We are fixated on our material stage of development. A hypothetical "couch" session between humanity and its therapist would include an emotional recounting of extreme neglect during our formative years. We were unable to depend on a stable food supply, exposed to the harsh elements and left vulnerable to invaders (both large and microscopic). No wonder we're so screwed up! Fulfilling our potential, and helping those still struggling to survive, requires that we overcome the fear and insecurity rooted in our past. Healing is possible, if we choose it.

We are like the elephant who, in its youth, learned that it could not venture beyond the reach of its leash. In its adult years it does not bother to test the holding power of the rope now tied around its own ankle. We continue to believe in limitations that no longer accurately reflect the real world. These limiting beliefs constrain our ability to experience fully the miraculous potential of our existence.

We (the authors) have overcome much of the material-oriented power and status seeking tendencies that characterized our young adulthood (to the chagrin of many of our friends and family members). We have chosen to focus more on creative exploration, adventure and relationships, and less on possessions and status. Our experience evidences the very real possibility of consciously choosing the being mode, and the conjoyment it enables. Indeed, we doubt it is a coincidence that the core of the ideas shared in this book came about during a watershed moment in our own experience of enthusiasm.

We have managed to reshape our lives for the better despite cultural norms. However, achieving conjoyment should not be a counterculture exercise. It is possible to create new social norms that define status in ways that foster real happiness and encourage the realization of our highest potential. The desire for power and status are important parts of human nature with deep evolutionary roots. However, *how* power and status are *achieved and measured* is determined by flexible social norms. Power and status (as we will see in the next chapter) are socially constructed facts that can be changed simply by altering our beliefs about them. When, for example, the most kind and generous people are held in the highest esteem, our biologically determined status-seeking drives can serve to improve the well-being of communities and guide us to the transcendence that awaits us at the top of the pyramid.

Homo Economicus (or the having mode writ large)

Market fundamentalism, the mainstream economic theory in the U.S. since Ronald Reagan introduced "trickledown economics" in the 1980s, is pretty firmly rooted in the having mode. It claims that the best use of resources results when people's economic choices are unconstrained by government. The core of this paradigm is a theory of human motivation typified by *Homo economicus*, a mythological version of *Homo sapiens* motivated solely by personal material utilitarian values. Homo economicus lives wholly in the having mode, he is a human *having* rather than a human *being*.

The relatively new field of behavioral economics combines psychology and economic theory. Researchers in this hybrid field are showing that many assumptions made by market fundamentalists about human motivation are seriously flawed. Thus, theories based on these assumptions are likely faulty. Unfortunately, these findings have done little to loosen the hold of market fundamentalist ideology on American minds.[18]

In his book *Predictably Irrational*, Dan Ariely, a professor of behavioral economics at Duke University, sets forth many ways in which human beings act "irrationally" as defined by conventional economics. One simple experiment, known as the "Ultimatum Game" illustrates the conflict between the assumptions of market fundamentalism and the actual behavior of human beings. It also shows the distorted reality seen through the lens of market fundamentalism. In the game a "sender" is given $20 to divide between herself and a "receiver." The sender can divide the $20 as she chooses – evenly (that is, $10 each) or unevenly (for example, keeping $19 and offering $1). The receiver either accepts the offer, and each gets the amount designated by the sender, or rejects the offer, and both get nothing. Market fundamentalists assume that receivers will accept any amount, since even $1 is better than none. However, unbalanced offers are often rejected. As evidenced by the title of Ariely's book, most mainstream economists consider the rejecting receivers to be *irrational*.

Defining rationality in a way that myopically focuses on money as the sole relevant factor ignores the diverse values held by human beings. In the Ultimatum Game, for example, the desire for money often takes a back seat to the values of fairness and justice. Money is a means to an end, a fact that many economists have forgotten, but their "irrational" test subjects intuitively remember. Money is a tool for ensuring fairness and justice, a way of keeping track of a complex web of reciprocal altruism spread throughout time and geography. [19] Losing sight of this truth warps our perception and blinds us to the critical importance of fairness and justice to a healthy society. From this holistic perspective, we recognize that it is the *experimenters*, not the players, who are irrational – they have mistaken the markers for the game.

Behavioral economists are like the quantum theorists of economics, probing the inner world of atoms and discovering that all is not as it seems. The gap is wide between the market fundamentalists' map of the world and the reality of the terrain it claims to represent. This significantly impedes our ability to function – the market turmoil that began with the subprime mortgage crisis in 2007 and continues to today is vivid evidence of this chasm.

It is likely that the gap is widening further as more of humanity is freed from the tethers of material survival. Analytic rationality, with its favored tool, the scientific method, is most powerful and useful in the material realm, which explains why it reigned supreme for the past 400 years. People facing threats to their survival (that is, those lower down on Maslow's pyramid) are more likely to behave like *Homo economicus*. A starving person playing the Ultimatum Game is much more likely to accept whatever amount is offered because money (specifically, the food money will buy) will take precedent over fairness and justice. Now that so many of us are relatively free of basic survival concerns, we have the luxury of focusing on our psychological and spiritual wealth (the higher levels of Maslow's pyramid). In this realm the material focus of analytic rationality is of limited use; here we need synthetic rationality.

Behavioral economics uses synthetic rationality. And while it is on the rise, it is not new. Decades ago, Maslow recognized the possibility of psychological insights into human motivation informing economics:

> And it can also be assumed that classical economic theory, based as it is on an inadequate theory of human motivation, could also be revolutionized by accepting the reality of higher human needs, including the impulse to self-actualization and the love for the highest values...
>
> [I]t is ... a clear confrontation of one basic set of orthodox values by another newer system of values which claims to be not only more efficient but also more true. It draws some of the truly revolutionary consequences of the discovery that human nature has been sold short, that man has a higher nature which is just as "instintoid" as his lower nature, and that this higher nature includes the needs for meaningful work, for responsibility, for creativeness, for being fair and just, for doing what is worthwhile and for preferring to do it well.[20]

Interestingly, Maslow's deep insights are similar to Adam Smith's view of human nature, which shaped his understanding of the evolutionary shift in economics he witnessed unfolding. However, many economists (particularly those who espouse market fundamentalism) aspire to the precision of physics and ignore these complex human values. Instead, they apply analytic rationality, and seek variables to plug into mathematical formulas, hoping to discover immutable economic "laws" that will enable them to predict and control economic forces. Thus, the fictional *Homo economicus* came into being – automata motivated by pure profit maximization satisfy the demands of mathematical precision. Because of this divergence of economic theory from reality we have maps that do not accurately describe the territory. These flawed maps are making it frustratingly difficult to get to our desired destination – a healthy, vibrant and just world.

Unfortunately, market fundamentalism (and its Frankenstein-like creation, *Homo economicus*) is not only a flawed academic idea, it has infected American political and cultural thinking. As described in the previous chapter, our beliefs shape our reality in powerful ways. The belief system of market fundamentalism includes the underlying idea that what the free market creates is just and right. Through this lens, poverty and wealth inequality reflect the moral and rational judgment of the market. The poor are poor because they have nothing of value to contribute. The rich are rich because they are superior to the rest. Thus, all is as it's meant to be; nothing needs fixing here. In this world, greed and envy are positive qualities because they drive the engine of growth.

A Native American parable highlights the corrosive effects of the market fundamentalist worldview:

> A grandfather talking to his young grandson tells the boy he (the grandfather) has two wolves inside of him struggling with each other. The first is the wolf of peace, love and kindness. The other is the wolf of fear, greed and hatred. The boy ponders this for a moment, then asks, "Which wolf will win,

grandfather?" Grandfather responds, "Whichever one I feed."

We do not choose which wolf to feed in a vacuum. Our society, the people and institutions with which we interact guide our decision, and often lead us to feed one wolf and starve the other. The ideology of market fundamentalism and the culture it has shaped encourage us to feed the wolf of greed and fear.

In the aftermath of the subprime mortgage crisis many accusing fingers pointed to "the greed of Wall Street." It's important to also recognize the greed of Main Street. All participants, including investment bankers, mortgage brokers and home buyers, were motivated by their personal financial interests. That unchecked greed and shortsighted profit seeking nearly toppled the global financial system wasn't enough to open the eyes of those who continue to espouse market fundamentalism. (Many of these diehards blame the crisis on government regulation rather than market failure, a testament to the difficulty of letting go of engrained thought patterns.)

The virtues identified by Thomas Jefferson – prudence, temperance, fortitude and justice – were notably absent throughout the economic and financial systems leading up to the crisis. From Main Street to Wall Street, virtually all the behaviors that contributed to the subprime crisis can be described accurately as the opposite of Jefferson's virtues: folly, desire, fear and deceit. An economic model that brings out the worst in human nature cannot coexist indefinitely with a political system, democracy, which depends for its success on the best in human nature.

As we will explore in greater detail, individuals and communities are shaped by social norms. Within the paradigm of market fundamentalism, greed, envy and material gain are primary values. These values create a society that fosters callousness, aggression, and psychological dis-ease (including the disempowerment and alienation described earlier). Witness the effects on public debate: right-wing commentators call for raising taxes on the bottom 50% of U.S. income earners, who currently do not pay federal income tax. Such a policy makes perfect sense to a market fundamentalist – the poor are freeloaders feeding off the material wealth of the worthy; justice requires that they pay their fair share.

An alternative approach that values human beings as ends rather than as means would see the situation differently, but no less rationally. When presented with the same facts, the first question would be "why do so many people earn so little that they are in a no-tax bracket?" The problem takes a very different form: it isn't that too many are not paying enough it's that the economic system is marginalizing millions. The solution is not regressive taxation, but reinventing the system so it empowers more people to contribute meaningfully to our collective efforts.

Striving for Better, Not More

Striving is an essential quality of life and, according to evolutionary theory, is a result of the drive to reproduce in a competitive environment. From these simple conditions miraculous complexity arises – our richly diverse planetary eco-system, our bodies and our minds. From this perspective, humanity's continuous striving for more and better is an expression of cosmic laws, and thus will never be satisfied for long (if even for a moment). Henry J. Ellsworth, the Commissioner of the U.S. Patent Office in 1843, failed to recognize that the momentum of the entire universe fuels human striving when he predicted: "The advancement of the arts, from year to year, taxes our credulity and seems to presage the arrival of that period when human improvement must end." What would Mr. Ellsworth make of our world today? (And in case you think our ideas tax credulity, consider Mr. Ellsworth's miscalculation.)

We will never be content with the status quo, it is written in our blood and in our bones – we are strivers. But striving can take on very different characteristics. In current Western culture and thinking, the having mode dominates: striving is focused mainly on the quantities of life – a bigger house, a more expensive car, a fatter bank account. The being mode looks quite different; one strives for the *qualities of life* – truth, beauty, and love. From here, everything becomes art, a manifestation of our striving to bring forth what is within us. We appreciate the efforts of those around us. The material needs – food, shelter and clothing – become opportunities to express truth and beauty. Those of us who have begun to shift from *having* to *being* are not very interested in eating at chain restaurants, listening to top 40 music, or buying mass-produced furniture and clothing. Rather, we enjoy the artistry of people sharing their creative passion and who are motivated, not by money, but by the higher values of love, beauty, justice, and transcendence.

Maslow foresaw the potential transformative power of this shift in values:

> I have a very strong sense of being in the middle of a historical wave. One hundred and fifty years from now, what will the historians say about this age? What was really important? What was going? What was finished? My belief is that much of what makes the headlines is finished, and the 'growing up' of mankind is what is now growing and will flourish in a hundred or two hundred years, if we manage to endure. Historians will be talking about this movement as the sweep of history, that here, … when you get a new model, a new paradigm, a new way of perceiving, new definitions of old words, words which now mean something else, suddenly, you have an illumination, an insight. You can see things in a different way.[21]

We are now at an evolutionary crossroads. We can continue to create a world shaped by fear, scarcity and a stunted vision of human nature; a world in which greedy individuals (that is, *Homo economicus*) hoard as much stuff as they can, thus creating a world in which fear and scarcity are the reality. In this reality, the human species will face continued tragedy and horror of our own making (though this tragedy is likely to be short-lived).

There is another way forward: we can consciously choose to seek, and find, a world shaped by wisdom, abundance and the full breadth and depth of human potential. As Maslow put it, "We have come to the point in biological history where we now are responsible for our own evolution. We have become self-evolvers. Evolution means selecting and therefore choosing and deciding, and this means valuing." This includes valuing the qualities – truth, beauty, justice, fairness – that money was meant to represent, rather than the money itself; it means not confusing the markers for the game.

6 – The Philosopher's Stone

The full depth and breadth of human nature is a priceless resource, a resource we must exploit if we are to meet the challenges we have created for ourselves. Ambition and altruism, passion and reason, nobility and profanity – all were passed down to us by our ancestors (that is, those who succeed in the game of life). These qualities are the innate toolkit from which we can create and recreate ourselves and society. Some traits are undoubtedly more useful than others, while some have likely outlived their utility. The question we face is *how do we reshape our society in a way that honors our nature while bringing out the best in each of us?*

But first, let's briefly sum up where we are: we are evolving individually on the level of consciousness and collectively on the level of culture and technology. Capitalism has served well as an evolutionary strategy. It has helped free billions from the tyranny of hunger and the elements. Liberal democracy has similarly freed many from the tyranny of authoritarian rule. Together, these social arrangements have enabled over half of humanity to climb the first levels of Maslow's pyramid, yet many are stuck solidly at the bottom.

We need new social norms that enable humankind to continue climbing, while also ensuring that those still stuck at the bottom of the pyramid have a chance to realize their full potential. We need new tools of collective organization suitable to the present task. Without them we risk continued stagnation or worse. By expanding and deepening individual consciousness, we free ourselves from the narrow confines of the human default operating system. From this liberated state, we can intelligently craft the necessary tools and intentionally choose our course toward true happiness. In designing these tools we would be wise to pull from the vast well of humanity's collected knowledge and insight. In the following chapters we draw from this wealth of wisdom and reveal a marvelous vision of our exceptional place in the unfolding universe.

Modern Alchemy

A significant contingent of past dreamers studied alchemy. Many, haven mistaken the alchemists' poetry for prose, dismissed it as a foolish and doomed effort to turn lead into gold, thus missing the ancient wisdom contained within the alchemists' cryptic teachings.[1] They were spiritual seekers on a quest for the Philosopher's Stone, the key to unlocking the secret to immortality and limitless wealth – not of the material, but of the spiritual kind.

In the days when the Catholic Church's dictate was law those on their own path to transcendence risked a torturous end in the hope of reaching higher spiritual planes. Therefore, prudent spiritual seekers expressed their knowledge through the complex symbolism of alchemy. This allowed them to communicate safely with one another and to pass their wisdom on to future generations. In the sixteenth century, Paracelsus hinted at this deception in his *Alchemical Catechism*: "Question: When the Philosophers speak of gold and silver, from which they extract their matter, are we to suppose that they refer to the vulgar gold and silver? Answer: By no means; vulgar silver and gold are dead, while those of the Philosophers are full of life."

Alchemists sought to transform the base material of egoistic man into the pure and radiant gold of beings transcending the illusion of separateness and freeing themselves from the prison of their personal desires. Much of their wisdom came from the Gnostics – early Christians who believed in the divinity of all life and self-knowledge as the surest path to truth and to the divine.[2] In the 4th century, the Church declared Gnosticism heresy and ordered all Gnostic writings destroyed. The Gnostics and their teachings were forced underground – alchemy was their cover. Alchemists saw the world as an interconnected miraculous whole, an expression of the divine, and sought to understand the secrets of nature to lift humanity to higher planes. This view of the world faded as the analytic rationality of the scientific method took hold in the 17th century. René Descartes ushered in this new worldview with his radical ideas about the search for knowledge, marking the rise of the materialist paradigm, and the separation of man from nature.[3]

The underlying unity of matter and spirit was the foundation of the spiritual alchemists' transformation. Alchemists viewed nature as the ultimate source of all existence and thus aspired to work in harmony with her.[4] In contrast, scientists steeped in the materialist worldview and the laypersons shaped by it came to see nature as an enemy to be conquered (though Descartes himself did not support this view).[5] We now face the daunting challenges created by Western culture's dualistic man versus nature view of the world. Thankfully, science is emerging from its fractured view of reality. Einstein redeemed the alchemical worldview with his great realization that energy and matter are two sides of the same coin. $E=mc^2$ is the supreme alchemical formula – proof of the underlying unity of existence.

Einstein's discovery (or rediscovery) of the unity of energy and matter marked the beginning of science's return to the synthetic rationality of the alchemists. This shift is still in its nascent stage, but it is reaching a watershed moment. The science of systems, the modern version of alchemy, goes by many names. Chaos theory, complexity theory, network theory, information theory, and fractal geometry all study complex systems. Economists, social scientists, biologists, chemists, computer scientists, engineers, and many others are applying its findings. The widespread application of the discoveries of systems science is strong evidence that it is describing something underlying all reality.

The insights of systems scientists are essential to building healthy social systems. These insights can play a critical role in lifting humanity beyond the limits of the materialist worldview. Armed with the wisdom of systems we can begin solving the problems caused by our irrational conflict with the natural world, and embrace our full potential as physical expressions of universal energy.

Systems Science – A Primer

Scientists have been pondering abstract ideas related to complex systems for over a half-century. But as an area of scientific inquiry it languished in the darkness of relative ignorance and abstraction because very little data was available with which to compare theories to reality. Real world nonlinear systems (that is, linear equations cannot predict their behavior) are complex and ever-changing. Thus, they are impossible to map even superficially without investment of a prohibitive amount of time and energy. Practical limits of human abilities also constrained understanding of these systems. As one early systems thinker put it, he needed an orchestra of mathematicians to perform the calculations necessary for his research. Computers supplied the solution to both of these constraints. Complex calculations became easy. Computer-simulated systems, and the rise of the Internet (a complex system that can be mapped with nothing but a software program) offered low-cost and detailed data for study. Revelations enabled by computers have been steadily streaming out of academia for several decades.

The systems we're talking about here are complex, adaptive and self-organizing, in other words, life. "Complex" simply means there are many parts interacting within the system. "Adaptive" means the system evolves in response to internal and external changes. "Self-organizing" means these systems arise from the interactions of the parts; there is no master engineer at work.

To understand complex adaptive systems, we have to use the tool of analysis. We break apart a system so we can communicate and think about it. What we end up with is a mere caricature of reality, but it makes visible features that would otherwise be lost among the details. The map is not the territory – our simplified *conception* of a system is not the *actual system*. As with all language, there is danger in forgetting it is simply a tool of thought. While an incredibly useful tool, it has limits that can seriously hamper our understanding of reality, and lead us astray, if not deliberately kept in check. This danger is heightened when dealing with complex systems because so much of the magic is in the *interactions between the parts*. These interactions are likely to be overlooked in the slicing and dicing of analysis.

Modern science is not the first to reduce the complexity of adaptive systems to a simplified map. Indra, a Vedic god, is said to have woven an infinite web and at each intersection he placed a faceted jewel each of which reflected every other jewel and the entire web. Indra's jewels are a metaphor for the Buddhist belief that all of existence is inextricably interconnected. Reality is made up of patterns within patterns within patterns (an ancient version of fractal geometry). As we will see in the following chapter, modern science is revealing the underlying truth of this belief.

In the language of systems science, systems are made up of two basic relatively stable units, links and nodes. Links are the connective tissue (Indra's web). Nodes are what is connected (Indra's jewels). In social networks, for example, relationships are links and individuals are nodes. In a telephone network, phone lines are links and telephones are nodes.

Some nodes have more connections to other nodes than average. (Nodes with many more connections than average are called "hubs" – the socialites of the system.) Some nodes are more connected to all other nodes in the system. (Kevin Bacon is a well-connected node in the network of movie actors, which is why the once-popular game, *Six Degrees of Kevin Bacon*, worked so well.) Nodes also have varying levels of fitness, which, like quality in general, is not susceptible to direct and precise distillation to mathematical terms. Thus, fitness is often a neglected feature of systems.

Links vary according to strength (for example, best friends versus casual acquaintances), capacity (that is, how much a link can carry and how fast) and directionality (for example, my webpage links to yours but yours doesn't link to mine). Links carry energy, matter and information. Then there is time – real world complex systems are dynamic. They evolve – new links and nodes are born whiles others die off. These are some of the basics of systems science. Simple stuff really, but there is magic hidden here.

The magic of complex systems is in the interactions between the parts. These interactions are driven by feedback loops. Feedback loops are made up of the energy, matter and information that flow across a system's links. How nodes respond to this energy, matter and information controls the behavior of the system. There are two kinds of feedback loops. Positive feedback loops make nodes to do more of what they have been doing, propelling a system forward (though not always toward progress). Negative feedback loops make nodes stop what they had been doing, thus applying the brakes. Well-functioning feedback loops help systems survive by adapting to changing conditions. Poorly functioning feedback loops cause breakdowns and spiraling catastrophes.

While nodes and links give structure to the systems of which they are parts. The system also *shapes* its nodes and links. The overall state of the systems of which we are a part – family, neighborhood, social circles, economy, nation and planet – is communicated to us constantly (though not always well). We respond to this information, consciously and unconsciously, by adapting to our ever-changing environment. This "downward causation" (the influence of the whole on the parts) arises from the whole-to-parts side of feedback loops. Downward causation is essential to understanding the art of scientific alchemy. We are constantly co-evolving with the systems in which we participate. It is this quality of systems that makes the future so unpredictable.

Now we have a shared language with which to communicate the nature of complex adaptive systems. We will apply this framework to real world human systems – societies – and see what we can learn. Not surprisingly, we are not the first dreamers to explore this territory.

Synergy

As an anthropologist steeped in the analytic rationality of academia in the first half of the 20th century, Ruth Benedict conformed to the standard of objectivity. Check your values at the door: if you can't measure it, it doesn't exist. Eventually, as the grip of objectivism loosened, Benedict began to explore questions of what it means for a society to be good and how such societies can be formed. She identified a quality she termed *synergy* (a word borrowed from medicine) as a key ingredient in societies that fostered well-being and nonaggression.

Benedict's investigation centered on a handful of Native American cultures (one of her areas of expertise). She chose the cultures intuitively, based on the sense that, though each was quite different from the others in most other respects, they were exceptional with regard to one quality – aggression. Half the tribes fostered a sense of security and self-worth and as a result its members were kind, happy, and nonaggressive. The other half of the tribes pitted individuals against one another, thus cultivating insecurity resulting in aggressive, acquisitive, tyrannous, and vengeful behavior. Her first study revealed no readily apparent explanatory variables (for example, physical wealth, geography, climate, size) that would account for the different cultural temperaments. Finally, Benedict identified the primary difference – the structure of their social arrangements. It wasn't in the parts as much as it was in the *interactions among the parts*:

> From all comparative material, the conclusion that emerges is that societies where non-aggression is conspicuous have social orders in which the individual by the same act and at the same time serves his own advantage and that of the group. The problem is one of social engineering and depends upon how large the areas of mutual advantage are in any society. Non-aggression occurs (in these societies) not because people are unselfish and put social obligations above personal desires, but when social arrangements make these two identical.[6]

Benedict called this quality of alignment between personal and communal goals "high synergy." While synergy can arise in just about any area of society, she specifically described synergy in the economic realm. Low synergy societies "funnel" wealth into the hands of a few, while high synergy societies "siphon" wealth in a constant flow, spreading it where it's most needed. In a low synergy funneling system no one is secure against severe poverty or starvation, since the winds of fortune can shift at any moment. In such societies the most rational and prevalent survival strategy is hoarding rather than giving. These cultures feed the inner wolf of fear and hate.

Abraham Maslow (recall, he was a student of Benedict) witnessed a high synergy siphoning arrangement in action while living among a tribe of indigenous Canadians called the Northern Blackfoot:

> At one point in the ceremony, in the Plains' Indian tradition, he strutted, and, we would say, boasted, that is, told of his achievements. "You all know that

I have done so and so, you all know that I have done this and that, and you all know how smart I am, how good a stock man I am, how good a farmer, and how I have therefore accumulated great wealth." And then, with a very lordly gesture, a gesture of great pride but without humiliating, he gave this pile of wealth to the widows, to the orphaned children, and to the blind and diseased. At the end of the Sun Dance ceremony he was stripped of all his possessions, owning nothing but the clothes he stood in. He had, in this synergic way (I won't say either selfishly or unselfishly because clearly the polarity has been transcended) given away everything he had, but in that process had demonstrated what a wonderful man he was, how capable, how intelligent, how strong, how hard-working, how generous, and therefore how wealthy.

The Blackfoot Indians' Sun Dance ceremony brought superficially conflicting human motivations into coherence. As Maslow explained it, this system transcended the dichotomy of "me versus them." The gift-givers innate desire for social status, recognition and influence was satisfied by the same act that gave expression to his equally innate compassion and generosity. The gifts thus fulfilled the givers needs while simultaneously providing comfort and support to his less fortunate brethren. The Northern Blackfoot found ways to bring potentially conflicting human traits into alignment, amplifying rather than canceling their transformative power – into a laser beam of positive human potential.

Synergy may be the Philosopher's Stone of the good society – the secret to sustainable social transformation. It transforms potentially disruptive elements of human nature, such as the desire for power and status, into forces for good. Synergy turns the lead of human ego into the gold of transcendent love and compassion.

From the view of systems thinking we can see social synergy as a well-functioning arrangement of nodes, links and feedback loops. These feedback loops circulate information, for example, information about the overall state of the tribe – who is in need and who is doing well. They circulate material (food and blankets) to where it is most needed. They circulate energy (status and influence) to those capable of putting it to use for the good of the tribe. What emerges is a pattern of coordination and cooperation (and some competition) that creates a vital and resilient community. This community nurtures its members so they can contribute what they are able to the tribe in a virtuous cycle of love and peace.

The wisdom Ruth Benedict gained from her study of Native American tribes is an illuminating example of the power unleashed by the fulfillment of human potential. She worked from the being mode atop the self-actualization pyramid of her protégé, Abraham Maslow. Benedict defied the orthodoxy of analytic rationality and risked her standing in the academic world by studying the subjective values of happiness and peace. Sadly, Benedict's work on synergy languished after the outbreak of WWII when the military needed her help in understanding Japanese culture. Ironically, a deeper understanding of the conditions under which peace and happiness can flourish was thwarted by war. Thanks to the efforts of Maslow and Margaret Mead who compiled and published her surviving lecture notes, her insights were not lost. Today we have the opportunity to apply Benedict's theory of social synergy in a way that, as we will see, holds the potential to transform civilization.

The Magic of Emergence

The terms "emergent systems" and "emergent phenomena" are the rage in a wide range of disciplines – artificial intelligence, sociology, and biology, to name a few. "Emergence," in a nutshell, is the spontaneous arising of a new behavior, movement, or ability in a system (computer program, a society, or a species, for example). "Spontaneous" means the new behavior, movement or ability was not a predictable result of preceding conditions. Life is a most ubiquitous emergent phenomenon. It arose from individual atoms joining into molecules, and after billions of years of intermediary and increasingly complex patterns, it gave rise to you and me. Emergent phenomena are the super-natural magic of alchemy.

Not surprising, those still holding strong to the materialist, analytic, reductionist, left-brain dominated outlook view this modern alchemy with suspicion. As one student of emergence put it,

> Although ... emergence is logically possible, it is uncomfortably like magic. How does an irreducible

but supervenient [i.e., arising from more basic elements] downward causal power arise, since by definition it cannot be due to the aggregation of the micro-level potentialities? Such causal powers would be quite unlike anything within our scientific ken. This not only indicates how they will discomfort reasonable forms of materialism. Their mysteriousness will only heighten the traditional worry that emergence entails illegitimately getting something from nothing.[7]

Let's unpack this dense statement. The dominant Western worldview (also known as "reasonable forms of materialism") assumes the whole can be understood by examining and understanding the parts. In this view, everything (except some yet unknown substance which makes up subatomic particles) is "supervenient" – the parts are all there is. This explains why physics is the king of science: from the Western perspective, if we can fully grasp the smallest, most basic units of existence, then everything else would be (at least theoretically) knowable. If this is not the case, then there must be something – or more accurately, no "thing" – at work, which science (at least in its current form) cannot perceive

> "It would be possible to describe everything scientifically, but it would make no sense; it would be without meaning, as if you described a Beethoven symphony as a variation of wave pressure."
>
> - Albert Einstein

and thus cannot measure directly. Such an idea is modern heresy. It is quickly dismissed with contempt by "discomforted" materialists as mysticism because it does not fit within their model of the world. But there is a hole in this reductionist worldview of cosmic proportions. According to materialist science's Big Bang Theory, *everything* in this miraculous universe emerged from a speck of infinitely dense matter (they don't even speculate where it came from). Why then does getting something from nothing seem illegitimate when *everything came from almost nothing*?

The magic of emergence is in the interactions between nodes through time. Interactions are what enable otherwise insular units (people, atoms, fireflies) to coordinate and cooperate in ways that give rise to ordered complexity. Information (a pattern of energy with a shared meaning within the system) flows through the parts and through the whole in a continuous current (a feedback loop) that enables orchestration without a conductor. The flow of energy, matter and information is what enables complex and ordered movement. The complex and ordered movement of nodes within a system depends on robust, resilient, sensitive and numerous links, as it is the links that carry the information to which the nodes are responding. We can think of the links as the sound system that carries the rhythms to which the whole system dances. If coherence and harmony are what we want, then we need a quality sound system to broadcast the rhythms loud and clear, we need some great tunes, and we need a crowd ready to dance.

Very often important "parts" of a system are not physical: they cannot be directly measured and dissected, and are thus outside of the realm of what counts as "real" to materialists. For example, in our social network the links are our relationships. Human relationships cannot be placed under a microscope or weighed on a scale. Quantifiable proxies (that is, indirect measurements) may have a high correlation with certain relationship qualities. For example, the number of times two people communicate over a given period may signal the strength of their bond, or it may not. Connections between people are changing, infinitely varied, and asymmetric (we often love people who don't love us back). These connections exist in our hearts and our minds and thus cannot be marked accurately on a map of the network or distilled to a precisely measureable variable, yet they are very real.

Complex adaptive systems cannot be understood by breaking them apart – weighing, measuring, cataloging and photographing the pieces. Nor can they be explained by mathematical models. The alchemy of emergence defies materialist logic. Market fundamentalism can be seen as an effort to explain capitalism (a complex adaptive system) in precise and quantifiable terms. To make their simplified model of reality work they have to ignore the inherent uncertainty of the complex adaptive systems that make up the economy, that is, human beings. We, who are often motivated by perhaps the most inexplicable and immeasurable force of all – love. The result is a dominant economic theory that bears scant likeness to the real world.

Phase Transition

Emergent phenomena arise from what scientists call "phase transitions." A phase transition is simply a big change in the state of a system, usually a change in the amount of order in the system. Common examples include the change of metal into magnets, light waves into laser beams and water into ice.

During a phase transition to a state of more order nodes coordinate their actions and as a result, the system as a whole displays new properties. Thus, when a critical mass of electrons in a ferromagnetic metal aligns its orbits around their atomic nuclei, magnetism emerges. When the valleys and troughs of light waves are coaxed into sync, a laser beam emerges. When H_2O molecules arrange themselves in a crystalline lattice, water turns to ice. The elementary parts of these materials – metal atoms, light waves and water molecules – do not undergo fundamental physical changes as these transformations take place; rather, the relationships between the parts shift. New properties emerge at the level of the whole, but nothing (or, more accurately, no *thing*) is added or destroyed.

Through the lens of emergence and the phase transitions that give rise to emergence, we can understand the strength of synergy as an organizing principle. Synergy describes the quality of social arrangements that align the potentially conflicting forces within human nature. When nodes align – electrons spin in unison, light waves undulate in sync, or Blackfoot tribe members give and receive –

new levels of complexity emerge, and new possibilities are born.

Synergy, our Philosopher's Stone, is the key to sparking a phase transition in humankind, a transition for which we are ready. Sometimes a system can be ready to undergo a phase transition, but due to specific conditions it does not take place. An extra push is needed to get the transition started. For example, when a fluid becomes supersaturated (it has exceeded its carrying capacity) sometimes the normal process of crystallization does not occur. It is as if the molecules are confused about what they are supposed to do. If a seed crystal – a few molecules that know the crystallization dance – is introduced to the fluid, the dance will spread and transform the fluid, as if by magic, into a solid crystalline structure.

Our species is the supersaturated solution in need of a seed crystal. The nodes and links in the system of humanity have been undergoing profound changes that make possible a phase transition in civilization. The form our global society takes will depend on the dance we (consciously or unconsciously) choose. The possibilities range from the monotonous, joyless march of Storm Troopers or the richly varied and joyful dance of a Broadway musical extravaganza (assuming, that is, we survive).

Mobius Flip

Biologists once believed that evolution happens gradually, but more recent evidence suggests that it sometimes occurs in leaps. This is especially so when a revolutionary adaptation is involved. Our species has come so far, and today, we are at a precipice; we can fly or we can fall. It would be tragic if we allowed our species to slip into a dark age, perhaps never to regain the great advances we've achieved. We are like children playing with fire – nuclear bombs, biological weapons, genetically engineered life – it's time to grow up and evolve. We have the means to begin the phase transition and catalyze our evolution to a higher level of being. Our choices in the near future may well determine whether our future will be one of peace and prosperity, or violence, scarcity and eventually, extinction.

A physical form called a mobius strip simply and beautifully shows the fundamental transformation that can result from a minor system reconfiguration. If we (the authors) could magically appear in front of you now, we would walk you through a demonstration. Instead, we highly recommend that you do this on your own rather than just read about it (an opportunity to exercise participation skills).

    1. Cut a half-inch strip down the length of a letter-sized piece of paper (resulting in an 11-inch long, half inch wide slice of paper).
    2. Tape the two ends of the strip together to form a ring.

3. Notice the features of this ring. There are two sides that never meet; like two independent systems, the nodes in one system will never interact or coordinate with the nodes of the other.

4. Carefully undo the tape and flip one end 180 degrees, and re-tape it. You are now holding a "mobius strip," a simple shape that was only "discovered" by August Möbius in the 19th century (though it is found in the artwork of many ancient cultures).

5. Notice the transformation to the system's fundamental features made by this small change; trace your finger along the strip surface and you will find there is only one side and one edge. Separation is only a local illusion, at the system level there is only one continuous whole.

Nothing was added or destroyed, but by rearranging the structure, unity was created out of duality. This simple demonstration proves that small changes, the equivalent of a "mobius flip," can have huge effects on a system. We are making such changes in our systems today – in ourselves, our communities and our civilization. These changes have the potential to take us to a new stage in the evolution of our species.

An Unfolding Pattern

Communication is a central thread in the unfolding pattern of human evolution: civilization has advanced in step with our ability to efficiently share information across an ever-expanding range of both geography and time.[8] Spoken and written language, currency, radio, television and the Internet – these are forms of connective tissue in our human network that link us to one another, and to those who came before. Technological innovations are expanding and strengthening these connective tissues, and are driving human evolution. Feedback loops circulate information, matter and energy through this tissue and hold the amazingly intricate and complex pattern of civilization together through time and space.

Without written language, oral tradition and ritual are the main ways information is passed from one generation to the next. These relatively unreliable methods increase the chance that valuable knowledge will be lost.[9] (Stamping this information with the gravity of religion – a message from God is less likely to be forgotten – was a method of increasing the strength of this otherwise fragile connective tissue.) Without written language, civilization would have fizzled in its youth.

Civilization flourished as communication technology improved, allowing our ancestors to increasingly specialize, resulting in a fantastic expansion of our understanding of the world. With this understanding came the ability to shape the world in accord with our imaginings. As specialization increases, so does the need to coordinate the efforts of an ever-growing number of people over an ever-widening geography; as complexity increases, so does the push for increasingly powerful forms of communication.

As Milton and Rose Friedman pointed out, it takes the knowledge of many people to make a pencil. No single person has the knowledge to log the trees, mine the graphite, harvest the rubber, and then shape these raw materials into the simple yellow "Ticonderoga No. 2" we take for granted.[10] This astounding truth is a vivid illustration of our interconnectedness and interdependence. It also provides purely materialist and utilitarian support for the urgency of making our human systems more robust. One unfortunate glitch can shake the whole system to its foundation. Life without No. 2 pencils may not be the end of the world, but the complex and critical systems of food production and distribution, information networks, and electrical grids are also vulnerable to disruption.

Venetian merchant bankers' adoption of Arabic numerals in the thirteenth century illustrates well the link between communication technology and the evolution of civilization. Arabic numerals are a far more convenient method of storing, manipulating and communicating quantifiable information than Roman numerals. (Try long division using the Xs, Vs, and Ms of the Roman system!) This advance paved the way for the Venetians' later adoption of double entry accounting. With the benefit of these advances, the Venetians created a financial system the likes of which the world had never before seen. This financial system allowed for an extension of credit that fueled the rise of exploration and global trade in goods and, more importantly, ideas. The Renaissance (literally "rebirth") of Western civilization was the culmination of these advances. The Renaissance revived thought patterns of the ancient Greeks, technological advances of the Roman Empire, and Gnostic wisdom disguised as alchemy that had lain dormant for centuries.

Another innovation, the printing press, highlights the importance of communication technology to the evolution of human systems. The heretical ideas of Martin Luther spread across Europe through the spread of his written works, leading to the first critical fissures in the Catholic Church's domination of Europe. Two centuries later, Thomas Paine's pamphlet, "Common Sense," helped propel the American Revolution: on its publication General George Washington ordered it read aloud to his troops to boost morale.

The 19th century historian, Thomas Carlyle, said, "The Printing-press may be strictly denominated a Multiplication Table as applicable to the mind of man. The art of Printing is a multiplication of mind, [and] pamphlet-vendors are the most important springs in the machinery of Reform." Martin Luther, Thomas Paine, and innumerable others used the printing press to multiply the mind of humanity. With it they reformed Western modes of social organization and laid the foundation for the changes brought by capitalism and liberal democracy.[11]

A Supersaturated Solution

Humanity is a system primed for a phase transition. Miraculous advances in communication technology are multiplying and strengthening our connections (that is, our links) and fundamentally altering the fitness of people (that is, our nodes).

The UN estimates that the worldwide illiteracy rate dropped 50% between 1970 and 2005 (from 36.6% to 18.3%). Literacy powerfully improves a person's ability to access and use the information flowing on the increasingly robust feedback loops in the system of civilization. Further, while literacy is important in its own right, it lays the foundation for other profound changes. One who reads is more capable of forming views different from those expressed by society and its leaders. Psychologists have shown that literate people tend to be better at abstract thinking and are thus more capable of developing and evaluating ideas beyond their direct experience. Thus, literacy spreads the Mind Shift Meme (that is, questioning the functionality of one's default operating system).

The links in the system of humanity are also undergoing significant transformations. Social networks, email and text messaging allow individuals to effortlessly develop and maintain more connections over longer periods of time with relatively little effort. Our links are multiplying (though the strength of these links may be weak, they are of critical importance to system dynamics). The quality of our connections is likely evolving as well: we are easily able to find people who share our interests, form groups and propel new ideas forward. Our new connections have a huge capacity to spread instantly vast quantities of data at a small cost and with no loss of fidelity. Also, connections that were previously one-way, such as between a constituent and a legislator are now more likely two-way, thanks to the ease of electronic petition signing or sending an email. These changes dramatically improve our ability to coordinate actions and to form new patterns in the complex adaptive system of human civilization.

Human connections are far less constrained by geography and language. Google's advances in language translation, largely enabled by the huge database of existing translations available on the Internet from which Google's artificial intelligence learns, is turning the 1s and 0s of binary code into a true universal language. According to the Bible, the last time humanity shared a common language we built a tower up to heaven, perhaps this time we can simply create a heaven here on earth.

These fundamental changes in the nodes and links of the human system are priming humanity for a phase transition. We have witnessed phase transitions of various kinds in our species before, of varying kinds, both good and not so good. Historically, war has been the most common and powerful seed crystal in human evolution. The transformation of Germany, in the span of a single generation, from a defeated and bankrupt people to a force that challenged the world is an example of a phase transition in humanity. There were many factors that contributed to the human failure that resulted in this phase transition. The German cultural belief in the glory of war, social values that placed obedience to authority above all else, and the harsh sanctions imposed by the victors of WWI – these left the German people vulnerable to manipulation by a demagogue.

Hitler's ideology of racial and national pride based on a story of manifest destiny captured the hearts and minds of the German people. This ideology aligned the actions of a critical mass of people who were able to compel the rest to step into line. Those who objected were silenced ruthlessly. This is a picture of phase transition gone horribly wrong.

Thankfully, there are powerful examples of phase transition lifting humanity toward a more just world: Gandhi's peaceful overthrow of the British Empire and the civil rights movement in the United States.[12] Martin Luther King, Jr. and Mahatma Gandhi inspired masses of people to embrace the power of love over the force of violence. They spread a wave of liberty and justice in the United States and India, with rippling effects still being felt across the globe, most recently in the Middle East. The astonishing success of these watershed movements shows the amazing potential of humanity when we align with our highest values. Powerful ideas that speak to the hearts of a people can transform societies in the blink of an eye.

It is difficult for us to realize the significance of our place in history because our default time horizon is short. By nature we focus on our immediate circumstances as they have, historically, tended to be more important to physical survival. Now that our technological abilities have wide reaching effects in time and space, we must learn to broaden our view. The sooner a critical mass awakens to this truth, the better our chances for survival – and for a world of peace and plenty for all.

Human beings have been dreaming of a future of peace and abundance for millennia. Our success so far is incontrovertible, but our best may be ahead of us. Synergy, the Philosopher's Stone, is the key to unleashing a resource far more valuable than vulgar gold and silver. Modern alchemists are uncovering the means by which we can create social arrangements that align our individual and collective interests to transform civilization and unlock the latent power of human potential.

Humankind has lived at the mercy of wars, economic cycles, and genocides – they happen to us, even though they are of our own making. But we now have the chance to become conscious creators of our future. Awareness of the importance of synergy to healthy societies, deeper understanding of systems, improved communication technology, and a spreading Mind Shift Meme are giving us the power to take control of our destiny. Heaven on earth is within our reach.

7 - Metamorphosis

So far we've studied our place in the unfolding story of life on this planet. From the emerging of multi-cellular beings, to the forming of civilization and the blossoming of capitalism, we recognize our unique place in the miraculous pattern called life. Now we will expand the view – to the extreme – and see our place from the perspective of the cosmos. There is a surprising amount of useful knowledge to learn from this lofty vista. (Be forewarned, the next few pages are rather dense, your full attention may be required.)

Until recently, a chasm separated the science of complex adaptive systems (aka life on Earth) from physics and its hard science siblings. This chasm is known as the Second Law of Thermodynamics. It states that the energy of the universe is becoming more dispersed, that is, spread out evenly, over time. The Second Law often manifests as a movement from order to disorder. From this view, the world is like a clock winding down. But clearly there is some other force at work: life emerged from a primordial stew and has continued to organize simple inert molecules into increasingly intricate forms. As part of this intricate network of systems, life represents a movement toward increasing order and complexity. From the perspective of physics and its Second Law, we are an inexplicable anomaly.

Science is building a bridge across the chasm of the Second Law (though its strength remains to be seen). Life appears to emerge at the edge of chaos, where order and disorder meet (the scientific term is "energy disequilibria"). Two kinds of familiar complex systems emerge when order (cold) and disorder (heat) converge in our atmosphere: tornados and hurricanes. But these are not *adaptive* complex systems. A storm fades as soon as the energy disequilibrium that gave rise to it dissipates. Life, in contrast, manages to stay at the edge of chaos – surfing the wave between order and disorder, using the flow of energy that arises from the Second Law of Thermodynamics to create and recreate itself in ever more complex patterns.

Science also has a theory about why complex adaptive systems can occur at the edge of chaos. Conditions there are well suited to storing, communicating and manipulating information (that is, patterns of energy with shared meaning within a system). This enables a system to hold together through time and adapt to changes – that is, to survive and reproduce in a tumultuous world.

The human body shows the importance of information storage, communication and manipulation in living systems. DNA can be thought of as a plan the body uses to recreate itself throughout a lifetime – it is the stored data of previous successes, through eons of evolution, expressed in physical form. DNA guides the creation of the brain. The brain also stores information, though of a different kind: comparatively new information about the recent past and the current state of the system (both internal and external). As we interact with our surroundings, new knowledge amasses in the patterns of our neurons and synapses. With our brains we communicate – see, touch, talk, gesture, exchange pheromones, read and write – and manipulate information – invent, innovate, create. In the process, we develop novel ways of shaping our world. Helpful manipulations survive and are carried forward (including the memes explored in Chapter 4). Thus, information storage, communication and manipulation enable the formation and continuation of complex adaptive systems. In fact, it may be more accurate to say that complex adaptive systems *are* the storage, communication and manipulation of patterns of energy. We are the dancer and the dance.

Life at the Edge of Chaos

The space between rigid order and turbulent disorder (picture ice versus boiling water) is where information can be effectively stored, communicated and manipulated. Storage requires stability – coded patterns of meaning must be preserved through time and space

> "We are nothing but whirlpools in a river of water that flows constantly. We are not habitable substance, but self-perpetuating patterns."
> - Norbert Wiener

(DNA or a computer hard drive, for example). Communication and manipulation require fluidity – not total chaos, but enough freedom to move and experiment with new patterns (the brain, or a computer's random access memory, for example).

All known life needs liquid water to survive. Indeed, the average human body is about 70% water. Fluid water exists in a relatively narrow range of temperatures – in the space between the rigid order of ice and the turbulent chaos of steam. Water affords life the conditions necessary to hold a pattern together while allowing the flexibility to communicate and adapt to new circumstances. Travel too far in the wrong direction, cold or hot, and life ceases. Our fluid bodies are held upright by bones made of rigid calcium and are sustained by a constant flow of ethereal gases. We are physical expressions of the idea that life needs a balance of rigid order and flexible disorder – a balance found at the edge of chaos.

The theory that life emerges at the edge of chaos aligns with thousands of years of ancient wisdom. The familiar symbol of the *Taijitu* (known in the West as the *yin-yang* sign) is a visual representation of the Taoist idea that existence arises out of a unity (the Tao) that divides itself into two. The yin is calm and ordered. The yang is turbulent and chaotic. According to Taoist philosophy, our universe arises from the interaction of yin and yang. This understanding of reality is laid out in the ancient Taoist text, the Tao Te Ching: "The Tao gave birth to one; One gave birth to two; Two gave birth three; Three gave birth to all things."[1] In other words, existence arises from yin and yang – if you are only counting two, you are neglecting *and* – the *relationship between the two* – which, as we have learned, is essential to understanding any complex system. The 13th century Sufi poet, Rumi, pointed to this common oversight when he wrote, "You think because you understand 'one' you must also understand 'two,' because one and one make two. But you must also understand 'and'." It is the "and" that the scalpel of the scientific method routinely destroys.

In sum, science is finding evidence to support an ancient understanding of the nature of existence: life is patterned energy that constantly reinvents itself in response to its ever-changing surroundings. Life surfs the energetic wave that arises in the dance between yin and yang. A particular form of life, a specific pattern of energy, survives only as long as it succeeds in staying in the space between order and chaos. What worked yesterday (the information we store about the past) is what we have to work from. It is the foundation as we experiment with new forms (the information we manipulate) that may be better adapted to current conditions at the edge of chaos. These conditions are in constant flux. To survive and to hold our patterns together through time and space, we must be alert to changes in the system, which we learn about through interaction (that is, communication of information).

The value of the Zen practice of beginner's mind (which is rooted in Taoist philosophy) is illuminated at the edge of chaos. The constant flow of changing patterns to which we must be ready to adapt, requires the openness, agility and creativity of beginner's mind. When we filter out too much relevant information because it is inconsistent with our worldview, we limit our perception of the system's current state. When we hold too tightly to the paradigms of the past ("paradigm" means pattern), that is, when our expertise narrows our notions of what is possible, we are unable to imagine new patterns and new solutions. These limits on our capacity to communicate and manipulate information constrain our ability to adapt to new realities, thus threatening our survival.

With the beginner's mind of a master chaos surfer, let's return to Earth and view our unique place, with all its possibilities, in the unfolding story of human evolution.

Civilization as Emergence

Human civilization likely began to emerge from small bands of hunter-gatherers about 10,000 years ago, a blip on the timeline of life on Earth. Specialization of labor arose in its nascent form shortly after humans discovered the art of agriculture in the Fertile Crescent (modern day Iran). People realized (consciously or unconsciously) that wealth multiplies when labor is divided. No head bureaucrat or central planning office had to order people to focus their efforts on a specific stage in the production of goods or provision of services, rather, it happened spontaneously. This trend continued on a gradual trajectory until the Industrial Revolution took hold and spurred specialization to new extremes.

Specialization is a relatively recent adaptation – a new pattern of coordination that has had a revolutionary effect on humankind. We have widened the edge of chaos by arranging ourselves in an increasingly intricate and complex pattern. This has allowed greater numbers to survive and thrive, as we learned to extract more energy from our surroundings and put it to efficient use. Adam Smith witnessed the beginning of this phase transition (that is, pattern change) in the system of civilization. The thread of specialization is a significant part of the fabric of modern capitalism.

In the previous chapter, we saw that civilization has been unfolding in sync with advances in communication technology. The edge of chaos theory clarifies the link between these evolutionary threads. The pattern of human coordination and cooperation (that is, civilization) increases in complexity only to the degree that we can store, communicate and manipulate information. From this vantage point, computers, the Internet, and smart phones are not mere tools of convenience and entertainment. Rather, they are means of creating new, more adaptive social arrangements with the potential to keep us balanced at the edge of chaos.

Improvements to our *external* abilities to store, communicate and manipulate information are many and clear. But dramatic advances in our *internal* abilities are equally important: increased literacy, improved education, and expanded consciousness result in more sensitive, creative, intelligent and responsive participants in the evolution of life. These changes help us create novel patterns, that is, innovations that can help us stay balanced in the sweet spot between order and chaos. The Arab Spring, the Tea

Party, and Crop Mobs are striking examples of these new patterns of cooperation.

Today, our metaphorical sound system is global and is increasingly capable of carrying frequencies most of us have never heard. People everywhere are composing new tunes (that is, memes) and sharing them with the world. Some are catching on. Not surprisingly, some tunes are not harmonious. For example, the London riots of August 2011, though even such destructive memes can carry important information about the state of the system. Too much of humanity is being cut off, atrophying and threatening the health of the rest of system. Good societies promote a healthy flow of energy, which is crucial to producing a truly transcendent Broadway musical extravaganza.

Starfish and Spiders Revisited

The edge of chaos theory explains the important roles played by the social arrangements metaphorically described as starfish and spiders. We can understand spider institutions as pattern holders. They are the relatively rigid, static arrangements of relationships and energy flow that hold the pattern of civilization through time as individuals come and go. Political, cultural and religious institutions store the information about what worked in the past, analogous to DNA in our collective human organism. Centralized, rule-based institutions anchor humanity in the order side of the edge of chaos, keeping us from flying into the flux of oblivion. If left unchecked, though, the "establishment" would drag humanity into ice-like rigidity that would eventually lead to extinction.

Starfish arrangements, on the other hand, are closer to the turbulent side of the edge of chaos. They are more fluid and flexible than spiders. Starfish tend to better communicate and manipulate information. Compare, for example, the rigidity of traditional corporations to the fluidity of Wikipedia. Decentralized, value-based organizations keep humanity perceptive and nimble so we don't freeze to death, but left to fly free, they would propel us into chaos where we would disintegrate into pure pattern-less energy.

In the unfolding of civilization successful starfish organizations naturally evolve into spider institutions. What worked yesterday solidifies into a new foundation from which future generations strive to adapt to changing conditions. Hippies become yuppies – not quite the same as their parents – but playing the same role in the rhythmic unfolding of humanity's story.

An attempt at educational reforms in Texas shows the backward looking tendencies of spider institutions. A think tank, seeking to address decreased graduation rates and higher tuition costs within the University of Texas, released a report suggesting seven changes.[2] It focused on improving the quality and availability of information (particularly about professors' teaching abilities) and offering students more and clearer options. In other words, they recommended introducing fluid democratic starfish qualities to a decidedly top-down spider institution. The backlash from within the University and its vast alumni was overwhelming. "The campus," said a report by the Liberal Arts dean "is not a marketplace."[3] The redistribution of power that would have resulted from giving students power in the form of information and choices threatened the interests of those within the institution – professors, administrators, and alumni. Not surprisingly, they used their clout to preserve the status quo. Of course, those opposed to the suggested changes likely did not consciously think they were putting their own interests ahead of progress. But their view of what higher education is *supposed to look like* precludes the systematic empowerment of students, whose proper role is confined to passively receiving knowledge from above. Put differently, the value rigidity of the spider institutions of Texas higher education is obstructing evolution.

From this vantage point, we see the importance of dreamers in the evolution of humankind. Every generation's dreamers push humanity toward the edge, where we must thrive if we are to realize our potential as a miraculous expression of universal energy. The frustration voiced in the Unites States, particularly by the Tea Party and the Occupy Wall Street movements, is at its core an expression of our failure to explore and reach for the edge. We yearn for a vibrant future but we are looking in the rear-view mirror. We hope our calcified institutions, the remnants of past successes, will miraculously liquefy into change-loving organizations that can propel us forward. The Tea Party blames government while the Occupiers fault large corporations, both are correct but they miss the underlying source of systemic dysfunction – the centralization of power. Merely rebelling against rigid centralized institutions will not give rise to the dynamic creative decentralized organizations that can rebalance society at the edge of chaos. Chapter 8 outlines a potential springboard from which well-intentioned Tea Partiers and Occupiers can launch a new wave of starfish organizations. Thus, they can spark a new pattern of civilization that reduces the role of governments and large corporations, and redistributes power to the people.

Downward Causation

Human nature has an amazing breadth: it encompasses the angry hateful wolf, and the peaceful loving wolf of the Native American grandfather. Indeed, the scope of our innate capacities allows us to survive in nearly every environment on the planet. Our adeptness at surfing the edge of chaos is matched by few, if any, species. As we mature, our natural potential narrows – some qualities expand while others shrink. The Nazis were just as human as you and me, but they were molded by their social arrangements, through feedback loops, into creatures having little resemblance to the human beings we consider ourselves to be. Blackfoot Indians were also just as human as you and me, but they were molded by the feedback loops formed by their synergistic social arrangements to be unattached to material possessions, generous and kind.

Modern capitalism and the emergence of the consumer culture that fuels it inflict powerful downward shaping forces on all who are exposed. The "greed is good" motto of *Wall Street*'s Gordon Gecko character is a vivid example of the not-so-subtle influence of the market fundamentalist worldview on our values. The current ad campaign of Coca-Cola, themed "open happiness," promotes the notion that a blend of caffeine, corn syrup, food coloring, and bubbles holds the key to fulfillment. Messages promoting greed and consumption as a viable path to true happiness pervade our society, molding us into the cogs and wheels the machine of capitalism needs to continue its blind growth. We do ourselves a huge disservice by confusing our true potential with the distorted caricature projected by this current of mainstream culture. Each time we click on the television or read a gossip magazine we add our personal power to this feedback loop – it is not being done to us we are doing it to ourselves. We (the authors) don't pretend to be immune to popular culture's allure; we do our best to limit our exposure – gossip magazines in line at the grocery store only!

Government policies also hold potent downward shaping forces. Welfare programs that are not carefully crafted to avoid misaligning incentives and to preserve values such as integrity and personal responsibility run the risk of warping the social fabric in unhealthy and unsustainable ways. Indeed, research suggests that government policies can, over time, erode the very foundation of welfare state programs. For example, reducing the social stigma of cheating the system to receive benefits to which one is not entitled.[4]

Donella Meadows, a pioneer in systems thinking, astutely describes results of well-intended system intervention that undermines important dynamics (including social norms) in her book *Thinking in Systems*:

> A corrective feedback process within the system is doing a poor (or even so-so) job of maintaining the state of the system. A well-meaning and efficient intervenor watches the struggle and steps in to take some of the load. The intervenor quickly brings the system to the state everybody wants it to be in. Congratulations are in order, usually self-congratulations by the intervenor to the intervenor.
>
> Then the original problem reappears, since nothing has been done to solve it at its root cause. So the intervenor applies more of the "solution," disguising the real state of the system again, and thereby failing to act on the problem. That makes it necessary to use still more "solution."
>
> The trap is formed if the intervention, whether by active destruction or simple neglect, undermines the original capacity of the system to maintain itself ... Why does anyone enter the trap? First, the intervenor may not foresee that the initial urge to help out a bit can start a chain of events that leads to ever increasing dependency, which ultimately will strain the capacity of the intervenor. The American health-care system is experiencing the strains of that sequence of events.
>
> Second, the individual or community that is being helped may not think through the long-term

loss of control and the increased vulnerability that go along with the opportunity to shift a burden to an able and powerful intervenor...

The problem can be avoided up front by intervening in such a way as *to strengthen the ability of the system to shoulder its own burdens.* This option, helping the system to help itself, can be much cheaper and easier than taking over and running the system – something liberal politicians don't seem to understand.

Understanding the power of downward causation is essential to mastering the complex art of weaving rich, strong, and sustainable social arrangements. Our failure to appreciate adequately the systemic effects of shortsighted policies at all levels of society (individual, governmental and corporate) severely undermines the strength of our society. For example, the systems perspective explains a basic flaw of market fundamentalism which is (at least in its current form) shortsighted (profits are measured quarterly) and thus chronically weaves an unsustainable pattern.[5] Similarly, U.S. politicians, with the ever-shortening time between campaign cycles, suffer from similar shortsightedness, resulting in choices that seriously threaten the long-term health of American society.

It is in our nature to favor immediate results over long-term progress, so we are left treating symptoms instead of curing diseases. Behavioral psychologists identify this tendency as a quirk in our cognitive processing. It is a quirk that makes sense given human beings' historically short life expectancy – saving for the future isn't a smart strategy if there is a high likelihood of dying in the near term.

We are now capable of dramatically affecting the force and direction of the wave at the edge of chaos, upping our needed surfing skills. Pollution and deforestation are causing climatic turbulence that will challenge our abilities to maintain balance, let alone simply stay afloat. Now that we are aware of our precarious position we must attune ourselves to the inherent wisdom of nature. Understanding the role of feedback loops and the downward causation they entail is essential to recreating healthy social arrangements. As we will explore in the next chapter, Ruth Benedict's social synergy may be the key to unlocking a treasure of new patterns that are better adapted to our current conditions at the edge of chaos.

Precision Bias

The materialist myopia that obstructs our understanding of system dynamics is an example of the more general cognitive flaw of *precision bias*.[6] We tend to focus on precisely measurable variables and neglect more difficult to assess elements, even though the latter are often of equal or greater importance. As Rumi taught, understanding *one*, doesn't amount to understanding *two* (the precise variables) without knowledge of *and* (the imprecise variable). This tendency results in maps that are intricate and thorough, but seriously flawed. We're better off with blurry but accurate maps. Unfortunately, the things many of us care about most (health, love, and meaning, for example) are not easy to measure precisely. Thus, because of precision bias we end up focusing on things that are secondary to our true fulfillment, which explains, at least in part, why we often confuse the markers with the game.

This seemingly academic problem has very real-world consequences. Government officials and the mainstream media myopically focus on gross domestic product ("GDP") as the measure of progress, rarely questioning whether this number is an effective proxy for what we are trying ultimately to accomplish. GDP includes cigarette production and the cost of medical care for smokers suffering from lung cancer, and foods laden with fat and sugar along with the cost of treating diabetes, cancer, and heart disease. The things we care about most – healthy relationships, the quality of the care of our children, the mental and physical well-being of loved ones, passion for our work, the beauty of our surroundings – are not reflected in GDP. In fact, corrosion of these values is often *positively* reflected in GDP. Paying divorce attorneys, treating preventable disease, hiring strangers to care for loved ones while we toil at jobs we dislike, erecting yet another strip mall on previously open space, cleaning up a toxic waste site – all are counted as progress. GDP certainly tells us something about the *speed* with which we are moving, but it tells us nothing of our *direction*.

Lest you think precision bias is a left-wing conspiracy theory, John Bogle, former head of The Vanguard Group and a titan of the investment world, warns that "In our society, in economics, and in finance, we place too much trust in numbers. But numbers are not reality. At best, they're a pale reflection of reality. At worst, they're a gross distortion of the truths we seek to measure."[7] Donella Meadows (an astute student of systems) echoes Bogle's appraisal: "No one can define or measure justice, democracy, security, freedom, truth, or love. No one can define or measure any value. But if no one speaks up for them, if systems aren't designed to produce them, if we don't speak about them and point toward their presence or absence, they will cease to exist."[8] We need to be smarter than the monkey with its hand stuck in the coconut, we must remember what it is we are really after and not allow precision bias to lead us astray.

Systems science offers a logical reason for the central role of quantifiable metrics in modern society. Expansive non-local systems are generally ill equipped to deal with qualitative values. For information to be efficiently and effectively communicated within a system, from node to node, well beyond direct connections, it must be expressed in a way that can be understood clearly throughout the system. The Internet, for example, could not have grown into the global network of today without the adoption of universal protocols that allowed anyone fluent in the language to participate. Nor would the Internet have been possible without the magic of the ones and zeros of binary code. The power of capitalism is likewise possible because of the language of numbers. Math is a universal language and is thus is an ideal means of communicating information in expansive systems.

Recognizing the role of numbers in expansive systems is essential to understanding the source of the limits of our current systems and developing alternatives that can bring us closer to the world we want to create for ourselves and our children. There are changes we can make to our systems that embrace the communicative power of numbers and expand the math-based language of economics to include more of the qualitative values that make life worth living. (The next chapter explores some specific ideas.)

Our criticisms of GDP, and other precise but inaccurate metrics, are not new and many economists would readily admit to their limits, but old habits die hard. News reporters and politicians seemingly lack either the will or the knowledge to shift away from the myopic focus on GDP. Despite its limited usefulness, we seem to be stuck with it for now. Perhaps one way to break this habit is to offer an alternative to supplement rather than replace GDP. [9]

The small Buddhist country of Bhutan assesses its policies based on *Gross National Happiness* ("GNH"). "Four pillars of happiness" form the basis of GNH – promotion of sustainable development, preservation and promotion of cultural values, conservation of the natural environment, and establishment of good governance. The pillars are tied to 72 specific indicators of well-being. GNH is an alternative measurement of progress that puts accuracy ahead of precision. It offers a means of tuning our system so it delivers more of what we really want – improvement in the *qualities* of life, not just the *quantities* of life. Of course, GNH can be adjusted to the values of a specific culture: for example, GNH for the United States would likely include a measure of personal autonomy. Introducing a GNH type metric in the U.S. (as a complement to GDP) would be a step in the right direction – a step many other countries, including France, Britain, China and Brazil are taking.

There is another source of precision bias: human beings (scientists and academics in particular) are not comfortable admitting our ignorance. By focusing on the narrow slices of reality about which we feel knowledgeable we can deceive ourselves into thinking we have a firm grasp on a universe that is very likely ultimately unfathomable to human consciousness. We need to get over this habit of self-delusion if we are to build accurate, if blurry, maps of our world, and thus more effectively choose and reach a destination.

The word "science" comes from the Latin "scientia" which means "knowledge.") However, more and more scientific knowledge is pointing to a place beyond the reach of our senses. We theorize based on the scraps of evidence we can perceive and build increasingly powerful means of extending the reach of our perceptive abilities (particle colliders and space probes, for example). Relativity theory, quantum mechanics and the science of systems are prime examples of this phenomenon. In fact, the science of systems arose in part

> He who thinks he knows, doesn't know. He who knows that he doesn't know, knows.
>
> -Taoist teaching

from the realization brought about by quantum physics that the nature of reality is far more complex, interconnected and, bizarre (from the view of common sense) than we ever imagined. Everything in this existence arises from a field of energy – this is not a mystical idea, but a scientific fact that has yet to be incorporated into most of our conceptions of reality.

Systems theory admits that our knowledge is relative, and that we are, by the nature of reality and our place in it, doomed to a significant degree of ignorance. Thus, systems theory integrates the bizarre-but-true revelations of physics into our everyday understanding of reality. It is here that synthetic and analytic rationality embrace – our new maps are made with both glue and scissors. With these tools we can reweave the pattern of civilization in a way that is in harmony, rather than in conflict, with the ever-changing web of life. Donella Meadows beautifully expressed this truth:

> Self-organizing, nonlinear, feedback systems are inherently unpredictable. They are not controllable. They are understandable only in the most general way. The goal of foreseeing the future exactly and preparing for it perfectly is unrealizable. The idea of making a complex system do just what you want it to do can be achieved only temporarily, at best. We can never fully understand our world, not in the way our reductionist science has led us to expect. Our science itself, from quantum theory to the mathematics of chaos, leads us into irreducible uncertainty. For any objective other than the most

trivial, we can't optimize; we don't even know what to optimize. We can't keep track of everything. We can't find a proper, sustainable relationship to nature, each other, or the institutions we create, if we try to do it from the role of omniscient conqueror.

For those who stake their identity on the role of omniscient conqueror, the uncertainty exposed by systems thinking is hard to take. If you can't understand, predict, and control, what is there to do?

Systems thinking leads to another conclusion, however, waiting, shining, obvious, as soon as we stop being blinded by the illusion of control. It says that there is plenty to do, of a different sort of "doing." The future can't be predicted, but it can be envisioned and brought lovingly into being. Systems can't be controlled, but they can be designed and redesigned ... We can't impose our will on the system. We can listen to what the system tells us, and discover how its properties and our values can work together to bring forth something much better than could ever be produced by our will alone.

We can't control systems or figure them out. But we can dance with them!

In other words, systems thinking tell us to put down our sandbags and start learning to surf.

Physics Envy

The notion of economics as "hard science" is being revealed as a fallacy. (Much as the idea of political science was discredited following its failure to predict one of the most dramatic political changes of the twentieth century, the fall of the Soviet Union.) Economic experts fall prey to precision bias. They make educated guesses, and shroud them in the language of physics – laws, mathematical formulas, and impressive sounding "econometrics" – to give their forecasts an air of certainty and precision. However, research has shown that the underlying assumption of modern economics – individuals act to maximize their own economic gain – is very often simply wrong. As economist John Kay explained, "The absurdities of rational expectations [that is, that people are motivated chiefly by economic gain] come from the physics envy of many economists, who mistake occasional insights for universal truths. Economic models are illustrations and metaphors, and cannot be comprehensive descriptions even of the part of the world they describe."

The desire to transform economics into a hard science distorts and limits the understanding of how human beings work together to shape our material existence. This desire is understandable given the reverence our world holds for physics, the hardest science of them all, and our yearning for certainty and control. Ernest Rutherford, the father of nuclear physics, pithily describes physics' place in the science: "All science is physics or stamp collecting." Who can blame economists for not wanting to be mere stamp collectors? Thus, economics and the study of capitalism, in particular, followed the logic of analytic rationality. This approach gave rise to market fundamentalism, that is, the notion that free markets follow natural laws that lead to the best allocation of resources. Synthetic rationality reveals the fallacy of market fundamentalist dogma.

For over two centuries academics has been searching for the ultimate, immutable laws of economics. While this approach may be helpful in understanding certain qualities of our economic system, it has also shaped our conception of reality. Capitalism is a product of the cumulative actions of human beings. We are not automatons. We cannot be distilled to a knowable and predictable set of variables. We cannot be efficiently molded to fit the precise requirements of a complex machine (though our education system keeps trying). We may be able to identify economic trends in our system, but it is unlikely that invariable laws await discovery. *Relative truths*, however, can provide practical insights that illuminate the way to a brighter future. We must keep in mind that trends and tendencies are manifestations of a dynamic system. Its structure is changing at an ever-increasing pace, making it foolish to rely excessively on past trends to predict the future (an easy pitfall given our precision bias).

Failure to recognize the systemic and dynamic nature of economics helped fuel the 2008 subprime crisis. Analysts, looking at history, concluded that real estate prices vary regionally, not nationally, so investors could be insulated from risk by diversifying geographically. The analysts did not adequately appreciate that by creating a national market for mortgages they rearranged the very system dynamics that had historically made real estate prices a regional phenomenon. The economy is not separate from us, it is us – when we change it changes. Economics is *not* like physics.

Imagine our cave dwelling ancestors trying to detect the laws governing the ebb and flow of their hunting and gathering success. Whatever trends they identified likely provided some seasonal predictability for a time, but precise predictions would have been impossible. Likewise, whatever "laws" may have governed pre-capitalist modes of production and exchange (feudalism, mercantilism, agrarianism) are obsolete today. Why should the "laws" of capitalism be any more permanent? Our economic system, unlike our DNA and the cosmos, is changing rapidly. Our understanding of it must account for the system's compressed time dynamics. The value rigidity of modern economics, reflected in the laws and mathematical formulas of market fundamentalism, hinder our ability to adapt to changing circumstances. This rigidity tends to make us slow and stupid – not helpful for balancing at the edge of chaos.

Silly Putty

Though letting go of our role as omniscient conqueror may at first feel dangerous and scary, ultimately embracing our place within the fabric of the cosmos is fantastically empowering. We have a choice between two alternative stories, the creations myths for the 21st century. The first is the one we've been telling ourselves and our children in various forms, over the past several centuries. We are Lilliputians caught in a mind-bogglingly vast and confounding universe, doomed to scarcity and eventual extinction at the hands of the Second Law of Thermodynamics. Meanwhile, we must amass ever more material wealth (sandbags) to forestall our tragic fate for a little while longer. The second story is far more optimistic. We are the most complex known material expression of the creative forces of the universe. All that we must do to live in abundance and harmony is align with these currents and they will propel us forward to new adventures! When we align ourselves with the forces out of which we arise, we are powerful beyond our wildest dreams. Currently much of our power is latent and we are squandering much of the rest in our fight against the very powers that are responsible for our existence.

The human mind is a miraculous emergent phenomenon. The human brain, the pattern that gives us access to consciousness, is an intricate and dense web of connections. Each neuron in the average adult brain contains about 7,000 synapses that link these neurons to one another. This profusion of connectivity points to the potential evolutionary quantum leap reflected in the advances in communication technology that are multiplying, strengthening and lengthening the connections among human beings.

The Internet, smart phones, and related advances are forming an increasingly intricate and dense web of connectivity, which may be the beginning of a collective human nervous system. We are learning to synthesize a *global human brain* and so far, most are playing with it like it's silly putty. We must awaken to the possibility that, with this emerging supra human organ, we have the capacity to bring new and powerful forms of emergence into being. There is magic here, not the *supernatural* stuff of fantasy, but the *super-natural* stuff of reality.

Humanity's future depends on inspiring the creative and productive use of this nascent super-natural magic. We are already witnessing the potential of this proto gray matter to transform the world. Twitter, Facebook, and the cell phones empowered Arab citizens to coordinate their efforts from the bottom up, bringing democracy to more of the world. But this is not destiny. It is a possibility; a delicate blossom that can be crushed by countervailing forces. The contest of alternative patterns is being played out across the globe. China, Syria and Bahrain prove that centralized power is the enemy of liberty and the authoritarian leaders who wield it are quite capable of using technology to crush the will of the people.

In Western democracies, politicians, bureaucrats and industrialists are moving toward controls that threaten to quash the evolutionary force of free and decentralized information flow. For example, bureaucrats at Bay Area Rapid Transit borrowed a move out of Mubarak's playbook when they recently cut off cell phone service to riders in an effort to thwart a planned protest. (Thankfully, the overwhelming public reaction caused officials to promise never to repeat this offense, but the lesson remains – institutional power seeks to preserve itself). The Cyber Intelligence Sharing and Protection Act, a bill that would give the federal government broad access to citizen's online activities with no judicial oversight, passed the House of Representatives on April 26, 2012. The Orwellian possibilities enabled by this act are truly terrifying.

Magic of Butterflies

It is said that for a caterpillar to transform into a butterfly, it must first give up being a caterpillar. For humanity to continue transforming from a species in conflict (with nature and one another) into a species in harmony, we must surrender our old ways. Caterpillars and butterflies have identical DNA – their cells contain an incredible range of possibility. Human beings have an equally, if not greater, miraculous range of possibilities. We have the power to consciously choose our individual and collective destinies – to become something new, more beautiful and free. We won't grow wings and fly (at least not biologically), but the possible transformation is no less transcendent.

There are signs of this nascent transformation: violent crime is declining, our stomach for the horrors of war is shrinking, and when nature inflicts tragedy on a population the world responds. Racism, sexism and other isms are more and more seen for what they are, a product of egoistic ignorance and small-mindedness. These developments are strong and encouraging evidence that we have the ability and the will to shape our reality. While human nature includes a strong dose of greed and envy, we can tip the scales and self-evolve into individuals who are more compassionate and generous: we can feed the wolf of love.

This possible transformation is of breathtaking and miraculous scope. In biological terms, it's similar to the first life venturing out of the primordial stew onto dry land, or that brave ancient reptilian creature who first took flight. Many are emerging from a cocoon of isolation into a world of connectedness, as we become aware of our privileged place in the unfolding story of our universe.

For centuries, Western minds have been shaped by an underlying and pervasive belief that we are separate from nature, and that our survival depends on conquering her. Under the influence of this distorted belief we have created a world of crisis – we have pushed our ecosystem to the bleeding edge of chaos. We are in danger of falling into an abyss. Everywhere we look essential systems are showing signs of disintegration, on the verge of utter destruction. We are slowly emerging from this nightmare of our own making, just in time to see that we had it all wrong: salvation lies in aligning ourselves with the cosmic forces of nature that created us and *that are us*. We may still have time to back away from the chasm and reestablish balance.

Balance, as we will explore in the coming chapters, involves recreating the pattern of capitalism so that it is aligned with nature and with our most humane selves. This pattern must include the right mix of spiders and starfish (and everything between). Spider institutions create stability and anchor us to the order side of the edge of chaos (so we don't go flying off into the abyss of anarchy).

Starfish organizations fluidly, creatively and (sometimes) intelligently adapt to the ever-changing reality on the edge of chaos; starfish keep us from descending into the icy death of static rigidity.

8 – The Art of Steering

We are explorers, surfers, dancers, singers and weavers – these are just a handful of the metaphors pointing to something we see on the horizon, something truly novel and thus beyond the direct reach of words. Our explorations of far-flung times, places, abstract ideas and philosophies have brought us to the here and now, where any world-transforming project must begin.

"Cybernetics" (that is, "the art of steering") is one of the earliest terms for the scientific study of systems. A deeper understanding of this art can aid in us in skillfully steering our civilization toward consciously chosen destinations. As we have seen, the current version of our most powerful collective system, capitalism, has as its aim material growth, rather than human happiness and fulfillment (or even long-term survival). As long as material growth is our overarching systemic goal, then we will continue getting more of the same – "progress" that deprives billions, now and in the future, of the opportunity to realize their full potential.

This chapter explores opportunities to change direction and move toward a future in which economic forces foster happiness and the expression of our full potential. Our new tools of navigation will include better maps, more precise compasses, responsive steering mechanisms and powerful propulsion. The philosopher, dreamer and pioneer of systems thinking, Buckminster Fuller, saw the possibility of small adjustments leading to major changes. He vividly expressed his vision in terms of the art of steering:

> Something hit me very hard once, thinking about what one little man could do. Think of the Queen Mary – the whole ship goes by and then comes the rudder. And there's a tiny thing at the edge of the rudder called a trimtab. It's a miniature rudder. Just moving the little trim tab builds a low pressure that pulls the rudder around. Takes almost no effort at all. So I said that the little individual can be a trimtab. Society thinks it's going right by you, that it's left you altogether. But if you're doing dynamic things mentally, the fact is that you can just put your foot out like that and the whole big ship of state is going to go. So I said, call me Trimtab.

The following ideas are trim tabs. These leverage points can empower a critical mass of dreamers to guide the unfolding pattern of civilization. With them we can reestablish balance at the edge of chaos, and create a future of peace, justice and vitality.

For Profiting Humanity Enterprises

Languages shape thinking, filters perceptions, and affects our ability to imagine novel responses to changing conditions. "Nonprofit" is a term that erects unseen barriers between humanity's current position and where we want to be. The word disempowers by only defining what it is not. Those in favor of women's reproductive freedom refer to themselves as "pro-choice" rather than "anti-life" while abortion opponents call themselves "pro-life," not "anti-choice." They understand the greater power lies with proactively stating what you are *for* rather than being defined by what you're *against*. At a basic level, it is the difference between being reactive, and thus letting your circumstances (the past) define you, and being proactive, and thus being the source of what you wish to create. The concise and poignant saying, "What you resist persists" explains this drawback of the "nonprofit" moniker.

More importantly, the etymological root of the word "profit" is the Latin "profectus" which means to progress, to advance or to succeed. Thus, the literal meaning of nonprofit is to "not progress, advance or succeed." Is it any wonder the nonprofit sector is unable to bridge the gap between what our economic system delivers and the world we would like to create? The conventional nonprofit model is a self-fulfilling prophecy of failure.

An alternative term that addresses these two flaws, "for profiting humanity," highlights the main difference between traditional "for profit" and "nonprofit" organizations. That is, who are the primary beneficiaries, a single owner, all of humanity, or something in between? The current framework separates individuals and organizations whose main purpose is improving the world from the dynamic and vital flow of energy and information of free market capitalism. They are relegated to dependency on donations. We put these "nonprofit" organizations in the position of beggars as they take on many of our most important challenges, such as preserving our environment and protecting the most vulnerable among us. The false dichotomy of for profit versus nonprofit seriously hampers our ability to shape our world for the better. System dynamics hinder efforts to overcome the limits of the present framework, such as social entrepreneurship and corporate responsibility. For profiting humanity ("FPH") enterprises can alter these dynamics in ways that can bring vital energy to individuals and ventures prepared to bridge the gap between where we are and where we want to be.

Moving away from rigid duality toward a continuum offers a more accurate and nuanced model of reality. It also illuminates previously obscured possibilities. Donella Meadows explains the value of conscious boundary drawing:

> Systems rarely have real boundaries ... We have to invent boundaries for clarity and sanity; and boundaries can produce problems when we forget that we've artificially created them...
>
> It's a great art to remember that *boundaries are of our own making, and that they can and should be reconsidered for each new discussion, problem, or purpose.* It's a challenge to stay creative enough to drop the boundaries that worked for the last problem and to find the most appropriate set of boundaries for the next question. It's also a necessity, if problems are to be solved well.[1]

Redrawing the boundaries *we have created*[2] between for profit and nonprofit enterprises is a relatively slight alteration in the patterns of commerce. But it is a change that can provide critical resources (energy, matter and information) to those experimenting with new patterns, addressing challenges and realizing opportunities. Experimentation is the key to discovering and developing the system configurations that can bring us into balance at the edge of chaos.

Carbon Neutral Travel

Imagine an environmentally conscious FPH investor (or group of investors) buys out the shareholders of *Orbitz.com*, and converts the company into an FPH enterprise. The business model is now focused on countering climate change. Travelers make online reservations the same way (and at the same price) but profits go to offsetting carbon emissions. This reinvented Orbitz could significantly impact the net effects of travel on global climate change.

The estimated cost to offset all online passenger air travel booked in the US is $853 million.[3] The estimated cash flow generated by online travel booked in US is $946 million.[4] Thus, a successful FPH Orbitz could counter all carbon pollution of its customers' air travel. Whether an FPH Orbitz would come to dominate the travel reservation industry is a matter of speculation. Our informal survey of friends and family suggests that (provided cost and quality are the same) people would be happy to switch from for-profiting-shareholder companies to an FPH Orbitz. Major corporations would not want to be seen on the (well-advertised) list of non-Orbitz customers.

One philanthropist or a group of like-minded, wealthy investors (or even a crowd-sourced venture) could purchase Orbitz today for about $400 million. The new owners could use its existing marketing budget to advertise its new mission, take market share from its competitors by offering a fundamentally better service, and make a sizable dent in America's carbon footprint. The same analysis holds for car rental companies: an FPH Avis could dominate the competition by offering carbon neutral rental car travel. Relative to other industries, travel reservations and car rentals are prime targets for the FPH model. Other than branding success, there is little to distinguish between the services of competing companies, thus, adding carbon offsets significantly improves the value offered to customers.

Of course, preventing carbon emissions in the first place, rather than offsetting them, may often be the most efficient means of combating climate change. Thus, providing suppliers of goods and services with incentives to lower emissions is a way to treat the problem of carbon emissions at its source. An FPH Orbitz could provide its users with a "carbon score" for airlines, hotels, and rental cars. This would create an information feedback loop within the travel industry to empower consumers to reward responsible corporate behavior that aligns with their ecological values. According to one survey, about half of U.S. travelers say they would more likely use an airline that offset carbon emissions, used newer, more fuel efficient jets, or recycled.[5] In other words, a significant portion of the nodes in this network is ready to respond to information related to an airline's environmental practices. The lack of this information in the system is hampering its intelligence, resulting in a poor use of resources. We are steering blindfolded.

The FPH Orbitz example shows that a minor shift in structure, a metaphorical mobius flip, can expand the economic system. Effects that were previously externalities (that is, external to the system of capitalism) such as carbon pollution can be included within, and responsibly dealt with by, the system. In other words, it moves us from fragmentation toward wholeness and integration. It gives people the power to effectively and efficiently steer the system in alignment with their ideals. An FPH Orbitz would improve the system's steering mechanism and enable us to move forward forcefully, propelled by the incredible power (that is, money) of free market capitalism. Thus, "we the people" could take an important step toward solving one of the most daunting challenges facing humanity, which is now inadequately addressed by governments and underfunded "nonprofits."

Pet Supplies

Americans spent over $50 billion in 2011 on their pets.[6] Little of this money goes towards animal welfare causes, even though many pet owners care deeply about the well-being of animals. This convergence of an industry and a charitable concern presents a prime opportunity to tap latent power within our system.

Imagine a group of philanthropists, motivated by animal welfare, launch a pet supply business (either online, brick-and-mortar or both). Their purpose is enabling customers to donate the profits from their purchases to the animal-related charity of their choice. The customer value proposition is compelling – buy pet supplies for the same price offered by other retailers and in the process improve the lives of animals. Also, by working with established animal welfare organizations, this enterprise could efficiently target its marketing to people who have already shown a willingness to support such causes. This enterprise could also offer pet owners reliable information about product quality and production practices. (You'd be amazed by the harmful stuff that ends up in pet food, even in brands that claim to be high quality.)

From the systems perspective, an FPH pet supply business empowers people to act in alignment with their values without sacrificing other aspects of their well-being (their financial position, for example). Pet lovers would be able to direct energy to the links and nodes dedicated to improving the lives of animals by making slight and painless changes in their buying habits. Wealthy philanthropists and concerned citizens could thus combine their power to create a better future for animals.

Nurturing Nutrition

The cost of poor nutrition to our personal health is beyond doubt, as is the threat of rising health care costs to national economic vitality. It is obvious to many people, who are aware of the importance of nutrition, that a major cause of Americans' poor food choices is the sheer profusion of junk food. In true systemic fashion, poor choices, both personal and legislative, contribute to the vast quantity and low-cost of junk food (a reinforcing feedback loop). Fast food and processed food are the norm – what some nutritionists refer to as the "standard American diet" ("SAD" for short). We (the authors) guess that over 90% of the food in a typical grocery store (outside the produce aisle) is not conducive to good health. "Faux food" producers highlight nutritional positives, even if their product's overall healthfulness is resoundingly negative. "No sugar added" is touted on products with high saturated fat; "a full day's supply of Vitamin C" distracts from astronomical sugar content. Standardized nutrition labels can help, but the average busy shopper doesn't have the time or knowledge to make sense of them.

Because most people buy the majority of their food from grocery stores, the grocery store is a potentially powerful leverage point in efforts to improve health and thus improve lives and lower health care costs. An FPH grocery store, with the main goal of helping customers improve their nutritional health, rather than maximizing financial profit, could tap a deep source of latent potential by making smart food choices easier and less expensive.

Consider this example: a smart phone app (and an alternative for those who don't have a smart phone) offers customizable letter grades for the food products a customer is considering. A diabetic can focus on glycemic load. Someone with high blood pressure can focus on sodium content. Thus, the best choices are easily found without the need to decipher cryptic nutritional labels one at a time. Also, since flavor is also important, the nutritional letter grade can be supplemented with customer ratings of the product's gastronomic quality. In short, complete, clear and personally relevant information can empower people to choose better.

An FPH grocery store would do well to honor customers' demands, including the continued offering of unhealthful choices. Profits from junk food sales might be used to subsidize the prices of healthier choices. This could help reduce the systemic imbalance created by artificially low junk food prices (due in large part to wrongheaded agricultural subsidies directed to low-nutrition crops like corn). Cooking and nutrition classes featuring healthy meal choices, prepackaged nutritionally sound school lunches, a separate section for junk food (allowing customers to avoid temptation), and discounts for financially struggling families are all likely features of an FPH grocery store.

This new kind of grocery store could change food production and consumption patterns. Specifically, by expanding the feedback loop carrying nutritional information, FPH grocery stores would empower people to adjust their choices to match their goals. Over time, new habits will form and healthy eating will become second nature: by making adjustments in our links we alter the quality of our nodes (that is, we get smarter). As more people make informed choices, the cost of healthy food will decline as economies of scale are created, leading more people to make healthful choices. Virtuous cycles abound.

E-Commerce for a Brighter Future

The FPH examples above take advantage of close link between the products and services offered and a charitable cause. But the model can be applied to any commercial venture, although businesses dealing directly with the public offer more powerful leverage. Imagine a consortium of philanthropists acquires an Amazon.com competitor, Buy.com for example. They convert it into an FPH enterprise. Besides offering the same service and pricing, it gives customers the opportunity to direct the profits from purchases to their charitable cause of choice. For better or for worse, the Internet has squeezed profit margins, so the percentage an FPH Buy.com could donate isn't as big as some might think. Getting people to change their buying behavior isn't a simple feat – we are creatures of habit. Thus, a big carrot is needed, bigger than giving 5-10% of sales to charity. One possible answer is not new, but it is powerful – donor matching. What if, through the generosity of wealthy donors, we could convince the rest of us to make the switch?

For example, let's say you plan to buy a new printer for $100. Normally you would buy from Amazon.com because they have all your information on record – it's easy. But now you have another choice, you can go to FPH Buy.com and buy the same printer for the same price with all profits directed to the charity of your choice. Assuming itis only $5 (not unlikely in the competitive consumer electronics market). You might decide that it's not worth the hassle of changing your buying routine, $5 isn't much. But today philanthropists supporting the Make-a-Wish Foundation have decided to match 10 to 1 all FPH Buy.com donations – your purchase triggers a $55 gift to the nonprofit. Only a dolt would pass up this deal. Now that you've taken the first step, hopefully you'll be more inclined to make future purchases through FPH Buy.com, even if the matching amount is less compelling.

By providing customers with the current "match rates" for various charitable organizations they are interested in helping we can motivate matching donors to give more. For example, let's say Bill and Melinda Gates supports the Global Fund (which fights AIDS in Africa). Thus, if they want to attract donations from FPH Buy.com users, then they will want to make sure the Global Fund has the highest matching rate.

From the previous example of a $100 printer purchase from FPH Buy.com, which generated a $5 donation to your cause of choice, the importance of having a high matching rate is clear. Although $5 is a small amount on its own, you see three of your favorite charities have current matching rates of 100%, 150% and 500%, respectively, boosting your $5 to a $10, $12.50 or $30 donation. You will likely choose the organization with 500% matching (perhaps it's the Global Fund). Thirty dollars is enough to buy nine potentially lifesaving meningitis vaccines in the developing world[7], feed a Malawian child for over half a year[8], or protect 2 hectares of rain forest in Paraguay.[9] The matching philanthropist leveraged her gift to influence your choice, and at the same time multiplied the effects of your altruism.

Wealthy philanthropists could energize the latent potential of the buying public and rearrange the pattern of capitalism. We've just described a synergistic mechanism – a Sun Dance Ceremony for the 21st century. This pattern of feedback and incentives aligns our best intentions with our material needs. Like the Sun Dance Ceremony, it allows us to transcend the tension between selflessness and selfishness. One source of the latent power unleashed by this synergistic arrangement is a largely unrecognized quality of giving – its value is multiplied when shared. When a philanthropist matches a customer's donation both experience the reward of having contributed to the well-being of others, and each giver's experience is deepened through their partnership. The philanthropist gives generously while, at the same time, enables the buyer to make a meaningful contribution. The buyer satisfies a material need and, in the same act, makes a positive difference in the world. Aligning interests and transcending the self versus other duality are hallmarks of synergistic social arrangements identified by Ruth Benedict as the key to good societies.

By reimagining the possibilities of business and commerce, humanity can expand the power of free markets. We can efficiently and effectively minimize negative "externalities" by making them internal, and provide more of the public goods and services we need to flourish. The FPH business model works, in large part, because it can dramatically improve our ability to steer our collective systems. First, by increasing the flow and quality of information (for example, carbon footprints of travel alternatives and the nutrition of food), FPH enterprises promote choices that reflect a person's goals and values. We will no longer be steering blindfolded. As we learned in the previous chapter, effective information flow is essential to the process of evolution (staying at the edge of chaos). Without it we lack awareness of the system's current state and thus cannot adjust our actions to maintain balance. Second, by making responsible choices convenient and financially painless, FPH enterprises increase the ability and willingness of people to align their behavior with their higher values.

Many Western minds will object to the idea that charity can be accomplished without sacrifice – it offends the guilt and self-denial orthodoxy of Christianity.[10] We don't disparage those who feel closer to their god when they forgo material well-being for the sake of others. However, it is foolish to rely on this small minority of humans to do the important work of creating a better future. Continuing to hope and pray for a wholesale transformation in human nature is not a rational plan for real change.

Real Karma

The notion of "humanity" has, until now, been a relatively abstract concept, something that existed more in our minds than in reality. Our ancestors were likely to identify themselves as members of a tribe, religion, or (more recently) nation-state; today many young people see themselves quite differently. Our 16-year-old relative recently volunteered that he doesn't think of himself as an American, but as an "Earthling." This reflects a fundamental shift in the default operating system of the latest nodes to emerge in the human network. We may be edging closer to Einstein's hope for a future in which humanity widens its "circle of compassion to embrace all living creatures and the whole of nature in its beauty." Communication technology is increasingly wiping away borders that defined the identities of past generations. It is thus bringing humanity into being as an organic, fluid and whole system. Something new is being born.

Facebook, LinkedIn and many specialized social networks, are playing a central role in this transition in the way we perceive ourselves and our place in the world. This new connective tissue in the human organism is giving rise to infinite possibility. In fact, the ideas in this book were sparked by a simple gesture of a friend sending Renée "good karma" on Facebook. A Buddhist-inspired icon appeared on her "wall" when she accepted the virtual gift. We wondered how this powerful tool for connecting people could be used to create *real* karma. What if we could offer our friends, our friends of friends, and their friends (that is, the whole of humanity) a way to do good without sacrifice to their own well-being (financial or otherwise)? Our first idea was to develop online games that generate advertising revenue, with profits going to players' chosen causes. Each user would have a meter on their profile, measuring the difference they've made in specific metrics, such as meals distributed, vaccines administered, or square miles of rain forest preserved. This display tool would also be a regular reminder of our power to positively impact the world.

We still think this is a great idea, but we quickly realized the potential was so much bigger. Imagine that every time you make an FPH enterprise purchase – groceries, electronics, pet food, or vacations, for example – your "difference meter" automatically updates and appears on your friends' "news feed"? Or that, when you make a purchase that comes with a charitable donation, you can choose to direct the funds to a friend's favored organization, thus giving her *real* karma? This Real Karma application could expand our 21st century Sun Dance Ceremony to include social recognition and community support. With it we might reweave our frayed social fabric in ways adapted to today's world. Such an application would help spread the FPH meme and awaken people to their power to shape the future.

A Real Karma toolbar widget could make it easy for buyers to find e-commerce companies that offer retail donations. As you surf the web (or shop in the brick and mortar world) the Real Karma application would display the donation offered by the company you're interacting with and the current matching rates for your favored charitable organizations. Think of it as an interface, like the dashboard of a car, allowing users to navigate intelligently toward a future aligned with their highest values.

Next we will explore the primary form of energy and information flowing through our economic system. Money may not make the world go round, but it has much to do with how fast it spins and in what direction. A basic understanding of the role of money clarifies major sources of our current inability to steer our collective systems, and points to possible solutions.

Making Sense of Dollars

Human cells communicate and influence one another through the exchange of molecules and electrical impulses; similarly, economic actors communicate and influence one another through the exchange of money. We most commonly exchange money to persuade others to give us material goods or to provide services (that is, time and talent). Money spreads from one node to another throughout the economy. Today these nodes are often on opposite sides of the world. Price informs the system about the amount of wealth (time, material, talent, attention) we are willing to trade for a good or service. Every economic choice echoes throughout the system, spreading a particular pattern of energy and information that shapes the structure of the whole.[11]

Price is a very efficient and powerful means of communication because it affords an objective and stable way to communicate subjective valuations. It is a universal language of sorts, with exchange rates acting as (more or less) efficient translators. In systems terms, we can think of *price* as the transmitter of *information* in the dominant feedback loop of the economic system. And *money* is the medium that carries *energy* (as action potential) through the system. Information and energy form a dynamic feedback loop, with the actions of individuals controlling the direction, velocity and volume of the currents. In biological terms, we can think of this flow as a muscle that moves the limbs of humanity - the neuroanatomy of the invisible hand.

As we mentioned, cybernetics means the *art of steering*. Successful steering involves a four-part process: perception, evaluation, formulation and action. Biological systems steer toward the destination of reproduction (with survival being an important step toward reproduction). By virtue of our consciousness, however, human beings have the unique ability to choose a different destination, such as achieving true happiness. Steering our systems, our societies, toward a chosen destination involves mastering the four ingredients of successful steering. Price as information and money as energy contribute critically to this process. Historically, these dual mechanisms have been rough guides – like navigating by the stars – but we're now able to refine these instruments to create the evolutionary equivalent of satellite powered GPS. With this new technology we can accurately steer our system toward goals of our conscious choosing.

Let's briefly examine the four parts of the steering process. Accurate perception involves not only the ability to receive incoming information about the state of the system, but a filter that will ensure the most relevant data is given priority. Our filters can become corrupted and fail to discriminate between important information and irrelevant information. Value rigidity (that is, unquestioned adherence to a particular worldview) is a major source of corruption. Beginner's mind is a means of ensuring our filters are operating optimally.

Simply facilitating perception by making relevant data widely available can dramatically improve steering. For example, in 1986 the federal Toxic Release Inventory required U.S. firms to report factory output of all dangerous air pollutants each year. (No penalties were imposed – this was purely an information gathering exercise.) In 1988 local journalists obtained information, available through the Freedom of Information Act, about plants in their communities and published lists of the biggest polluters. Within two years, chemical emissions nationwide (as reported, and hopefully in fact) had decreased by 40 percent.[12] The Toxic Release Inventory, combined with a free and diligent press, improved the steering ability of our system. It also showed that latent potential can be unlocked by simply delivering relevant data to the right parts of the system. Feedback is the key to learning, it's why we give treats to puppies when they behave and scold them when they don't. We're not so different from puppies, and that's good news.

Evaluation involves comparing incoming information on the current state of the system to an imagined ideal state (real happiness, for example), and predicting the likelihood of possible future conditions. Is the system on track, or is corrective action needed? Accurate forecasts require an understanding of relevant system dynamics (often achieved by noticing patterns in past system states, though, as we have seen, overreliance on this method can be dangerous). For instance, in this book we predict possible future courses of human evolution by looking at the patterns formed by past adaptations, which, in turn, offer clues to the underlying dynamics of human civilization. However, the future will not look like the past, so prediction also involves imagination, creativity and intuition.

Successful formulation includes an important predictive component. Similar to evaluation, it requires the ability to foresee how alternative courses of action (or inaction) will reverberate through the system. Intelligent formulation demands both short-term and long-term foresight. Steering failure in human systems often occurs when anger, envy, pride and prejudice influence plan formulation. The Mind Shift Meme offers a solution to these common speed bumps and detours.

Finally, successful steering requires action in alignment with formulation (unless the plan is not to act). The movie character, Forrest Gump, said it best, "stupid is as stupid does." Inertia and fear are two common sources of inaction in human systems. Anyone who has decided to follow a healthy diet only to be derailed by a pint of ice cream, knows that pleasure and habit are two additional forces that can disrupt a well laid plan. Put simply, successful steering demands follow through.

With the steering process as our guide, we can more fully appreciate the pivotal roles of price and money in our navigation system. We can also see opportunities for exciting improvements in this system that can deepen and expand the intellect and consciousness of the invisible hand.

Price and money are means of sending information that enables accurate perception. Based on our perception we predict patterns and make informed decisions (for example, home prices are declining, so I will wait to buy). We act on our choices with relative ease, thanks to the universality of price and the fluid medium of money. Price is a primary means by which we perceive important changes to our environment far beyond the range of our physical senses, and by which we coordinate our activities across the globe. Thus, price is critical to successful steering. The price of oranges will rise whether or not we know frost damaged Florida's citrus crops; the price of gas will fall whether or not we know OPEC increased crude oil output by 10%.

Prices provide information that forms the basis of intelligent steering: a farmer in rural India decides to plant potatoes instead of beans because the price of the tubers is rising. He doesn't need to understand the complex market dynamics of potato futures. College students choose to study nursing based on high salaries in the field, rather than on the demographic pressures underlying the high value placed on nursing skills. Our collective resources are allocated far more efficiently through market pricing than any central planning committee could ever hope to do.

The value of a good or service to us at any given moment arises from an ineffable mix of utterly subjective, mainly subconscious, and continually changing preferences and needs. Price allows us to distill this mix to a definite, objective and universally understandable term.[13] However, price is a relatively unsophisticated language – like the grunts and crude gestures that made up our ancestors' first forays into the realm of speech. Our inability to create a world that reflects our highest ideals is partly due to the constraints of our economic language. Imagine the difficulty of building a house if your only means of communication were grunts and body language.

Price is rooted inextricably in perhaps the most universal of all languages – mathematics. When Newton, and later Einstein, sought a broader understanding of the cosmos they first had to push the limits of mathematics. Newton invented calculus; Einstein worked with cutting edge non-Euclidean geometry. We need a similar refinement of the mathematics of price to illuminate new possibilities.

As we have seen, modern Western civilization is based on the underlying belief that if something cannot be measured (that is, distilled to a mathematical variable) it does not exist. The technological progress of the past two centuries vividly proves the power of this worldview. Math can be understood *precisely* across time and geography. The strength of mathematics is in its precision, universality and constancy, which allows knowledge and information to flow past temporal, political and cultural borders. Because information storage, manipulation and communication are the lifeblood of complex adaptive systems, math is an incredibly useful adaptation.

As with all language, mathematics shapes and limits our conception of reality. It is fragmentary; it separates reality into discrete categories. But unlike other languages, mathematics is deliberate and conscious in its fragmentation. Every variable must be defined – mathematics is the most precise language we've invented (or, as some would argue, discovered). However, as previously discussed, *precision* is not the same as *accuracy*. Many of the problems we face today have their roots in this limitation. We focus on the measurable, the easily countable, and neglect the messier parts of life, where much of the good stuff hides.[14]

Can we use the tool of math without letting it dominate us? Put another way, can we include the precise rhythm of numbers in our Broadway extravaganza while still fully expressing our empathy and the fluid artistry of our creative joyful selves? Finding this balance has proven elusive. We strongly gravitate towards precision – but like the dreamers who came before us, we may be able to expand and deepen the language of numbers, uncovering new ways of viewing our world and its possibilities.

A True Cost Index

As we've discussed, price is a tool of perception through which we know something about the state of the system far beyond our direct experience. However, prices currently reflect only a narrow range of information. Specifically, price tells us about the direct and immediate economic cost of a product or service. It generally does not tell us about the environmental, psychological or spiritual toll. In other words, the tool of price is limited because it communicates only a narrow band of information, so we are left to make our decisions with woefully incomplete knowledge. Not surprisingly, our limited perception constrains the decisions we make and the possibilities we see.

Our system has produced alternatives that address the myopia of price, but they are not nearly as efficient. The "leaping bunny" means a product is animal friendly, fair trade certifications signify social responsibility, and various organic certifications signal environmentally friendly agricultural practices. These efforts to communicate about important values are no match for the power of price, but they're better than nothing and, until recently, were the best we could do. The most obvious limits of these solutions are that they are, (1) an either/or proposition (there is no credit for incremental improvements), (2) they require an understanding of the certification (that is, a shared language), and (3) they need a chain of trust that may be weak or nonexistent. Compared with the precise and universal language of price, these alternatives are akin to smoke signals.

The widespread five-star ratings gleaned from customer reviews on the Internet have filled much of the void about product and service quality. It is increasingly difficult for makers of shoddy goods or rude, incompetent people to remain in business. Business is increasingly lucrative for those creating fundamentally better products and delivering superior service. Customers are eager to share their experiences (a result of our social nature) leading to far more complete information about the consumption phase of the economic process. In market fundamentalist terms, the increasing availability of information about product and service quality is creating a more efficient market. This leads to a better use of resources (in other words, less money wasted on disappointing goods and services). However, the production side of the process remains largely hidden from view. Thankfully, technology is providing the means to expand the communication power of price. What might such an expansion look like?

First, we need to rethink conventional boundaries. We have deliberately avoided using the word "consumer" as it does not align with our view of the customer's role in the economy. The notion that buyers are simply "consuming" (from the Latin "consumere" meaning "to use up, eat, waste") obscures the reality that how we, as individuals, choose to spend, or not spend, our money shapes the physical world. Consumption is not (or, rather, should not be) a passive thoughtless exercise. We are not at the mercy of heartless capitalists – we are the ones who make the fundamental choices that ripple across the globe. Corporations supply what we demand. We suggest an alternative word, "prosumer" to refer to people who recognize the importance of their buying choices in *pro*ducing the world and take *pro*active steps to ensure the world they are creating is aligned with their highest values.

We have at our fingertips the technological infrastructure to collect, compile, analyze, synthesize and deliver the vast quantity of information prosumers need to make informed choices. The Internet, smart phones, and tablets provide the basis for a robust prosumer platform. Consider the revolutionary advantages of a True Cost Index. Companies across the globe respond to (electronically distributed) surveys detailing supply chain, production, distribution and human resource practices. Answers are available online for public review, comment, supplementation and correction. This transparency could prove to be an efficient alternative to top-down auditing – current and former employees, contractors, competitors and other insiders play the role of auditors and help ensure integrity and veracity. Companies earn extra credit by certifying their responses, posting a bond that guarantees information accuracy. Breaches (inflated numbers, flagrant inaccuracies) result in substantial negative points. Additional information, such as the results of government inspections, could be included in a producer's profile.

The rapidly decreasing cost of video and Internet broadcast could provide another means of monitoring operations. For example, the public could remotely view slaughterhouse activities (so we're not dependent on animal rights activists secretly recording dangerous and inhumane practices). The pitifully feeble supervision of underfunded government agencies would be greatly enhanced by a watchful concerned public. (Just the threat of video oversight, accessible to all, might improve regulatory compliance). In short, technology is providing low-cost alternatives to ineffective top-down government regulations and industry self-policing. Technology can increase the flow and reliability of information, which is vital to efficient market functioning and reflects the depth and breadth of our true values.

On the prosumer side, users would complete a survey (shorter or longer depending their interest) to discover their values with respect to environmental and social concerns. Users would be asked to rank these values relative to their personal financial concerns. Based on the information from producers and prosumers, a software program adds a number (positive or negative) to the actual market price of a product, resulting in a customized True Cost to the user.

For example, let's say you highly value environmental conservation (that is, you're willing to make significant financial sacrifice for the sake of the health of the planet). You use a True Cost Index smart phone application while shopping for laundry detergent. Which of the available brands has the lowest True Cost? Important factors include: place of origin (measuring transportation related pollution), the ingredients' environmental impact, the source of ingredients (including upstream supply chain information), and packaging efficiency. Another buyer might have little concern for these issues, thus that buyer's True Cost will be different from yours. Brand X has a True Cost of $9, but it retails for $7 (signaling significant negative environmental impact). Brand Y has a True Cost of $5 and retails for $7.50 (indicating that Company Y pays considerable attention to the environment). Brand Y's laundry detergent is a far better deal *for you* than Brand X's even though it is $0.50 more in conventional terms. You may not choose to buy the lowest True Cost detergent because of temporary budgetary concerns (long-term financial concerns are built into your True Cost), or because of personal preferences that are not reflected in your True Cost (scent, for example). But your decision will reflect much more information than it would have otherwise. You will have the information you need to make a fundamentally more intelligent choice. Your choice will echo throughout the economic system, altering its course ever so slightly in response to your action.

A systematic and widely used True Cost Index would encourage producers to adjust their products, procedures and policies to bring them into alignment with the values of prosumers. Further, prosumers could make their True Cost values public, allowing others to compare their value matrix with friends, celebrities, and their communities. Seeing that a friend or an admired public figure cares deeply about a subject to which you give little or no weight may inspire you to reconsider your position and perhaps lead you to expand your values. Parochial concerns and viewpoints may thus begin to give way to a broader and better-informed perspective. The system evolves through shared knowledge and experience.

A True Cost Index can vitalize a critical feedback loop that currently suffers from chronic and severe anemia – the information flowing from providers to buyers. Currently this information is usually limited to purely economic data – the reptilian concerns. The end result of our economic system reflects this constricted flow. A True Cost Index can expand and deepen the language of price to include noneconomic data. By counting the human concerns of love, compassion and the desire for a better future our system can produce outcomes more aligned with the full depth and breadth of our values. Simply put, a True Cost Index can expand the vocabulary of price to include the physical and spiritual health of one another and our planet. We, the prosumers, can steer our economic system toward the horizon of health, happiness and justice, and away from the rocky shores of pollution, destruction and injustice.

If this sounds like a pipe dream, consider a program Wal-Mart is spearheading. Yes, Wal-Mart. Spurred by customer surveys showing the importance of environmental sustainability, especially among younger buyers, Wal-Mart is partnering with academics to bring information about products' environmental impact to its customers. To this end, Wal-Mart has requested that its suppliers provide information about their practices, which will be translated (eventually) into ratings displayed on store shelves.

Thankfully, Wal-Mart is not treating this "Sustainability Index" as proprietary. Rather, it is using its pull to get the ball rolling on a program that it hopes will eventually be run by an independent nonprofit. The company's recognition of the importance of sustainability to its customers and its decision to act on its customers' preferences is a very encouraging sign. It is also a vivid example of how power dynamics in a complex system can result in surprising twists. Wal-Mart's possible transformation from dark side villain to environmental savior is exactly the type of counterintuitive development that continually fascinates and inspires systems thinkers. Wal-Mart's approach to the Sustainability Index is, not surprisingly, on the spider end of the spectrum, with its reliance on experts and a single score. In contrast, the True Cost Index we imagine is more starfish-like, relying on crowd sourcing, transparency and flexible customized ratings.

Wikipedia provides an exciting example of the potential of crowd sourcing information. Ten years ago, no one fathomed the prospect that Encyclopedia Britannica and Encarta (a project of Microsoft) would be left in the dust by a free online encyclopedia written and edited by a worldwide network of volunteers on a platform provided by a charitable organization. Wikipedia is a testament to the collective power of our desire to share what we know with the world. A True Cost Index would harness this power and give rise to a free flow of deep and expansive information delivered to prosumers in a convenient format.

Distilling environmental and social values down to a specific number will doubtlessly be fraught with potential pitfalls and will be a continual work in progress. It is a marriage of accuracy and precision, synthetic and analytic rationality, art and science. If civilization is to adapt to rapidly changing conditions, then we must improve the system's ability to store, communicate and manipulate important information. With these improvements we can more intelligently apply our energy to creating new, more beneficial, patterns of behavior and relationships. Our economy is increasingly global and dynamic, so we need an equally expansive and resilient way to communicate information throughout the system. A True Cost Index can be an important part of an improved system-wide communication network. The choice is clear: we can put a price on the priceless – clean air, our children's health, old growth forests, human rights – or we can allow the current system to continue treating the priceless as valueless.

An ounce of prevention is worth a pound of cure. A True Cost Index could prevent rather than correct negative externalities, resulting in more intelligent use of resources. For example, the cost of cleaning up a toxic dump is far higher than dealing responsibly with the waste from the outset. A True Cost Index could also resolve the inherent conflicts of interest faced by socially responsible companies. An increasing number of entrepreneurs and investors are pursuing business models that seek to "blend" the conventional profit motive with social and environmental responsibility.[15] The term "double bottom line" aptly describes this approach (that is, people and entities aimed at maximizing profits and doing social good).[16]

While this trend is a step in the right direction, there are fundamental problems with current efforts at blending in the present state of the capitalist system. A company with one owner, or a few like-minded partners, can navigate the gray area between monetary gain and social good on an ad hoc basis. However, when ownership is diffuse (multiple shareholders with differing views) this careful balancing act can prove difficult. If a double bottom line company chooses responsible action *only* when its financial bottom line is unaffected, then it isn't really challenging the existing paradigm.

A prime example of the conflict that can result from diffuse ownership is eBay's dispute with Craigslist (of which eBay became a minority shareholder in 2004, after buying shares from a former Craigslist employee). Craigslist explained the source of the dispute thusly:

> As those who know us best will recognize, every measure we have taken has been for the sake of protecting the long term well-being of the Craigslist community. Sadly, we have an uncomfortably conflicted shareholder in our midst, one that is obsessed with dominating online classifieds for the purpose of maximizing its own profits.

The majority shareholders in Craigslist have chosen to place community benefit above financial profit. If eBay was not a shareholder, this blend of priorities would not be problematic. However, the presence of an owner in disagreement with the primacy of social goals throws the whole thing out of whack. The Delaware Chancery Court recently sided with eBay and explained that under Delaware law (by far the most favored state of incorporation in the U.S.) monetary profits trump all other values:

> Jim and Craig did prove that they personally believe craigslist should not be about the business of stockholder wealth maximization, now or in the future ... The corporate form in which craigslist operates, however, is not an appropriate vehicle for purely philanthropic ends, at least not when there are other stockholders interested in realizing a return on their investment.

In other words, "double bottom line" is likely synonymous with "breach of fiduciary duty" if you're an executive in a Delaware corporation.

"Beneficial corporations" as an alternative legal structure designed to accommodate double bottom line enterprises is gaining traction in some states. However, the ability of such companies to raise capital in any significant amount is dubious. Most investors, first and foremost, want monetary returns for their investment dollars. The "B Corp" may be helpful to bootstrapping entrepreneurs who want to protect the future integrity of their vision, but it will not likely prove viable for start-ups in need of significant financial capital.

This constraint limits the growth of truly blended companies. Their need for capital comes into direct conflict with their social objectives. Given current system dynamics, most double bottom line enterprises face a tradeoff between growing (with the help of outside capital) and staying true to their ideals. Thus, companies devoted to their social objectives will generally not become large enough to compete with the big boys.

Socially conscious investors recognize the untenable challenge faced by genuine blended businesses: "financial value and return [come] first. As investors, they [cannot] justify investing in ideals above returns. Many [socially conscious investors] reported that the toughest lesson they had learned was not to fall in love with the social side and overlook the fundamental business drivers and risks of their investments."[17] In other words, for many socially conscious investors, the double bottom line really means, do as much social good as you can without hurting the *real* bottom line – financial gain. Unfortunately, in our current system, responsibility is often inadequately rewarded in terms investors understand – dollars – and so is given lip service. Money is energy in our economic system – we can steer all we want, but without forward propulsion we will never arrive at the chosen destination. Thus, transformational change requires arrangements that guide the flow of money toward enterprises that are pointing in the direction we want to move.

The flow of capital to socially responsible ventures dwindles even more as conventional corporations increasingly jump on the responsibility bandwagon (often only at the level of lip service). If mainstream companies actually placed responsibility on par with monetary profits, there would be little or no loss associated with this trend. However, diffuse corporate ownership is unsuited to a true double bottom line approach. Corporations can pursue responsibility, but never *at the expense of monetary gain* – when responsibility and profit conflict, the latter will prevail. As conventional business makes inroads into social responsibility, they will take market share from truly responsible ventures.

A hypothetical explains the challenge. The large multinational "Corporation X" launches a "green line" of household cleaning products touted as healthy for the planet and people. Because of economies of scale, well established distribution network and access to low-cost capital, Corporation X can produce its purportedly eco-friendly products less expensively than its smaller environmentally motivated competitor, "Company E." Corporation X creates a logo and trademarks a green-sounding name, like "Green Certified" and puts it on its product line (even some that aren't all that green). (S.C. Johnson put its "Greenlist" logo on products containing ethylene glycol, a toxic ingredient.) Corporation X and Company E sell very similar end products, but their social and environmental footprints (that is, their True Cost) may diverge considerably. Also, the profits made from Corporation X products may fund research into pesticide development, or some other environmentally harmful product. However, because of its lower price, wider distribution, and superficially similar product offering, it will have a significant competitive advantage over Company E. In short, truly responsible enterprises currently face serious disadvantages because buyers don't have the time or expertise to carefully vet every product they buy.

The Body Shop was an early adopter of corporate social responsibility.[18] Anita Roddick opened her first store in 1976, selling all natural beauty products. In 2006 she sold the company for £652.3 million to L'Oréal, the French cosmetics giant. Here lies a poignant example of the difficulty of making informed and responsible decisions in our current system. Nestle *S.A.* holds over 26% of L'Oréal's shares, while wielding an infamously horrific social responsibility record. The Body Shop continues to offer environmentally responsible products, such as 100% recycled containers. But its profits roll up into the corporate coffers of a global giant whose business practices can only be described as atrocious. Nestle routinely flouts WHO International Code standards, selling infant formula (or products that look like infant formula). This practice causes 1.5 million infant deaths each year. Nestle also has a history of buying chocolate from sources using child slave labor.[19] These are just two practices that evidence Nestle's psychopathic behavior – a sobering example of the reptilian nature of many conventional corporate enterprises.

The Body Shop website offers this message about its relationship to its parent company: "It retains its unique identity and Values ... It operates independently within the L'Oréal Group and is led by the current management team of The Body Shop reporting directly to the CEO of L'Oréal." Where do we, as prosumers, draw the line? Do we accept the notion of corporate personhood and thus recognize The Body Shop as an independent entity? One laudable effort to aid consumers in making informed choices – Better World Shopper – apparently buys into the notion that a subsidiary can maintain an identity distinct from its owner. It rates The Body Shop an "A" while L'Oréal receives a "D" and Nestle an "F."

The corporate form was created to disrupt a feedback loop – to prevent responsibility for corporate conduct from flowing back to shareholders. There is a rational basis for this choice of system boundaries: the capital that flows throughout the increasingly global economy depends on cutting the link between money and legal liability.

Prosumers can correct some of the most dire effects of this disrupted feedback loop by holding owners responsible for the actions of all of their varied enterprises. Put differently, the corporate form draws system boundaries that make sense when the goal is enabling free flow of capital. However, these boundaries do not make sense when the goal is empowering prosumers to positively shape the world in alignment with their highest ideals.

Given our purpose, what system boundaries are most suitable? We believe responsibility should follow the money. (A True Cost Index could offer prosumers the option of drawing their own lines.) Because dollars motivate investment decisions and business judgment, it makes sense to let the boundaries recognized by freely flowing money set the parameters. In this framework, responsibility flows from subsidiaries to parent corporations to shareholders (whether other corporations, institutions, or individuals). On the buyer side of the equation, prosumers must be given the means to judge conveniently and accurately the companies they choose to support through their buying choices. Thankfully, the same information that will enable prosumers to choose better will enable investors and business executives to choose better. Price (information) and money (energy) form a single integrated feedback loop. Information flow improvements (a True Cost Index) and prosumer decision making on one side of the loop will spread through the rest of the system, affecting investment choices and business practices. As a critical mass of well-informed prosumers forms, wise choices for prosumers, and wise choices for investors and businesses will converge.

The role of divestment in persuading South Africa to end apartheid shows the wisdom and power of intentionally redrawing system boundaries. Western investors withdrew their financial support (the energy in an economic system) from firms doing business in South Africa, regardless whether these companies had any official role in apartheid policies. Pressure was applied on a part of the system that held power, eventually triggering change. Concerned investors used their leverage to realign incentives so a powerful force in South Africa (its business community) had a strong financial interest in ending apartheid.

How can conventional for profit enterprises become genuinely socially responsible? Can a critical mass of prosumers, armed with a True Cost Index, fundamentally change market dynamics? Let's return to Company E from the previous hypothetical, with its environmentally friendly line of cleaning products. Company E will likely regularly face decisions that place social responsibility in direct conflict with its profit motive. For example, the choice between buying more expensive local ingredients and reducing the environmental damage caused by transport, or buying cheaper but otherwise identical ingredients from China and thus increasing the company's profit margin. In our current system, a money-maximizing enterprise would not consider buying from the local supplier to maximize good to the detriment of its bottom line. Indeed, if an executive from a Delaware corporation with profit-motivated shareholders chose to buy local, she may very well be in breach of her fiduciary duty. However, in a system that includes a critical mass of prosumers using a True Cost Index, using local ingredients will be reflected positively in the True Cost of environmentally concerned buyers. Thus, the responsible choice will be rewarded financially, making Company E's difficult decision much easier.

Prosumers armed with a robust True Cost Index will have the power to change fundamentally the old-paradigm cost-benefit analysis that pits narrowly defined monetary profit against the good of humanity and the planet. In the new paradigm, the conflict between maximizing shareholder profit and doing good disappears.

Unfortunately, so far, many mainstream companies are more apt to focus on the marketing benefits of being *perceived* – too often *mis*perceived – as a socially responsible enterprise. A recent spate of Dow Chemical Company advertisements espousing its socially progressive stance is proof that even the biggest environmental offenders covet a positive public image.[20] This "greenwashing" is a deliberate attempt to misinform consumers. Clearly, a complex adaptive system cannot function well when too much misinformation about important matters spreads through the network. A True Cost Index takes social responsibility out of the marketing department and puts it squarely on the CEO's desk. Responsible buyers, provided with relevant, accurate, reliable, convenient and timely information can directly influence corporate decision making, and thus powerfully shape the world in alignment with their values.

When companies are forced to compete on price, quality, *and* responsibility, social good becomes an important factor in the basic equation of all economic activity. We will no longer depend on financially privileged philanthropists, underfunded nonprofits, well-intentioned entrepreneurs and overburdened government regulators to spread the ethos of responsibility. Instead, prosumers will *demand* that companies act responsibly, and wise businesses will *supply* products and services that meet this demand. Undoubtedly some companies will continue competing mainly on price and/or quality, but responsible buyers will have options that reflect their values. Social pressures will likely come to bear, influencing the buying choices of even apathetic people who are nonetheless concerned about how they are perceived by their peers. Also, mere lip service will no longer fly with prosumers when the corporate hype doesn't match the facts.

A True Cost Index would solve a dilemma many charitable foundations find themselves struggling with – how to invest endowment funds in ways that do not conflict with their charitable purpose. In 2007 the Bill and Melinda Gates Foundation briefly tried to align its endowment investments with its charitable purpose. It quickly gave up, deciding instead to aim for conventional profit maximization. Many other foundations with endowments find themselves similarly positioned: as shareholders in companies that are contributing to the very problems their charitable efforts are aimed at correcting. In other words, they are helping to cause the illness, then paying for a pound of cure rather than an ounce of prevention – not an efficient approach. The complexities of aligning profit maximization with big-picture charitable objectives from a top-down approach are simply too daunting to handle effectively. The True Cost Index creates a bottom up systemic solution to the problem.

In a future where a critical mass of buyers uses the True Cost Index to guide its buying choices, profit maximization and responsibility will be aligned. The pressure to act responsibly will come from the base of the system – the individual buyers – rather than just a few unusually conscientious business owners at the top. Thanks to advances in communication technology, the True Cost Index is a relatively simple systemic change – a mobius flip. But it can transform competing goals into complementary goals (a hallmark of synergy) allowing us to remove systemic friction that is hindering our evolution.

Additionally, a True Cost Index holds the possibility of overcoming another limiting duality, namely, the seemingly endless and fruitless debate of free market fundamentalism (that is, less government) versus neo-Keynesianism (that is, more government). This vertigo inducing ping-pong match has held public policy captive for nearly a century. Both sides of the debate agree that transparency combined with well-distributed, reliable information is necessary for markets to be free and efficient. (Those who disagree are likely among the beneficiaries of opacity, that is, those whose position in the system receives more than it contributes and who veil their unmerited gains in areas that lack transparency.) Past failures of free market principles have often resulted from systemic opacity, where corruption inevitably takes root, leading to instability, inefficiency and injustice.

A True Cost Index is an example of a nongovernmental solution that could systematically increase transparency and information flow. It can empower us to shape a future in alignment with our highest ideals, free from (or at least freer from) corruption, widespread ignorance, and centralized power. A True Cost Index would bring us closer to realizing the dreams of free market proponents by creating what has never before existed – a free and well-informed base of concerned and empowered prosumers making *truly* rational choices.

As we've seen, systems with a strong bottom-up dynamic (starfish systems) are generally more adaptable than hierarchical systems that are, by their nature, conservative (as in conserving the progress of the past). Our collective frustration with the inability of our rigid institutions to move us forward is rooted in a failure to recognize their inherently rigid and backward looking nature. Evolutionary progress is far more likely to arise in systems powered by grassroots forces. The True Cost Index, and the FPH enterprises discussed earlier are means of spreading vital energy (money) to the democratic, flexible, adaptable, responsive and local organizations most capable of creating the future we seek.

When we awaken to the realization that our world is shaped by the choices of billions of people, we awaken to a source of immense power. If we want to shape a future that is different from our past, then the key is to empower people to make smarter choices. We know the dangers of using authoritarian institutions to force these changes – power corrupts, top-down solutions often lead to systemic dysfunctions, and bureaucracies are inflexible, static and backward looking. Of course, not everyone will make responsible choices, even when given clear and relevant information and better alternatives. All we need is a critical mass of people to alter their behavior and the systemic changes can be dramatic.

It is easy to be cynical about the motives and will of others. Often when we (the authors) share our ideas with people their response is, "well, I would do it [for example, buy from an FPH company or use a True Cost Index] but I don't think most people give a damn." Maybe we surround ourselves with uniquely caring people. But we suspect that this cynicism has its roots in a failure to recognize that the sorry state of much of our world is not the result of masses of heartless people (or even a few elite villains). Rather, it is the natural result of the current arrangement of our economic system, within which intelligent steering is nearly impossible. Granted, there are some nasty people out there (which any well-functioning society must recognize and manage) but their numbers are small, and they are not the main cause of our most significant problems. As long as those who seek change focus their efforts on demonizing a few or tinkering with the mechanisms of government, then we will continue to get more of the same (or worse).

As we will see in the following chapter, these relatively simple alterations in the pattern of capitalism (Fuller's trim tabs) hold the possibility of sparking a phase transition and spreading changes that can solve many of the most frustrating and debilitating effects of our current economic paradigm.

9 – Ripple Effects

We've coined a term for our vision of the future evolution of human systems. *Eco-nomics* is an alternative model for understanding and shaping the system with and in which we collectively and individually respond to and shape our material world, and are, in turn, shaped by it. Eco-nomics is based on the wealth of wisdom coming out of the science of systems. Through the eco-nomics lens, the economy is seen as *"a living system* composed of human beings and social organizations in continual interaction with one another and with the surrounding ecosystems on which our lives depend."[1] Thus, it is more expansive than the conventional notion of economics.

An Eco-nomics Paradigm

The eco-nomics model applies systems thinking to create societies that foster true happiness and the fullest expression of human potential. Human beings are treated as ends, rather than as means to the end of narrowly defined material profit. Human well-being – physical, psychological and spiritual – is the center of the eco-nomics paradigm. Eco-nomics empowers us to put the full force of capitalism at the service of humanity.

"Eco" comes from the Greek word, "oikos," for household. "Economics," from "oikonomikos," means "practices in the art of managing a household." Safe to say, modern economics has drifted far from its roots. Today, the "household" of the dominant theory of economics is extremely dysfunctional. Market fundamentalism paints a picture of isolated individuals acting in their narrowly defined material self-interests rather than cooperative communities, like families, working together toward shared goals. In contrast, the household of eco-nomics achieves harmony and coherence through synergistic arrangements, by aligning (as much as possible) self-interest with the interests of the community. Synergy applies the art of being yielding to curing the malaise of alienation and disempowerment with a strong dose of community and power.

A strong force within the eco-nomics household is healthy, striving-centered competition. This healthy competition helps ensure that we collaborate on the best projects (that is, the most effective at creating material, psychological and spiritual well-being). Competitiveness is an essential driver of the innovation needed to balance on the edge of chaos. The competition of eco-nomics is not the ego-centered competition that is as satisfied with an opponent's failure as with one's own achievement. Indeed, in today's fast-paced world of technological innovation, those who waste time looking backwards and sideways to check their position vis-à-vis other players in the game are likely to lose. Success today depends on first out-dreaming the competition.

For profiting humanity enterprises, a True Cost Index, and a Real Karma synergy mechanism are just a few ways we can subtly, but powerfully, bring about an eco-nomic shift in our human systems. The previous chapter outlined some ideas that, if put into practice, can help us steer our system more intelligently toward the world we want to create. This chapter details the possible ripple effects of these small changes to our economic system.

Our Funneling Society

Karl Marx may have gotten a lot of things wrong, but on one point his theory has stood the test of time: capitalism tends to concentrate wealth in the hands of a few. In the iconic game of Monopoly, the lone winner ends up with all the money – that's the nature of the current version of capitalism. In the US, this flaw is rarely the subject of rational dialogue. Rather, it is often the subject of righteous moralizing from both sides of the political spectrum. From the right, we hear blustering about the unfairness of progressive taxation and the rights of individuals to the fruits of their labors (for example, recent calls for taxing the poor). From the left, we are likely to get an earful about evil corporations and greedy Wall Street types. Ignored in the debate is the fact that, regardless of merit or motives, our economic system funnels wealth.

The funneling tendency of capitalism can be understood in systems terms: it arises from a bundle of reinforcing feedback loops that bring wealth to the wealthy. Current wealth inequality in the U.S. is similar to the divide that existed just before the Great Depression. The top 10% of Americans own about 85% of (economically defined) wealth, while the bottom 40% own 0% (or less because of debt). The international situation is no better: the wealthiest 1% control 43% of the world's assets; the top 10% control 83%; the bottom half control only 2% of the world's assets.[2] This dynamic is not the work of a cabal of elitist bankers and industrialists; it is a natural result of the system's structure.

Evidence of the deep systemic roots of the reinforcing nature of success is found in the Bible: "For to every one that has shall be given, and he shall have abundance. Whoever does not have, even what he has will be taken from him." A materialist reading of this passage describes a wealth to the wealthy feedback loop that predates capitalism. (However, a spiritual reading is much more encouraging: generosity and compassion – wealth of spirit – creates abundance, while ingratitude and selfishness – meanness of spirit – produces scarcity.)

Many underlying dynamics fuel the wealth to the wealthy feedback loop in both subtle and not so subtle ways. The ability of wealthy parents to secure a top-notch education for their children greatly improves the odds of success. Consider legacy admissions such as George W. Bush's attendance at Yale and John McCain's admission to Annapolis despite their less than stellar academic records. Public education goes some way toward correcting this source of inequality. However, states' public school funding is often raised through local property taxes. Schools in wealthy communities receive more funding per student than those in poorer areas (despite the added challenges of educating children disadvantaged by poverty). Spending varies dramatically; wealthier states such as New York spend over double the amount per student as poorer states such as Oklahoma. Thus, the reality of public education funding cancels much of its potential to balance the wealth to the wealthy feedback loop. (This is not to say that money is everything when it comes to quality education, but it is certainly a factor.)

The importance of social and family connections in the business and political realms is another element that fuels the wealth to the wealthy feedback loop: knowing the right people is critical to success. Earning a degree from a top-school opens doors, but the alumni network that comes with the degree is highly valuable in its own right. In networks terms, having wealth connects you to other wealthy people, thus increasing your access to information and power within the system. The investment world offers a vivid example of this dynamic. Entrepreneurs in need of financing send business plans to venture capitalists, many of whom will not accept unsolicited plans and require a personal referral before they will review an investment. In other words, the path to funding is blocked for many, regardless of intellect and dedication, simply because they are not connected to the "right" (that is, wealthy) network of people.

Further, cultural hallmarks of wealth, such as driving an expensive car and wearing designer clothing, cause people to respond more positively in making decisions such as hiring and giving money to charity.[3] It seems we assume that if someone has attained success, or at least the cultural indicators of success, that she must be worthy of it. An acquaintance of ours who recently lost his job in the entertainment industry immediately *upgraded* his car, knowing that projecting success could help him land a new position.

Additionally, wealth equals power – the power to lobby (or simply buy) politicians, to avoid inconvenient laws, and to influence public opinion. Evidence of this power at work is the fact that the top 1% of earners, who average over $1 million a year, actually pays a smaller percentage of personal income to taxes than the 9% just below them.[4] It appears the wealthiest use their influence wisely.

The most obvious way wealth begets wealth is by growing – money earns interest, businesses expand, real estate earns income and (often) appreciates. The power of financial leverage multiplies this dynamic. The more assets you have, the more others are willing to lend you at low rates, thus allowing you to invest even more in wealth expanding opportunities.

Why are we concerned about the wealth to the wealthy feedback loop? Other than the seeming unfairness, wealth inequality severely hampers the health of humanity – potential is squandered and resilience is undermined. A vast supply of human creativity and generosity goes untapped because so much of the lifeblood of the system – money and the energy it represents – isn't being circulated well. Much of humanity is left on the sidelines.

A biological analogy explains well the problem posed by wealth inequality. If a human body fails to circulate glucose (that is, energy) according to the needs of its various organs and extremities, then those parts that do not receive it will begin to atrophy. In a genuine famine, it makes sense to give glucose to the most essential bodily functions; however, if there is plenty of nutritious food, then starving parts of the organism isn't smart. A bloated brain attached to a weak body is not well adapted to survival. If the predator catches up because the legs gave out, the brain dies too. That the Great Depression followed on the heels of extreme wealth inequality is evidence of the danger posed by poor energy circulation in a society. Simply put, our malnourished legs gave out and our recovery was a long one.[5]

Like most analogies, this one is imperfect. Humanity is not a single biological entity; the wealthy can survive, physically if not spiritually and psychologically, as the poor die of starvation. Yet as global risks like nuclear proliferation, the spread of disease and climate change worsen, our fates seem to be ever more intertwined. However, we now have the ability – in terms of consciousness, knowledge and material wealth – to move from dog-eat-dog survival to a thriving mode of abundance and compassion. Most of us, including those in the top of the wealth distribution, would gladly flip a switch to redistribute wealth fairly, systemically and sustainably, if the results contributed to peace, plenty and happiness for all.

From the perspective of the Second Law of Thermodynamics (the universal tendency to dissipate uneven distributions of energy) we can better understand the danger of today's extreme wealth inequality. Money is a form of energy – like the glucose that fuels muscle contractions and brain activity that set us apart from the inorganic world of rocks. Money circulates between and among human beings, carrying information and the means to act – work, study, eat, rest, move, etc. When money collects within the system in a small area or group of areas, the remainder starves atrophies and begins to die. But systems have ways of rebalancing such extreme disequilibrium. Earth naturally dissipates energy variances through quakes, volcanic eruptions, hurricanes, tornadoes and thunderstorms. The system of humanity disperses energy imbalances through revolutions, riots, and wars.

The summer 2011 riots in London were a sign of dangerous levels of wealth imbalance. Disaffected youth, left out of the vital system of wealth circulation, showed their power in the only way they knew how. The rioters, whatever else might have been their personal motivations, succeeded in reducing energy disequilibrium in their immediate vicinity. They forcibly took energy where they could and destroyed it where they couldn't take it for themselves (breaking windows and destroying cars). They were the human equivalent of a hurricane: an expression of the Second Law of Thermodynamics. The Occupy Wall Street Movement spreading the world over is a similar, though more peaceful (so far), expression of the Second Law.

Understanding the systemic danger of wealth disparity illuminates another insight. Too little disequilibria, that is, a too even distribution of wealth is not necessarily an ideal system state. Systems that reach static equilibrium die. Life *is* the flow of energy; stagnation is death. The Marxist ideal would stultify humanity. There is such a thing as too much equality (apart from the loss of freedom enforced equality entails[6]). Though, given our current state we need not worry over this eventuality too much. In imagining our ideal future it is nonetheless important to remember.

Extreme wealth disparity and the energy disequilibria it represents do not serve the human system well, including those fortunate enough to be among the very wealthy. Many at the apex of the money pyramid, including Bill and Melinda Gates, Warren Buffet and George Soros work hard to ameliorate inequality and address the most acute suffering caused by extreme poverty. But their amazingly generous contributions are a mere drop in the bucket. They alone cannot transform our funneling system into a siphoning system without addressing the underlying systemic structure that causes the funneling.

The inefficiency of our current economic circulatory system is illustrated by the U.S.'s current unemployment rate of nearly 10% (and much of Southern Europe, which is suffering far higher levels of wasted human potential). There are innumerable, important unmet demands in our country: teacher-student ratios are too high, mentally ill people are homeless, working parents struggle with inadequate childcare, vital infrastructure is crumbling. This is an obvious waste of human potential, yet our system cannot adapt and put people to the task of doing important and valuable work. Millions of human beings are left out of a system that desperately needs their contribution.

Government efforts to address the problem of wealth inequality tend to be shortsighted interventions. Policies such as protectionist tariffs, rent control and living wage ordinances focus on the desired result (imposed by top-down bureaucracy) rather than encouraging fundamental systemic changes. While it's true that core adjustments to the system may take time to bring about the sought after goal, and demand a deeper understanding of system dynamics, these are the only way to create real and sustainable positive change. Superficial fixes often distort incentives, unjustly favor one special interest over another, sacrifice principle to expediency, and create new power centers that hinder future adaptation – all of which contribute to systemic breakdowns that damage our ability to bring forth a better world. Such policies favor short-term distributional goals (material equality) at the expense of longer-term freedom and overall well-being. Many government efforts ignore the importance of aligning means and ends – that *how* we get to our chosen destination is as important as getting there.

Progressive taxation is the most common government policy to address the funneling effect of capitalism. Indeed, in the past it was probably the best large-scale solution available. Evidence suggests that such tax policies can be an effective means of reducing wealth disparities. However, the impact on creating wealth is debatable. Progressive taxation tends to equalize the size of our pieces of pie, but it does not necessarily make the pie bigger or, more importantly, better.

Progressive taxation does nothing to create the synergy Benedict identified as the holy grail of healthy societies. Not many people enjoy a deep sense of altruistic satisfaction when they send a check to the IRS – our contribution is stripped of its meaning. Our tax schemes turn one form of funneling into another, with its own set of inefficiencies. Capitalism is a force of nature while government bureaucracy is a consciously designed institution. Our current tax plan is like taking the fuel out of a 400-horsepower machine to fill the tank of a Trabant (the East German two-stroke car that epitomizes the failure of centralized state planning). It is not a solution worthy of our present abilities. Put simply, using threat of force to take wealth from some and give it to others (that is, our current solution) is one way of addressing wealth disparity, but it is not the best way.

Here are a few obvious flaws. Government inefficiency and waste are rampant. Welfare programs pervert incentives and often foster resentment and mistrust among citizens. The sheer cost of administering and complying with our cumbersome tax system is staggering (over $400 *billion* a year).[7] Others, such as the risks to individual liberty of an expansive government and the human costs of welfare dependency, are subtler and potentially more severe.

The example of the Northern Blackfoot shows an important ingredient in the creation of a good society – liberty – that is notably absent in the tax solution to capitalism's funneling effects. Maslow explains that he, remember[s] my confusion as I came into the society and tried to find out who was the richest man, and found that the rich man had nothing. When I asked the white secretary of the reserve who was the richest man, he mentioned a name none of the Indians had mentioned, that is, the man who had on the books the most stock, the most cattle and horses. When I came back to my Indian informants and asked them about Jimmy McHugh, about all his horses, they shrugged with contempt. "He keeps it," they said, and, as a consequence, they hadn't even thought to regard him as wealthy.

Jimmy McHugh was not compelled to give away his material wealth. Participation in the Sun Dance ceremony was woven into the tribal social fabric. Nonconformity came with a social cost, but no legal consequence. This distinction is important – the alignment of altruism with self-interest requires the freedom to choose. Compulsion severs the link, turning an act of generosity into a submission to authority. The former honors individual freedom, the latter destroys it. This is not to say compulsion does not have a place in a good society. But we must remember the founding fathers chose liberty as the cornerstone of their political paradigm, and for good reason – freedom is essential to the realization of human potential and the attainment of happiness.

Major past efforts to counterbalance the wealth to the wealthy feedback loop have not been fair, sustainable, and social progressive. From the extreme of Soviet-style nationalization of all material wealth to more moderate progressive taxation paired with redistribution (employed by most Western countries) superficial, symptom-focused solutions cause their own serious systemic problems. State sponsored communism crushed the human spirit, creating a dystopia in which people pretended to work, and the state pretended to pay them for their efforts. The effects of progressive taxation coupled with redistribution aren't nearly as dramatic, but they are serious: often unintentionally, state assistance creates and reinforces dependence and disempowerment among recipients. This is not just right-wing libertarian drivel. We have seen it in our own families – existing for too long on the receiving side of the contribution-empowerment dynamic stunts a person's potential for self-actualization and happiness.

Additionally, our system feeds another dysfunctional feedback loop – power begets power. Over the past four decades, the quadrupling of federal spending shows the gravitational pull of tax-fueled government power. The United States' "tax and spend" approach to wealth redistribution has created a monstrous bureaucracy that uses its political pull to feed its own growth. Now that we cannot afford to support our spending habits we turn to other countries, China first among them, to finance our debt – the power feedback loop pays no heed to national boundaries. The U.S. is now closely tethered to the epicenter of centralized authoritarian power. Americans today live in a bloated, unsustainable bureaucracy with an insatiable appetite for power. This leviathan is now mortgaging the future of freedom and democracy to finance its addiction.

(Liberals quick to decry the austerity measures currently being imposed on Greece at the hands of central bankers would do well to take a broader view and see that top-heavy government is the true source of the current debt crisis.)

The matrix of eco-nomic changes outlined in the previous chapter – FPH enterprises, a True Cost Index and a Real Karma system – can form the basis of a wealth redistribution system that is fair, sustainable, and socially progressive. Currently profits of commercial business go disproportionately (80% to 90%) to the top 10% of wealthy individuals,[8] who by-and-large reinvest their wealth into other "for-profiting-the-few" enterprises. (As a percentage of income, the wealthiest Americans donate less than half as much as the poorest Americans.[9]) This means that money in the hands of the wealthiest tends not to re-circulate into the economic system in the most wealth-expanding manner. In conventional economic terms, money in the hands of the wealthy has a relatively low "multiplier effect."

In economics, the multiplier effect measures how spending choices impact the growth of the economy. Wealthy people tend to spend less on goods and services: conventional shareholders spend between 5% and 15% of their income and save or invest the rest.[10] On the other end of the spectrum, the poorest among us spend 100% or more (if they have access to credit) of their income on goods and services. Similarly, charitable enterprises lacking large endowments quickly spend what's in the coffers.

The people and organizations that tend to spend incoming cash generate higher total demand for goods and services (what economists call "aggregate demand"). On the other hand, the more money that ends up in the hands of the wealthy, the lower the total demand for goods and services.

Put differently, the multiplier effect refers to the rate at which energy (money) circulates, which varies based partially on the differing spending habits of market participants. A higher multiplier effect signals a higher rate of energy circulation and thus more economic activity. A lower multiplier effect signals a lower rate of energy circulation and less economic activity, that is, less coordination and cooperation. Thus, mechanisms and dynamics that increase the overall multiplier effect will circulate more energy, creating a more vital, robust and resilient economy.

An organism with a well-functioning metabolism will distribute its energy resources intelligently and thus be active and healthy. On the other hand, a life-form with metabolism problems (for example, storing energy even when it's desperately needed to fuel cell regeneration or toxin removal) will suffer from lethargy and illness. Our collective human organism has a faulty metabolism. Given the insanely fast growth of humanity in the past two centuries (during which we've gone from 1 billion to over 7 billion people) it is not too surprising that we are having some difficulty adjusting.

A vivid example of our faulty metabolism is that our collective human organism is storing much of its energy in the form of gold – a rare mineral with scant practical uses. As a result, gold prices are soaring and previously shuttered mines in Nevada are now booming. People are employed to remove gold from the earth so it can be melted into ingots and stored in vaults. Imagine what a crew of aliens might think about our choice of resource use. Billions of people suffer from a lack of basic education and infrastructure while we waste precious time and energy removing relatively useless minerals out of the ground. If the aliens could speak English they might say, "These poor humans have obviously mistaken the markers for the game."

Eco-nomic mechanisms offer a fair, sustainable and socially progressive means of improving the metabolism of the human organism by *intelligently* increasing the multiplier effect. Technology can empower prosumers and wealthy donors to efficiently siphon money out of the for-profiting-the-few sector and direct it toward for-profiting-humanity ventures. These funds will be spent on solving critical social problems, and will expand our economy so it delivers essential goods and services where they are most needed. Charitable organizations' money, in general, quickly flows back into the economy, often in ways that continue to circulate. For example, when a nonprofit group funds a new job for a teacher, nurse or social worker, the ranks of the middle-class expand. This new job increases the total demand for goods and services – cars, food, healthcare, etc. – because, on average, the middle-class spends more of their income than wealthy shareholders.

This wealth circulation effect satisfies the criteria of fairness, sustainability and social progress. First, the process is fair because it works from the bottom-up with individual prosumers and philanthropic donors freely and independently making choices. There is no compulsion involved, only pressures created by free and well-informed market participants. Thus, liberty is honored.

Second, because eco-nomic mechanisms work in harmony with system dynamics, they are sustainable. These mechanisms increase the flow of information and energy, decentralize power and contribute to a more intelligent and resilient system. FPH enterprises, a True Cost Index and a Real Karma system are a form of economic jujitsu. They harness the power of the system in order to change it and thus do not waste energy by creating unnecessary friction. Legislation, civil disobedience or threats of imprisonment are unnecessary to transform our current system into a new, more intelligent and evolved form of capitalism. This is evolution, not revolution.

Third, eco-nomic reconfigurations are socially progressive. As Ruth Benedict found in her study of Native American cultures, there is magic in aligning altruism, status, generosity and individual freedom. There is power in transcending the duality of self versus others. Synergy is the key to a society that fosters human potential and true happiness. We now have the ability to create synergy in a powerful, world-transforming way.

Taming the Leviathan

The increasing centralization of power poses a severe threat to liberty. The more we look to government to provide the services we need to flourish – education, healthcare, pensions, unemployment insurance, environmental protection, financial regulation, poverty relief, defense, etc. – the greater the danger. Eco-nomics offers a way to get what we need that spreads rather than concentrates power. FPH enterprises, a True Cost Index and a Real Karma interface are ways *we the people* can do much of the work being done by government. As we prove we can do a better job than Washington, the federal government will shrink. The best way to reduce the power of politicians, bureaucrats, and the special interests who feed them is not by direct resistance, but by making them irrelevant.

Eco-nomics can spark a renaissance in the art of associating identified by de Tocqueville as the key to healthy democracy. As energy flows to community organizations aimed at serving the common weal, opportunities to associate will multiply, precious social capital will grow, and democracy will thrive.

The tangled knot of campaign contributions, lobbyists, special interests and political corruption has us bound tightly. Untangling the knot is not the way out (especially now that the *Citizens United* decision grants corporations unlimited influence in political campaigns). Instead, we must use our flexibility and ingenuity Houdini-style to break free. Our *ballot votes* are powerless to change the status quo, but our *dollar votes* hold the power to bring real progress. But to use our dollar votes wisely, we must have accurate and relevant information that a True Cost Index would give.

Automation Dystopia

In developed countries there is a strong jobs trend away from manufacturing and toward the service sector. Automation is a major contributor, whether it's the grocery store self-checkout, ATMs, or robotic vacuum cleaners. Machines streamline our lives and in the process lessen the need for human labor. But they also create a conflict between the goals of efficiency and cost-effectiveness on one hand and the goal of full employment on the other. This friction is illuminated by a conversation said to have taken place as Henry Ford II and a veteran UAW leader. As Ford showed off his newly automated factory, he asked the union leader, "How are you going to get those robots to pay union dues?" He replied, "Henry, how are you going to get them to buy your cars?"

A thought experiment clarifies the nature and systemic implications of the conflict. Imagine a scientist named Maya, having toiled for years in her private laboratory, unveils the revolutionary "Maya Machine." Using nanotechnology, it takes raw materials (the elements from the periodic table) to manufacture finished products quickly and cheaply, from tennis shoes (in whatever shade you choose) to a perfectly ripened strawberry. The Maya Machine can replicate items, including itself, or it can create new products based on provided schematics. Thus, within weeks the world is home to tens of thousands of Maya Machines where you can go to buy items (whether mass-produced or customized) at a small fraction of the former cost. A handful of raw materials businesses will be busy, but the vast majority of people and companies that formerly earned their livelihoods by producing material goods will be out of work.

Now consider the broader implications. Soon the huge numbers of the unemployed will sap their savings, eventually unable to afford even the low-cost goods produced by the Maya Machine. Nor will these unemployed people be able to patronize the service providers (artists, designers, counselors, hairstylists, etc.) whose employment was not affected directly by the Maya Machine. Thus, this amazing new technology that holds the potential to free human beings from doing work they don't enjoy doing ends up creating poverty. Absent significant adjustments, Maya and the handful of raw material providers will hold all the material wealth, leaving everyone else destitute and at the mercy of the privileged few. (Kurt Vonnegut depicted just such a dystopia in his novel, *Player Piano*, in which automation leads to a chasm between the minority of engineers and managers whose skills are still needed, and the masses whose skills have been rendered useless by technological progress.)

This illustration reveals an underlying systemic challenge we face today (though in a less extreme version). As technology frees people from the drudgery of work, our system continues to function based on the unspoken assumption that we will always need more stuff. Thus, there is always more work to be done (work of the making stuff variety). Conventional economics strives simultaneously for improvements in productivity (the amount of work one person can do) and full employment. It never notices that in a finite world such as ours these two goals are, ultimately, contradictory. For two centuries this conflict has been kept at bay. New products and services, helped along by rampant consumerism, have, so far, filled the gap that otherwise would be caused by job-eliminating automation. But there are unnerving signs, such as the jobless recovery from the 2008 recession, that this equilibrium is coming unhinged. Indeed, one analyst has suggested that roughly 50 million American jobs (40% of all employment) could be filled in whole or in part by software.[11] While this estimate may be overstating the situation, increasingly intelligent computer programs (such as Google's translation software) will undoubtedly eliminate many knowledge-based jobs soon.

Automation is contributing to the wealth concentration discussed earlier – the few are benefiting as the many are marginalized. But it's because of our system structure rather than attempts at world domination by the privileged. We have been slow to adapt to our changing reality, and thus we have created significant systemic dysfunctions. We must use our intelligence and wisdom to reshape the system in ways that promote a healthy circulation of wealth that advances the well-being of humanity.

The eco-nomic catalysts outlined in the previous chapter offer examples of possible system adjustments that can ease our transition into an increasingly automated world. Each has the ability to expand the parts of our collective system aimed at improving the well-*being* of humanity (rather than its well-*having*). People will have the opportunity to use their talents to help others. As we shift focus away from making things, to helping people we create jobs that cannot be done by robots or shipped overseas – jobs that require compassion, connection, love and creativity. A software program cannot replace a counselor and your masseuse can't do her job from Hyderabad, India. In terms of Maslow's pyramid, the eco-nomic model shifts our collective human system up – helping all rise to new heights of creativity, community and purpose. Said differently, eco-nomics offers a path that transcends the tension between automation and full employment by adjusting our systems to adapt to our changing reality

Kindness Changes Us

It is no coincidence that every major spiritual tradition stresses selfless giving as the primary path to transcendence. Modern neuroscientists are finding the biological foundation of the saying, "it's better to give than to receive." Charitable giving activates the areas of the brain associated with pleasure – quite simply, it feels good to give. Human beings have thrived in large part due to our strategy of social living and the reciprocal altruism it entails. Our cooperative tendencies are hardwired. (Indeed, some evolutionary biologists say humans are a combination of primate and bee (the quintessential collaborator).)

In saying that selfless generosity is evolutionarily useful, we are not saying that a Machiavellian cost-benefit analysis drives people to give because it's a good survival strategy. Rather, the vast majority of humans are descendants of people who enjoyed giving and who, because they gave and were thus a valued part of their community, lived to reproduce. Survival is a happy by-product of love and generosity.

The link between survival and giving offers a clue to the mysterious magic of the Sun Dance Ceremony and its ability to transcend the self versus other duality. As Maslow explained it, in the Sun Dance Ceremony the opposition between selfishness and generosity evaporates. Our Western individualism highlights our separateness and thus creates a reality in which self and other are opposites. But this is not necessarily the most accurate, or the most helpful, way of viewing our world. In a world seen through the lens of Western individualism charity is a sacrifice. Neuroscientists, using cutting edge FMRI technology, are seeing a different reality: giving triggers pleasure, not pain – there is no sacrifice.[12] This points toward a reality in which self and other, though separate, are potentially complimentary parts of a unified whole, no more in conflict than your hands are in conflict with your feet. Thus, Western scientific empiricism, our culturally favored tool, is discovering that our self versus other conception of the world is inaccurate. Neuroscience is catching up with Ruth

Benedict's insight. The social systems most conducive to our well-being are those that align the interests of self and other. Thus, helping people overcome the optical illusion of separateness and achieve at-one-ment.

Kindness tends to make us happy and happiness tends to make us kind. In a study of Japanese undergraduates, researchers asked students to count their acts of kindness for a week. The students experienced a significant improvement in subjective happiness, and those who reported more acts of kindness experienced greater improvements in their happiness.[13] Social scientists have repeatedly found happy people more inclined to help others.[14] In system terms, we have a reinforcing feedback loop. This is an exciting loop!

Much of the eco-nomics paradigm is about integrating kindness and generosity into our everyday lives. Such integration offers enormous potential to improve our happiness, and the well-being of those we help. By tapping into and strengthening the kindness-happiness feedback loop, we can put capitalism to the task of creating societies that empower people to shape the world in alignment with their highest ideals, and foster true and lasting happiness.

In particular, a Real Karma mechanism can nurture kindness. Prosumers will have an opportunity to give to others regularly. Contributions – whether from wealthy donors or less wealthy prosumers – will be channeled in a way that changes the configuration of our collective human system making a real and lasting difference. With this power, we expect the most fortunate among us (beneficiaries of the wealth to the wealthy feedback loop) will be more inclined to use their affluence for good.

Unleashing Our Potential

The examples of eco-nomic catalysts we have described deal mostly with prosumer-facing areas of the economy because that is where we, as buyers, have the ability to shape our world immediately and profoundly. However, the potential long-term effects of these changes can reach deep into the fabric of human civilization. Awakened to the joy of giving, more people will step away from 40-plus hour workweeks that mainly benefit a few at the top. Instead, we will look for opportunities to earn a living and contribute to the creation of a better world simultaneously. That is, to do well and do good at the same time.

Science has confirmed that financial incentives, while effective in some situations, are fraught with pitfalls (like encouraging unethical behavior) and can be counterproductive.[15] Intrinsic motivators such as mastery and purpose unleash creativity and enable focused attention. As Bill Gates explained, "Young people today – all over the world – want to work for organizations that they can feel good about. Show them that a company is applying its expertise to help the poorest, and they will repay that commitment with their own dedication."

An eco-nomic system is filled with enterprises committed to making the world a better place. Money (energy) flows to those who are doing the work that prosumers, matching philanthropists, and for-profiting-humanity entrepreneurs consider most important. Thus, scientists, managers, executives, designers and others will have far broader opportunities to earn a good living while putting their talents to work for companies and organizations dedicated to positive change. Meaningful contribution will be an integral part of our lives, and we will be happier for it. Not only will we be happier, but by fostering the intrinsic motivator of purpose we will unleash the latent human potential needed to address the mounting challenges facing our species.

While we hold great hopes for a future guided by economic principles, we are realists. No human system will insulate our species from the natural, rhythmic ebb and flow of existence – we are, after all, surfing at the edge of chaos. As with a single human life, when we cease breathing we return to the stardust from where we came. An optimal human system will be inspired by our understanding of humanity and our planet as living, breathing organisms that adapt to changes, or go extinct. We must always have an eye on our ultimate objective – empowering life in its fullest and most joyful expression, and the attainment of true happiness that emerges when we strive for new and richer experience in harmony with one another and with nature. This human system is being born as you read these words – to thrive it must be nurtured.

10 – Twenty-First Century Dreamers

Eco-nomics is all around us. Our world is full of dreamers who have begun writing the first chapter of our hero's journey. These dreamers are like groups of neurons firing in the collective human brain giving rise to a new pattern, a new paradigm. It is not being made from scratch – that way has been tried and it failed miserably. Instead, it is being shaped from the quality work and deep insights of our predecessors. Small changes made in alignment with our most noble goals and informed by the collective wisdom of humanity is how the new pattern is emerging.

Many dreamers are helping others understand their role in the larger system of humanity and the planet, so they are less likely to follow blindly traditional values rooted in racism, nationalism and a host of ugly isms. Among this group we find writers, counselors, life coaches, parents, caregivers, spiritual teachers, yoga instructors, musicians and other artists. These generous souls practice and teach the arts of inner technology – the development of the inner evolution of human beings.[1] In systems terms, this shift improves the fitness of the nodes in the human network and increases energy flow to previously neglected areas critical to the success of humanity's evolution. They are deepening and strengthening the roots of our system, laying the foundation for new growth in the branches.

Other dreamers practice the arts of outer technology, helping to shape our material world. These artisans (often helped by inner technologists) follow their passions, scale their personal pyramids, and in the process express a unique vision of truth and beauty. They create or rearrange the architecture of our social arrangements, develop innovations that help us live harmoniously within our ecosystem and help those who are struggling simply to survive. These dreamers are all around us, inspiring us with their enthusiasm for life and passion for bringing forth a better world. These outer technologists are branches, leaves and flowers striving toward the farther reaches of human potential.

The eco-nomics shift emerges before our eyes, forming the edges of crystallization; the players are the first storm troopers to begin twirling and humming. This pattern is beginning to take shape, worth recognizing and repeating. If we choose wisely, a beautifully intricate, strong and resilient tapestry will form the likes of which this world has never seen.

Root Expansion

Many people, fortunate to live amid material abundance, have heard their inner voices calling out for spiritual meaning. While many of our parents and grandparents satisfied this calling with faith in conventional religious dogma, we have the privilege of searching more deeply and broadly to find our own truth. A wealth of fellow travelers generously shares their insights into the nonmaterial realm, helping us transcend the material fixation that dulls the thrill of living and threatens our continued survival. Among these travelers are two who have played an important role in our (the authors') inner evolution.

His Holiness the 14th Dalai Lama of Tibet embodies ancient Eastern spiritual wisdom blended with Western modernity. His popularity around the world evidences the yearning of so many for spiritual enlightenment and political justice for all (which is a logical result of recognizing our shared divinity). The Dalai Lama's teachings reflect synthetic rationality: he integrates Buddhist philosophy with the insights of modern science. His readiness to let go of those aspects of traditional Tibetan Buddhist philosophy that conflict with current knowledge of the nature of existence distinguishes him from many religious leaders. He is not touting a particular creed; instead he aspires to expand his own understanding and share his insights with others.

The Dalai Lama is concerned with the lack of consciousness among scientists. He calls on them to accept moral responsibility and recognize the impact of their actions on the world.[2] He echoes the sentiments of Albert Einstein who observed, "It has become appallingly obvious that our technology has exceeded our humanity." It is precisely this imbalance between our outer technologies – nuclear proliferation, genetic manipulation, chemical engineering, etc. – and our humanity that inner technologists strive to correct.

The Dalai Lama is also concerned about the dominance of the having mode, and the danger of confusing the markers for the game:

> In the frenzy of modern life we lose sight of the real value of humanity. People become the sum total of what they produce. Human beings act like machines whose function is to make money. This is absolutely wrong. The purpose of making money is the happiness of humankind, not the other way round. Humans are not for money, money is for humans. We need enough to live, so money is necessary, but we also need to realize that if there is too much attachment to wealth, it does not help at all.[3]

Modern social science is proving the truth of Tibetan Buddhism's ancient wisdom – happiness flourishes when we contribute to the well-being of others, and atrophies amid selfishness. It is not surprising that the teachings of the Dalai Lama echo another great spiritual teacher, Jesus: there is substantial evidence that during his "lost years" Jesus traveled throughout the East, visiting the Tibetan holy city of Lhasa. This theory helps explain the source of Jesus' unorthodox teachings of peace and humility which contrast starkly with previous Western traditions ("an eye for an eye" versus "turn the other cheek"). Peace and humility are deeply held values in Buddhism.

The spiritual teacher, Eckhart Tolle, catapulted to mainstream stardom when Oprah Winfrey featured his book, *A New Earth: Awakening to Your Life's Purpose*, as the first and only nonfiction work in her book club. She also posted on her website a chapter-by-chapter conversation with Tolle, an effort she called "the most rewarding experience" of her career. Tolle's impact on millions of students cannot be distilled to simple numbers. He speaks to the inner voice of people who realize that mainstream culture offers little in the way of true purpose or a path to the top of the pyramid.

Tolle's teachings are steeped in the Eastern philosophies of Taoism, Buddhism, Hinduism and the mystical branches of the Abrahamic faiths (Gnosticism, Sufism, and Kabala). As such, his philosophy finds a natural affinity among the growing number of yoga practitioners in the West. Yoga, with its emphasis on the union of mind, body and spirit ("yoga" literally means "to yoke" or "to unite") naturally aligns with the eco-nomics paradigm. Its inward focus and teachings of discipline and kindness are a powerful answer to the dangerous imbalance between our technology and our humanity.

The popularity of the Dalai Lama and Eckhart Tolle can be understood as a continuation of the human potential movement begun by Maslow and his contemporaries, including Aldus Huxley, Carl Rogers and Viktor Frankel. These early visionaries' ideas are woven into the fabric of our culture. In true evolutionary fashion, what was once fringe is now core. Indeed, many Fortune 500 companies regularly feature seminars that teach inner technologies to employees.[4]

Psychologists and therapists are finding that mindfulness – the practice of being present to the moment, observing reactions to thoughts, emotions and circumstances – is a helpful treatment for anxiety and depression.[5] Through mindfulness we become aware of our default operating system and can then consciously choose to rewrite it. Mindful people are likely to be scaling their personal pyramids, less constrained by ego-centered fear and envy, and less attached to the lifeless things of this world. In our (the authors') own experience mindfulness is not just a key to a more contented life, but is a doorway to living in harmony with others and taking personal responsibility for our responses to whatever life throws our way. Put simply, the inner technology of mindfulness powerfully transcends egoistic reactions and desires, and offers a path to true happiness.

The evolutionary shift in the system of humanity depends on people distancing themselves from the whims of ego through mindfulness practice or other inner technologies. Those who succeed are likely to practice the Zen "beginner's mind" so critical to recognizing opportunities and correcting flaws in our operating system. Egos tend to give beliefs the gravity of identity, making us rigid and static, and putting us in conflict with the flexible and fluid world.[6] Donella Meadow's "omniscient conquerors" (that is, ego-driven people) are ill suited for the surfboard shaping approach to life. Put differently, nodes controlled by ego are of an inferior quality to mindful nodes. Thus, transforming nodes through inner technology is critical to improving the intelligence of the human system.

The Dalai Lama, Eckhart Tolle and many other contemporary spiritual teachers are helping guide the way beyond our hedonic, materialist culture (and the alienation and disempowerment it causes). They are leading toward a future in which human relationships and experience are central. From the "omniscient conqueror" perspective this transition is terrifying. It means letting go of old, entrenched ideas and ways of being – ideas and ways that for many are infused with identity. It need not be a painful transformation. The pain comes from resisting the future, of struggling against evolution, of insisting on control. We need to do is let go of our rigid ideas about how things are supposed to be. We need to dance, not march.

Reaching for the Sun

Outer technologists are bringing about growth at the branches, leaves and blossoms in an infinite variety of ways. The following are just a handful of the seed crystals spreading the eco-nomics pattern in ways that can put capitalism at the service of humanity.

The Giving Pledge

Billionaires are jumping on The Giving Pledge bandwagon by promising to give most their wealth to philanthropic causes. Bill and Melinda Gates were among the first to take the step publicly in recent years, Warren Buffett followed. Mark Zuckerberg is a recent convert. There are too many generous billionaires to list. The tradition of the Rockefellers, Carnegies, Mellons, and other wealthy industrialists continues to inspire the United States' strong philanthropic spirit. As a percentage of GDP, Americans give more to charitable causes than any other nation by a factor of over two. These givers, and their less well-off brethren, recognize that material wealth multiplies when shared with those in need. They, like Adam Smith and the countless Sun Dance Ceremony benefactors, know that financial net worth is not an accurate measure of true wealth.

Billionaire givers are influencing their wealthy friends to give. In many circles, it is no longer fashionable to flaunt one's riches through conspicuous consumption. This is evidence of the truth of Maslow's hierarchy – when psychologically healthy people have all they need to fully satisfy the bottom rungs of the pyramid they shift their focus to the higher level needs of love, belonging, community and meaning.

Bill Gates stresses the need to apply capitalism's strengths to the challenge of extreme poverty. What he calls "creative capitalism" is a significant step toward economics. Mr. Gates' identification of the roots of our problems, and the need for systemic solutions that draw on the power of capitalism parallel much of the authors' thinking. Though his reliance on established system boundaries (the nonprofit versus business framework, for example) seems to limit his perception of the full richness of the opportunities:

> As I see it, there are two great forces of human nature: self-interest and caring for others. Capitalism harnesses self-interest in a helpful and sustainable way but only on behalf of those who can pay. Government aid and philanthropy channel our caring for those who can't pay. And the world will make lasting progress on the big inequities that remain – problems like AIDS, poverty and education – only if governments and nonprofits do their part by giv-

ing more aid and more effective aid. But the improvements will happen faster and last longer if we can channel market forces, including innovation that's tailored to the needs of the poorest, to complement what governments and nonprofits do. We need a system that draws in innovators and businesses in a far better way than we do today.[7]

Mr. Gates stepped down as CEO of Microsoft to apply his business sense to the issues of poverty, health and education through the foundation he and his wife set up. He is setting an example for other baby boomers who have talent and knowledge that can be put to use creating a more just and peaceful world.

Panera Cares

The Panera Bread Foundation (a 501(c)(3) organization funded through donation boxes at Panera Bread bakery-cafes) has, so far, opened three Panera Cares restaurants, which operate on a donation-only basis. Financially well-off patrons often pay extra (about 20% do so), others pay the suggested donation (about 60%), and those in need pay what they can afford.[8] Offering a menu similar to Panera Bread's conventional outlets, the goal of Panera Cares "isn't about offering a hand out. It's about offering a hand up to those who need it. The cafes also offer the option of volunteering an hour of time for a meal. The Panera Cares cafe model is designed to be self-sustaining with support from the community."[9] This model is proving sustainable with sufficient revenue to more than cover operating expenses. Profits fund job training for disadvantaged youth and other community programs.

Panera Cares is a beautiful example of joining the force of capitalism with our most noble goals. It is an inspiring eco-nomics seed crystal. By not drawing stark lines between givers and receivers it recognizes and honors our common humanity and the importance of supportive community. We live together in this "oikos," the household of humanity. Panera Cares gives prosumers the choice to use their buying power – their dollar votes – to create positive change locally on a daily basis. Thus, it brings generosity and compassion into the heart of our economic system. Panera Cares also aligns ends and means – people are fed by feeding people!

Like Gates, Panera's founder, Ron Shaich, stepped down as CEO (keeping his Chairman position) to dedicate his time and talents to the foundation he helped create – another baby boomer making a real difference. He too recognizes the need to bring the intelligence and force of capitalism to the task of solving our most intractable human problems:

> Imagine a world in which Walmart did all the distribution for the food banks. Who knows better how to do that than a company like Walmart? Think about a world in which the banks, JP Morgan and Bank of America, [are] as worried and involved about people getting foreclosed and how they avoid foreclosure as in foreclosure … Think of a world in which the energy companies so big and with so much resources are not only dealing with

remediation after the oil spill, but helping us with this energy crisis that nobody can deny ... Think about our largest companies, Ford, AT&T, HP, you name it, GE, the management talent that exists ... think about if they took on real responsibilities with NGOs ... in places like Haiti where there are horrible, horrible problems. If our companies understood that their broader interests are the communities in which we operate.[10]

Eco-nomics is not a pipe dream. It is a way of seeing the world shared by many of the titans of capitalism. Bill Gates and Ron Shaich are dreamers. They offer proof that the dream of a better world – where the compass of compassion guides the forces of human creativity and ingenuity – is becoming reality.

Looking forward, one has to wonder at what point the duty of Panera Bread Co. to maximize profits (it is a Delaware corporation, so there is no doubt that its primary duty is to maximize shareholders' financial value) will begin to conflict noticeably with the charitable goals of Panera Cares. Surely shareholders will balk at opening a Panera Cares franchise anywhere near the for-profit version. Since they averaged opening two new for-profit cafés each week in 2010, the potential for conflict is more than hypothetical.

Micro Finance – Kiva

The economist and philanthropist Muhammad Yunus won the Nobel Prize in economics for his groundbreaking work in microfinance. Yunus saw the impoverished people of his native Bangladesh had extremely limited access to the credit they needed to lift themselves out of poverty. The usurious interest rates attached to typical loans made it all but impossible for the borrower to come out ahead. Yunus began Grameen Bank with the objective of bridging this gap, offering micro loans at reasonable rates to poor aspiring entrepreneurs (mostly to women, who turned out to be far better credit risks than men). The loans came with basic business education and membership in a close-knit community of other business owners. Yunus' microfinance idea has spread across the globe and is lifting millions out of abject poverty.[11]

Kiva.org, an online charitable organization, combines the microfinance revolution with the digital age. Kiva enables individuals to make micro loans to people in need all over the world. A prospective lender can use Kiva's website to make a loan of as little as $25 to a specific person or group enterprise. Kiva coordinates with local microlending organizations that facilitate loan distribution and repayment. Thus, Kiva and its partners use communication technology to connect people in need with those who wish to contribute. It offers the opportunity to siphon wealth and thus systemically treat the roots of poverty rather than only its most obvious symptoms.

Kiva enables person-to-person economic interactions that satisfy our basic need to contribute to the well-being of others. Its network of specialized connectivity widens and strengthens our human community. Its structure is designed to empower rather than control: individual lenders and borrowers make their own decisions about the best way to use their respective capital and talents. Kiva and its local partners facilitate the transactions, and maintain a platform, allowing a dynamic flow of participants.

The goal of microfinance generally (and Kiva in particular) is to empower people to lift themselves out of poverty. Thus, it is fundamentally about a bottom-up transformation of humanity. The experience of Ethiopia underscores the need for such transformative programs: its population has doubled since the 1980s famine that seized the world's attention. The global response treated the symptoms of poverty with handouts, which has led to unintended consequences, creating dependence and worsening the underlying conditions that gave rise to the earlier disaster. Food aid programs aggravated the problem of a population that outstripped its agricultural capacity and lacked sustainable solutions to bridge the gap. The lesson here is not to ignore starving people. Rather, we would do well to take action *before* disaster strikes, anticipate the unintended consequences of our actions and take steps to address them. We need to become savvy system choreographers rather than shortsighted interveners.

Our tendency to focus on shortsighted symptom-treating solutions (rather than system adjustments that go to the source of a problem) may be rooted in our metaphors. In a machine, if a part breaks you can repair or replace it and the problem usually will be solved. But, if part of a living system breaks there is usually an underlying cause (unless some physical trauma is involved). If only repaired, and the cause isn't addressed, then new manifestations of the underlying problem will arise. Thus, fixing parts is usually an inefficient, shortsighted and often self-defeating approach to problem solving in our human systems.

Product (Red)

Product (Red), an initiative started by Bono (of the famous rock and roll band U2) and Bobby Shriver (a member of the Kennedy clan), embodies the values of eco-nomics. Product (Red)'s goal is to engage public-facing businesses in raising awareness and money for the Global Fund to help eliminate AIDS in Africa. The initiative works, in part, because the Bono "coolness factor" has made Product (Red) a recognizable cause among a demographic that retailers are eager to attract. Well-off buyers use their buying power to encourage corporations to include contribution in their products. By offering a Product (Red) branded item, a company attracts the attention of affluent young prosumers and builds goodwill. An impressive list of companies has joined in: American Express, Apple, Converse, Gap, Emporio Armani, Motorola, Hallmark, Dell and Microsoft. These partners have (RED) product offer-

> People see a world out of whack. They see the greatest health crisis of 600 years and they want to do the right thing, but they're not sure what that is. (RED) is about doing what you enjoy and doing good at the same time.
>
> – Bono

ings (often in the color red) that usually sell for the same price as the regular version, but a portion of the sale price goes to the Global Fund. Thus, Product (Red) allows buyers to contribute without sacrifice. The success of this idea is evidence of its power – as of May 2012 it has raised more than $190 million since its March 2006 launch.

Bono's role in Product (Red) and other Africa-focused initiatives shows the eco-nomics paradigm in another way – art is integrated into the larger tapestry of human endeavors. The compassion and appreciation for harmony and beauty that are the ground from which great art arises are qualities we desperately need throughout our human systems. In a world in which the eco-nomics pattern takes hold we will all be encouraged to find our inner artists and bring truth and beauty to all.

Causes

Causes is a Facebook application with over 2 million active monthly users (as of May 2012). Users create or join any cause they care about and the application facilitates donations to tax-exempt organizations. While this potentially satisfies a person's need for contribution and belonging, the limits are clear: attracting people willing to join a cause often does not translate into fundraising success. Only a handful of nonprofits have raised more than $100,000 through the Causes application.[12] This shows that although people and Facebook users in particular, care enough to join a cause and invite their friends to join, they often don't get past the hurdle of making the financial sacrifice needed to donate.

One comment from a Causes user illustrates both the need being satisfied, and its limits:

> Causes is great!
> by Leanne Campbell at 9:52pm on August 6th, 2008
> I love this application because I can do something small for my causes any time of the day or night and feel that I have contributed to the world. I usually do it when I am feeling down and it lifts me up. I just wish there were more ways we could help via this application.

The inability of Causes to translate concern and connection into concrete action illuminates the limited utility of network connections alone – connectivity must be paired with a means to act. This is not to say that connections are not essential, but they are not sufficient on their own to reshape the world.

Causes has another weakness – it is a conventional for-profit enterprise. It has investors who expect it to maximize their financial returns. We (the authors) hope that by this point you know that we are not anti-profit – we want people to make as much money as their abilities and desires allow provided it is done so responsibly. However, a business model that has *at its core* the leveraging of altruistic and generous inclinations of others and involves making more than a fair salary (or a fair return on a non-equity investment[13]) can muck-up system dynamics. For-profit status of such giving-oriented efforts tends to dampen, rather than amplify, charitable momentum.

Problems arise when one party is taking money off the charitable table for more than reasonable operating expenses, or when there is a lack of clarity about an organization's motives. Researchers studying the effects of mixing social and market norms (that is, altruism and money) have concluded that market norms can drive out social norms. Said differently, when profit is mixed un-artfully with altruistic giving, the altruism tends to dry up. In other words, it is the *opposite* of the synergy identified by Ruth Benedict, because the whole is worth *less* than the sum of the parts.

In one experiment Dan Ariely and a colleague asked subjects to perform a boring, but easy, 5-minute computer task (dragging circles from one side of the screen into a square on the other side). Some participants were paid $5, others $0.50 and a third group was asked to volunteer. The volunteers performed best, moving on average 168 circles, the $5 recipients did second best, moving 159 circles, and the low paid subjects did the worst, moving an average of 101 circles. Simply stated, no one is motivated when they feel used. From an evolutionary perspective this makes perfect sense. People too easily walked on tend to get trampled to death. Since the goal is to amplify generosity, not to funnel more money into the hands of a few, an ideal synergistic Real Karma application would be an FPH enterprise, with all profits going to cause positive change in the world (that is, a 501(c)(3) charitable organization).

Freerice

Freerice.com began with visionary computer programmer and humanitarian, John Breen. He put his skills to use by creating a simple computer program that tests a user's English vocabulary ability, with multiple-choice questions that automatically adjust in difficulty based on performance. Freerice.com brings together people who want to expand their vocabulary, marketers who are eager to display their brands to these studious people, and the UN World Food Program whose mission is to feed the hungry throughout the developing world. Breen gave the Freerice website to the UN World Food Program in March 2009. It has since expanded to cover a range of topics including geography, chemistry, mathematics and more languages. Today knowledge seekers can help expand the waistlines of people around the world - each correct answer sends ten grains of rice to those in need. Since its start in October 2007 over 95 billion grains of rice have been donated (as of May 2012).

Getaround

Getaround.com one of several Internet platforms enabling people to offer their own cars for rent to other (pre-vetted) members. Users set an hourly price for renting their car. GPS facilitates locating vehicles, and a secure box holding the keys can be opened using a smart phone app. According to Getaround's website, each shared car takes 10 cars off the road and reduces personal carbon emissions by over 40%.

Getaround.com is an example of a wider phenomenon called the "sharing economy." People are offering spare rooms on CouchSurfing.com, or whole apartments on Airbnb.com. Technology facilitates the networks of trust needed for the sharing economy to work well. Resources – idle cars, empty guestrooms, vacant vacation homes – that were previously wasted are being put to good use. Underlying the sharing economy is a subtle shift away from the having mode – it's not about possession, it's about enjoyment and experience.

Kickstarter

Kickstarter.com is an Internet platform that facilitates crowd sourced funding for creative projects – films, books, plays, websites, start-ups can tap their friends, family, and supportive strangers for money to get their dreams rolling. Donors are enticed with rewards (invitations to opening events, signed copies of the finished work, etc.) in addition to getting the satisfaction of being a part of the realization of another's dream. Kickstarter.com is creating a global community of people who are interested in scaling Maslow's pyramid and helping others reach their fullest potential.

InnoCentives

InnoCentives is an Internet platform that facilitates crowd sourced problem solving by linking organizations with a fluid global network of millions of problem solvers in a wide range of fields. Booz Allen Hamilton, Eli Lilly & Company, NASA, Nature Publishing Group, Popular Science, Procter & Gamble, Roche, Rockefeller Foundation, and The Economist have partnered with InnoCentive to solve problems cost effectively and efficiently. InnoCentives brings the power of starfish to the research and development efforts of spider institutions.

Celebrating at the Top of the Pyramid

The Giving Pledge, Kiva, Panera Cares and others are reconfiguring capitalism in ways that transcend the self versus other duality. Philanthropists, social entrepreneurs and prosumers are coming together to weave an incredibly varied and rich pattern. Other outer technologists bring their inner beauty and truth into our material world in the form of art, thus creating an environment that connects us with the magic of life and reminds us of our place in the unfolding of the cosmos.

Technology is enabling the emergence of what author Chris Anderson refers to as "The Long Tail." When people choose to buy unique products rather than mass-market hits, it allows artisans to make a living plying their craft. No longer satisfied with merely functional or mass-produced stylized offerings, ever more buyers are searching for goods that reflect their personal taste and values. Etsy.com, the online marketplace for handcrafted items, is an example of how the Internet allows artisans to take their one-of-a-kind wares direct to customers, while simultaneously empowering consumers to find the artists whose works reflect their values and tastes. Visual artists, musicians and writers are now able to skip the intermediaries and, if they can find a niche, make a living (or at least supplement their living) doing what they love. Our material surroundings are increasingly reflecting the awe-inspiring diversity of human creativity. With this expanding focus on artisanal work we are awakening to the preciousness of materials that come from the earth, and thus, many are moving away from a disposable mass-market mind-set.

Agriculture is another area showing signs of a paradigm shift that values quality over quantity. The spread of community supported agriculture and farmer's markets are sparking a comeback of small farmers specializing in organic or semi-organic produce. The heightened interest in heirloom varieties of plants reflects the movement away from generic toward specialty. Local seed libraries are popping up, allowing community gardeners and small farmers to develop collectively varieties of produce naturally evolved to thrive in a local environment. Their efforts can lead to highly localized varieties in far less time than it would take a single gardener to develop the same varieties – an example of the synergistic power of cooperation.

The Crop Mob described in the introduction is another example of the increasing interest in the art of local agriculture. Popular writers such as Barbra Kingsolver and Michael Pollan are contributing to a deepening awareness of our food production and distribution system's fundamental dysfunctions. This trend toward localization and diversification can be seen as a reflection of the wisdom of aligning structure and purpose. Supporting life through healthful and flavorful food is the fundamental purpose of our food system. But supporting life includes preserving our environment that is maintaining clean air and water, stabilizing our climate, and ensuring the long-term sustainability of our agricultural practices. If wrong-headed government subsidies did not support large agribusiness, and if it had to actually pay the price for the pollution and increased disease virulence (due to antibiotic use in farm animals), then local sustainably produced food would be price-competitive. But as things stand, agribusiness gets to put the burden of its unsustainable practices on the public and future generations, while reaping the rewards for a privileged few.

Qualitative values such as land stewardship and the humane treatment of farm animals are best protected and promoted in systems that maintain a close link between people (that is, those capable of evaluating quality) and production. The simplest way to preserve this connection in agriculture is to grow and buy locally whenever possible. When it's *your* water being tainted by petrochemicals, as a farmer you're far less likely to shrug off effective responsible alternatives. As a buyer you're more likely to be willing to shell out a couple extra dollars for organic produce. Quite simply, those nasty externalities aren't so external and that's a good thing for intelligent decision making.

On a related front, the Slow Food movement's focus on high-quality local and sustainably produced food is finding supporters across the country, and across the globe, who celebrate the joy of food. The wildly popular British celebrity chef, Jamie Oliver, has brought a simple style of healthful cooking to the masses. His latest book, *30 Minute Meals*, broke the UK record for fastest selling work of non-fiction (735,000 copies in just over two months). Oliver and his ilk bring artistry to our tables, teaching us to savor the simple yet profound pleasure of food that is as good for our bodies as it is for the our planet. They remind us that an intelligent food system is life-sustaining at every level.

A Slow Money movement is emerging to financially support the values of local and sustainable food production. As its founder, Woody Tasch, explains, "We need to roll up our sleeves and collaborate with our friends and neighbors to begin fixing the economy from the ground up. We need to begin investing in small food enterprises near where we live."[14] Instead of using huge amounts of valuable energy to take gold out of the ground, we would be far wiser to plow our investment dollars into the creation of local and sustainable sources of a commodity crucial to survival – food.

Our morality, our compassion for one another and all living things, exists only at the level of the individual. Systems can foster individual morality by valuing compassion and integrity, or they can stifle it by devaluing compassion and integrity. One powerful way of preserving and fostering morality within a system is to keep actions and consequences closely linked. Local decentralized systems are far better at maintaining such links than expansive centralized ones. There are certainly times and situations that call for expansive centralized systems, but as conscious architects of future human systems we should keep in mind that decoupling cause and effect tends to degrade our moral fiber in ways that often leads to extreme instances of unintelligence.

The 2007-2008 financial crises and its continuing aftermath provide a vivid case study in the dangers of decoupling cause and effect. Every player in the system – brokers, borrowers, lenders, investors, investment banks, regulators, and rating agencies – were, to one degree or another, leveraging the mismatch between their personal costs and benefits.[15] This was a problem for *both* Wall Street *and* Main Street. The end result was a breathtakingly unintelligent allocation of resources that has yet to fully unravel.

We are witness to the birth of an alternative way of creating our world, which celebrates our most human qualities of compassion, creativity and striving. The Dalai Lama, Eckhart Tolle, and the millions who are opening their hearts and minds to a deeper life purpose are growing the roots of the system. They are laying a firm and stable foundation for a resilient, enduring and higher pyramid of human achievement. Philanthropists, social entrepreneurs, and prosumers build upward and empower people to climb to new heights of self-actualization and express their full potential. Still others are revealing the beauty and abundance that is unleashed as people follow their creativity and passion in harmony with one another and the natural world of which we are a part. Together we are beginning to move to a new rhythm and the emerging dance celebrates freedom and gives rise to new and beautiful forms of coordination and cooperation.

Hippie Redemption

To many baby boomers looking back on the time of their youth the hippie counterculture was a hiccup in the timeline of American history, a temporary disruption in the otherwise smooth ride of mainstream conservative values. "Conservative" means to maintain the status quo – it is inherently backward looking and value rigid. While the hippie counterculture was largely reactionary (its values were defined in opposition to the mainstream) it found a rich source for its unconventional worldview in Eastern thought. We have the hippies to thank for opening our minds to the wealth of ancient wisdom of Zen, Taoism, Buddhism and related philosophies.

It is not unusual for change to take on a pattern of reaction followed by synthesis. An initial reflexive rejection followed by a reflective integration of new and old. A pendulum swing of sorts morphing into a dynamic equilibrium. (We can see a similar pattern occurring in China where absolute communism (at least in part a reaction against a long history of Western imperialism) is softening into a mix of state-control and capitalistic entrepreneurship.)

This process is seen in the evolution of biological systems. More robust organisms result when a sudden cleavage divides a line of development, allowing parallel independent progress, followed by a reunification during which the two separate lines interbreed. This often results in offspring that embody the best combination of innovations from each lineage (though maladaptive misfits also arise in the process). Genetic programming, which mimics evolutionary biology to create computer code, uses this technique.

Many today are hostile to change. Some view the world through the prism of ideology and see the erosion of their place of privilege. Some view the world through the prism of fear and see change as a threat and technology as a monster to be slain. These groups fail to recognize that we cannot turn back the clock. Fighting against the currents of change is devolutionary – we must always adapt to the new conditions at the edge of chaos. While progress is not inevitable, change is. Failure to accept this truth is dangerous, as it deprives us of the opportunity we may actually have to shape our future. We have a choice – we can walk backwards into our future, tripping and getting lost along the way, or we can turn around and face our future head-on, striding confidently, carefully and hopefully forward.

The pendulum is swinging and it is time for the Hippie Generation – a major contingent within the biggest demographic wave to hit the U.S., the baby boom – to take the next step on their journey. To shift from reaction (and for many from resignation) to creation and bring about the world of love and peace they imagined in their youth. Baby boomers are beginning to hit retirement age, threatening to stretch our social fabric to its breaking point under the financial stress of this historic demographic shift. But there is a potential to transform this threat into an opportunity. The parents of the baby boomers, called "The Greatest Generation" by some for their sacrifices during WWII, made their mark on history through their efforts during wartime. Now their children have the opportunity to make their mark on history by creating lasting and sustainable peace. The abilities and knowledge of the baby boomers are far too precious to let slowly evaporate on golf courses and in senior centers. Of course, they have earned their retirement, but they have the option of choosing something much more exciting – a chance to put their talent and energy towards proving that the optimism of their youth was not misguided, it was just a bit premature.

Imagine the possibilities if a significant fraction of the 76 million U.S. boomers decided to follow the lead of Bill Gates and Ron Shaich, to contribute their talents and energy to social causes they care about. Imagine experienced engineers, artists, doctors and entrepreneurs devoting time to teaching and mentoring young people, establishing or developing community groups dedicated to positive change, or founding and running FPH enterprises. This could be the opening chapter of a heroic saga of peace, hope, and (like all good tales of heroism) a healthy dose of redemption.

11 – An Invitation to Dance

You may consider this book to be a rather long-winded invitation to join the ranks of the Conspiracy of Dreamers. If you are reading these words, then there is a good chance that you will accept the honor. As you likely have figured, this is not a conspiracy of intrigue and subterfuge, but a conspiracy of dreams, and the means of turning dreams into realities. Throughout history our members have been called, among other things, heretics, traitors, revolutionaries, radicals and utopians – all have challenged the status quo and dreamed of a better future. We are among those who believe in the possibility of universal opulence, peace, and liberty, not in a someday maybe kind of way, but here and in our lifetime. Thankfully, because of the noble and daring efforts of our predecessors, most of us no longer risk being beheaded, tortured, or burned at the stake for our dreams.

"Conspire" means to "breathe together." Conspiracies succeed when their members coordinate their efforts, pool their talents and resources, and work toward a common goal. In the past, conspiracies were constrained by the limits of communication, and the need to keep disruptive plans secret to avoid the wrath of the powerful. But now we are empowered by technology to breathe together across great distances. And dreamers who are fortunate to live in liberal democracies can shout their subversive plans from the rooftops (at least for now).

This has been a whirlwind invitation, but we assured you that in the end the disparate and varied threads would be woven into a resilient and rich tapestry. It's now time to review the results of our efforts, tie up loose ends, tighten the weave, take in the big picture and see what's to be done next.

From the view of the cosmos we are patterns of energy held together through time and space. How we do this is a mystery yet to be solved (perhaps never to be solved, at least while we hold this particular pattern). The scientific detectives looking into this mystery are following an exciting trail of clues: it seems we are a miraculous dance of energy that happens in a special place in the universe, the space between order and chaos. Only here, at the edge of chaos, can energy hold a pattern together through time while also rearranging itself to form new patterns that can survive and even thrive in the flux. (This is what is, more conventionally, referred to as "life.")

Evolution has a direction: life is surfing a wave (and *is* the wave) moving toward higher levels of complexity. Humanity will continue to survive and thrive only to the degree it can stay atop this wave. Our balance is threatened. Environmental destruction, abject poverty amid a profusion of material wealth, and the modern malaise of psychological and spiritual discontent evidence our vertigo. Crisis is a natural part of the evolutionary process. Species and whole ecosystems are continually losing their balance, falling off the edge and disintegrating. As new patterns arise to adapt to new circumstances, old patterns die out. Abrupt changes, like huge meteorites hitting Earth, or cataclysmic catastrophes such as those threatened by human technology, may set the evolutionary process back hundreds of millions of years. The relative comfort of our current conditions in the developed world, and our innate inclination to think the future will look similar to the recent past, has lulled many into a pleasant, but dangerous, slumber of complacency. Let's not sleepwalk into extinction.

Evidence suggests we may have unintentionally turned the wave at the edge of chaos into a tsunami. The Paradox of the Destruction of the Fittest has its roots in the very nature of life. What worked in the past does not necessarily work in the present, especially when past strategies powerfully effect the environment. Humanity's past and current strategies are wreaking astounding changes to our world; we must develop new strategies to adapt intelligently to our new conditions (and avoid causing excessive future turbulence). If we are to triumph, then we must harness the full potential of humanity – our intelligence, our compassion, and our creativity. We need all hands on deck.

Much present discontent is rooted in the disempowerment and alienation inherent in expansive centralized spider-like institutions. It is in the nature of such institutions to deny meaningful contribution and autonomy to most participants. In the U.S. we have witnessed, over the past half-century, a gradual intertwining of large corporations (many of which are part of the military industrial complex), and an increasingly centralized and powerful federal government. People on all points of the political spectrum recognize the danger posed by this two-headed Leviathan, though proposed solutions differ greatly. On the right, the Tea Party calls for a dramatic shrinking of the federal government. But they fail to recognize the very real human costs of cutting critical social programs, and the inherently destabilizing effects of the wealth to the wealthy feedback loop. On the left, the Occupy Movement (having arisen as we write this closing chapter) calls for a dramatic shrinking of corporate power and an accompanying (though largely implied) expansion of government. But they fail to recognize the threat posed by dependence on a centralized power. Freedom is illusory when one's education, healthcare, savings and income all come from government, no matter how graciously paternalistic that government may seem at the moment.

The potential threat of centralized institutions with the power to withhold essential services is increasing daily. Unmanned drones, GPS tracking, widespread video surveillance, electronic banking and DNA profiling lay the foundation for an Orwellian science *nonfiction* dystopia. Whatever the short-term rewards of vesting government with more power to redistribute wealth and provide critical services to ever more of the populace, it is not worth the risk to our hard-won freedom. We have the intelligence and knowledge to create systemic, long-term, balance inducing, wealth (material, spiritual *and* psychological) expanding, and freedom strengthening solutions.

De Tocqueville, nearly two centuries ago, pointed to the keystone of a healthy democracy – the art of associating. The old patterns of association, based as they were on community voluntarism, have been disintegrating over the past four decades as ever more of us have become entranced by television. New patterns are needed. We can see new patterns beginning to sprout: crowd sourcing (Wikipedia and Kickstarter), Internet enabled organizing (Change.org), and social entrepreneurship evidence the potential of new patterns to replace the old. The eco-nomic trim tabs described in Chapter 8 – for-profiting-humanity enterprises, a True Cost Index and a Real Karma application – offer ways of increasing the flow of energy to these new patterns of association.

The eco-nomic trim tabs are relatively small system reconfigurations can move us toward harmony and balance, in harmony and balance (means and ends are aligned). These reconfigurations provide relevant information and practical everyday opportunities for positive action. They are powerful leverage points that can alter the circulation of energy and information in our collective human organism. By increasing energy flow to starfish organizations at the edge of our collective striving we can empower them to discover new patterns of cooperation and coordination, some of which will be better adapted to our current circumstances. Evolution takes place among the starfish – shouting, protesting, and imploring a spider to change is not an effective approach. (Nor is threatening to cut off its

An Invitation to Dance | 317

head and replace it with another.) We must nurture and support the starfish.

Ruth Benedict pointed to the keystone of healthy societies – synergy, that is, the alignment of individual and community interests. The eco-nomic trim tabs are synergy enhancing as they enable people to give without sacrifice and act in line with their ideals. By using the generosity of wealthy philanthropists to amplify the good intentions of the buying public, and channeling both toward creating new economic arrangements, we can convert the funneling effect of capitalism's current version into a siphoning system. For-profiting-humanity enterprises, a True Cost Index and a Real Karma application are the equivalent of a modern-day Sundance Ceremony. They are siphoning mechanisms that can nurture the vitality and resilience we need to reestablish our balance on the edge of chaos.

The future we create will reflect who we are as human beings. Envy, anger and distrust create a world of scarcity, injustice and corruption. The change in our patterns of thought from conflict to compassion, from judgment to forgiveness, from scarcity to abundance, from passive cynicism to proactive optimism, from doubt to possibility, from having to being, that is, the Mind Shift Meme is essential to the success of our Conspiracy. No amount of system reconfiguration can create a whole that does not reflect the qualities of the parts. If we are not willing to dance the dance and sing the songs, no amount of expert choreography and direction (or shouting from the peanut gallery) will give rise to a Broadway musical extravaganza.

As Gandhi famously taught, we must be the change we want to see in the world.

The Mind Shift Meme is not new – it is at the core of many spiritual traditions – but its spread has thus far been modest. The eco-nomic paradigm can give those who have adopted the Meme the power to push forward. With it we can use the energy of economic forces to bring a new consciousness in humanity that will bring forth a phase transition of peace and possibility.

Ever more of us are listening and responding to the rhythm we hear on the horizon and feel in our hearts. We are finding one another and giving up the monotonous drone of the lifeless mechanical march. Your task, as a Dreamer, is to listen to your rhythm and find others whose rhythm resonates with your own. You will find your rhythm becomes louder and richer when you turn down the noise around you – television, video games, advertising, and consumerism are distractions. Find and surround yourself with people who embody the qualities you want to see reflected in the world, contribute your time and talent to their efforts, emulate them – breathe with them. Connect with your passion – bring forth what is within you, and it will save you.

Find hope and power in the knowledge that you, as a human being, are at the leading edge of the cosmic forces of evolution – the unimaginable power of the universe is propelling you forward. You are the latest in a dynasty of champion chaos surfers dating back billions of years. The knowledge and the abilities required to thrive, here and now, is within you.

Listen to the sound of your breath, feel the beating of your heart, notice the signs of life all around you. We are all here for a brief stint. What awaits us is up for debate. What is clear is that this moment we are sharing here in this seemingly insignificant corner of the universe is miraculously pregnant with infinite possibility. What you make of this incredible confluence of energy and consciousness is up to you.

༄

Imagine masses of humanity marching in lockstep to the hypnotic drone of heavy footsteps (picture the machinelike Storm troopers from Star Wars – George Lucas is definitely a Dreamer). A few brave souls begin to hum a tune, it's catchy and the humming spreads. Nearby a few others start working in a couple of twirls between steps and the twirling spreads. Suddenly the entire cast of humanity breaks out in a number from a Rodgers and Hammerstein musical … "The hills are alive with the sound of music …" The marching disintegrates and the music diversifies into a cacophony of folk, classical, hip-hop, jazz and rock. The seemingly disorganized throngs begin to seek and find like-minded people. From the chaos emerge new forms of collaboration, rich with the vitality and talent of humanity. The monotony of a rigid march liquefies into a kaleidoscope of sound and movement. Stoic faces morph into the joyful expressions of children. A most magical and human form of alchemy emerges as the machine of capitalism experiences its own phase transition giving rise to a whole new level of intricately beautiful complexity. We cordially invite you to join us as we dance and sing with the millions of others who are breathing together – *conspiring* – as we give birth to a new world

Epilogue

As of July 30, 2012 we (the authors) have formed a California nonprofit corporation, Zagfly, Inc., to provide a platform for executing many of the ideas shared in this book. The Internal Revenue Service has refused to acknowledge Zagfly's status as a tax-exempt organization, claiming that its intended activities are "too commercial" and thus it does not quality for exemption. We are taking the Service to court to fight this unconstitutional use of executive power. We hope to have a positive decision in hand sometime in late 2012 or early 2013 (though the exact timeframe is out of our control). Please visit our blog, ConspiracyofDreamers.com for more information about the Zagfly, Inc. project and legal developments.

Acknowledgments

We are deeply indebted to our supportive tribe of family and friends. Many patiently waded through various incarnations of our work, offering invaluable feedback and encouragement: Shelley Harrison, Teresea Horn, Keith Horn, Andy Hoye, Michael James McElligott Jr., Michael James McElligott Sr., Julie Orth, Theresa Stewart, Chris von Roy, Todd Walker, Emma Weda, and Soon Yetasook. Our dear friend, Dr. Henning Kreke, contributed generously to our efforts to spread the Conspiracy of Dreamers. The editing skills of James O'Connor were a tremendous help in turning Renée's "lawyer language" into readable prose. Stephen Weiner helped iron out the final kinks. Silviu Nica translated our ideas into inspiring cover art.

Renée's mom, Sharon Forbes, and step-father, Len Forbes graciously shared their inspiring oasis where much of this book was researched and written. Paul's mother, Babette Behrman, is an enthusiastic supporter of all her son's endeavors, this book was no exception. Our fathers have passed on to the next-big-adventure, but they are with us in our hearts and the lessons they taught us are reflected throughout these pages. Renée's grandfather, George Gratton, her first and favorite editor, gets brownie points in heaven too.

No single idea in the book is completely novel; we are merely two synapses firing in the collective brain of humanity. We thank those, past and present, on whose shoulders we stand.

Endnotes

Introduction

[1] Genesis 11:6.

[2] Hagel, John, John Seely. Brown, and Lang Davison. *The Power of Pull: How Small Moves, Smartly Made, Can Set Big Things in Motion*. New York: Basic, 2010.

[3] Among the "Six Acts" passed by Parliament in 1819 in response to popular discontent was a provision expanding the existing stamp duty to publications which had previously avoided stamp duty by publishing opinion rather than news. The purpose of the stamp duty was stated as follows: "Whereas Pamphlets and printed Papers containing Observations upon public Events and Occurrences, tending to excite Hatred and Contempt of the Government and Constitution of these Realms as by Law established, and also vilifying our Holy Religion, have lately been published in great Numbers, and at very small Prices; and it is expedient that the same should be restrained."

[4] Ariely, Dan. *Predictably Irrational: the Hidden Forces That Shape Our Decisions*. New York, NY: Harper, 2008; Lehrer, Jonah. *How We Decide*. Boston: Houghton Mifflin Harcourt, 2009.

[5] Kaczynski, Theodore. *Unabomber Manifesto: Industrial Society and Its Future*. Theodore Kaczynski (aka The Unabomber) had much to say in his Manifesto about the misalignment of human nature and modern society. His

own descent into homicidal psychosis can be seen as, at least in part, a symptom of this misalignment. While we don't in any way condone his methods, his message is not without insight.

[6] Taylor, Jill Bolte. *My Stroke of Insight: a Brain Scientist's Personal Journey*. New York: Viking, 2008. Taylor provides a mind-expanding explanation of the differences between our left and right hemispheres. If you don't have time to read her book, then at least watch her TED talk, available at www.ted.com.

[7] Pirsig, Robert M. *Zen and the Art of Motorcycle Maintenance: an Inquiry into Values*, New York: Morrow, 1974. If you have read ZAMM (and we highly recommend that you do) you may recognize in the duality of analytic and synthetic echoes of Pirsig's duality of classic and romantic. This is no accident: Pirsig's insights inform this work throughout.

[8] See Pink, Daniel H. *A Whole New Mind: Why Right-brainers will Rule the Future*. New York: Riverhead, 2006.

[9] Jung, C. G. *Synchronicity; an Acausal Connecting Principle*. Princeton, NJ: Princeton UP, 1973.

[10] Among the works we are familiar with in this line of thought: Ferguson, Marilyn. *The Aquarian Conspiracy: Personal and Social Transformation in the 1980s*. Los Angeles: J. P. Tarcher, 1980; Tolle, Eckhart. *A New Earth: Awakening to Your Life's Purpose*. New York: Plume, 2006; Capra, Fritjof. *The Turning Point: Science, Society, and the Rising Culture*. New York: Simon and Schuster, 1982.

[11] Bstan-'dzin-rgya-mtsho, Dalai Lama XIV. *The Universe in a Single Atom: the Convergence of Science and Spirituality*. New York: Random House, 2005. In this work, His Holiness the Dalai Lama addresses the need to develop quickly the moral capacity to balance scientific advances with ethical awareness, especially in the area of genetics.

[12] Zabelina, Darya L., and Michael D. Robinson. "Child's Play: Facilitating the Originality of Creative Output by a Priming Manipulation." *Psychology of Aesthetics, Creativity, and the Arts* 4.1 (2010): 57-65.

[13] *Id.*

[14] Pirsig, Robert M. *Zen and the Art of Motorcycle Maintenance: an Inquiry into Values*, New York: Morrow, 1974.

[15] Kofman, Fred. "Double-Loop Accounting: A Language for the Learning Organization," *The Systems Thinker* v. 3, no. 1 (February 1992).

[16] Huxley, Aldous. *The Doors of Perception & Heaven and Hell*. New York: Harper Perennial, 2009.

[17] Pirsig, Robert M. *Zen and the Art of Motorcycle Maintenance: an Inquiry into Values*, New York: Morrow, 1974.

[18] Goethe, Johann Wolfgang Von, and Douglas Miller. *Scientific Studies*. New York, NY: Suhrkamp, 1988.

[19] Lakoff, George, and Mark Johnson. *Metaphors We Live by*. Chicago: University of Chicago, 1980.

[20] Thibodeau, Paul H., and Lera Boroditsky. "Metaphors We Think With: The Role of Metaphor in Reasoning." *PLoS ONE* 6.2 (2011).

[21] Fromm, Erich. *The Art of Loving*. New York: Continuum, 2000.

[22] Pirsig, Robert M. *Zen and the Art of Motorcycle Maintenance: an Inquiry into Values*, New York: Morrow, 1974.

Chapter 1: You Are Here

[1] Bloom, Howard K. *The Genius of the Beast: a Radical Revision of Capitalism*. Amherst, NY: Prometheus, 2010.

[2] "Nuclear Weapons: Who Has What at a Glance." *Arms Control Association*. Web. 22 Sept. 2011. http://www.armscontrol.org/factsheets/Nuclearweapons whohaswhat.

[3] Capra, Fritjof. *The Turning Point: Science, Society, and the Rising Culture*. New York: Simon and Schuster, 1982.

[4] Krolicki, Kevin, and Kiyoshi Takenaka. "Radiation Hotspots Hinder Japan Response to Nuclear Crisis." *Business & Financial News, Breaking US & International News*. 15 June 2011. Web. 22 Sept. 2011. http://www.reuters.com/article/2011/06/15/us-japan-nuclear-hotspots-idUSTRE75D1JT20110615.

[5] Roosevelt, Margot. "Global Warming: Critics' Review Unexpectedly Supports Scientific Consensus on Climate Change." Los Angeles Times 04 Apr. 2011. Web. 22 Sept. 2011. http://articles.latimes.com/2011/apr/04/local/la-me-climate-berkeley-20110404.

[6] Harte, Mary Ellen, and Anne Ehrlich. "Overpopulation: Perpetual Growth Is the Creed of a Cancer Cell, Not a Sustainable Human Society." Los Angeles Times 21 July 2011. Web. 22 Sept. 2011. http://www.latimes.com/news/opinion/commentary/la-oe-harte-population-20110721,0,715317.story.

[7] Hager, Thomas. The Alchemy of Air: a Jewish Genius, a Doomed Tycoon, and the Scientific Discovery That Fed the World but Fueled the Rise of Hitler. New York: Harmony, 2008.

[8] Zweig, Stefan. The World of Yesterday: an Autobiography. New York: Viking, 1943.

[9] "The Rise and Rise of the Cognitive Elite." The Economist (US) 22 Jan. 2011.

[10] "Food Stamps: The Struggle to Eat." The Economist 14 July 2011. Web. 22 July 2011. http://www.economist.com/node/18958475.

[11] McPherson, Miller, Lynn Smith-Lovin, and Mattehew E. Brashears. "Social Isolation in America: Changes in

Core Discussion Networks over Two Decades." *American Sociological Review* 71 (2006): 353-75. Print.

[12] A report prepared by The Economic Mobility Project (an initiative of the Pew Charitable Trusts) found that children of divorced families were less economically upwardly mobile than children of married or never been married mothers. While the degree to which economic mobility is evidence of realized potential is uncertain, it is likely to be directionally correct. *Does Divorce Hurt Children's Economic Mobility?* The Pew Charitable Trusts. Web. 27 Sept. 2011. http://www.pewstates.org/research/reports/family-structure-and-the-economic-mobility-of-children-85899376379.

[13] Pepitone, Julianne. "U.S. Job Satisfaction Falls to Lowest Level in 22 Years." *CNNMoney* 05 Jan. 2010. Web. 27 Sept. 2011. http://money.cnn.com/2010/01/05/news/economy/job_satisfaction_report/.

[14] Robbins, Tom. *Skinny Legs and All*. New York: Bantam, 1990.

[15] Pinker, Steven. "We're Getting Nicer Every Day: A History of Violence." *The New Republic Online* 20 March 2007. Web. 26 April 2010.

http://pinker.wjh.harvard.edu/articles/media/2007_03_19_New%20Republic.pdf.

[16] Pinker, Steven. *The Blank Slate : the Modern Denial of Human Nature*. New York: Viking, 2002. We're oversimplifying here just a bit – the 50/50 split refers only to the portion of our personality and intelligence that is variable.

[17] Hesman Saey, Tina. "Human Gene Count: More Than a Chicken, Less Than a Grape : Discovery News." *Discovery News* 20 Oct. 2010. Web. 22 Sept. 2011. http://news.discovery.com/human/human-gene-count.html.

[18] The Age of Enlightenment took different shapes in Continental Europe on the one hand, and Britain and the U.S. on the other with the former having strong communal tendencies which are still quite apparent in the values of the French populace, and the latter manifesting strong individualist tendencies.

[19] While human on human violence is declining, humanity has far to go in valuing the lives and well-being of other sentient beings. The rise of material affluence has had the unfortunate effect of greatly increasing the numbers of non-human animals subject to horrific conditions as livestock.

Chapter 2: Capitalism as a Force of Nature

[1] Smith, Adam. *The Theory of Moral Sentiments*. New York, NY: Penguin, 2009.

[2] Maslow concluded that these needs are hierarchical. While the degree to which these motivations are absolutely hierarchical is doubtful, it is directionally accurate. Maslow added enlightenment to his hierarchy in the later years of his career.

[3] Hawkins, Jeff, and Sandra Blakeslee. *On Intelligence*. New York: Times, 2004. This is not to say computers are categorically incapable of manifesting human-like intelligence, but that past efforts fell short in part due to the centralized top-down nature of their structure.

[4] Morsch, Laura. "Government Salaries vs. Private Sector Salaries." *CNN.com - Breaking News, U.S., World, Weather, Entertainment & Video News*. 11 Oct. 2006. Web. 18 Sept. 2009. http://www.cnn.com/2006/US/Careers/10/11/cb.government/index.html.

[5] Greenspan, Alan. *The Age of Turbulence: Adventures in a New World*. New York: Penguin, 2007.
[6] Bogle, John C. *The Battle for the Soul of Capitalism*. New Haven: Yale University Press, 2005.

[7] Bronowski, Jacob. *The Ascent of Man*. Boston: Little, Brown, 1974.

[8] Weatherford, J. McIver. *Genghis Khan and the Making of the Modern World.* New York: Crown, 2004.

[9] This criticism of capitalism explains the psychopathic nature of corporations highlighted in the 2003 documentary film *The Corporation.* Dir. Mark Achbar and Jennifer Abbott. 2003. DVD.

[10] Biologists separate cooperation into several categories, including mutualism (helping myself simultaneously helps another), reciprocal altruism (I make a sacrifice now with the expectation that you will make a later sacrifice for my benefit), and kin altruism (I make a sacrifice for you because you carry a sufficient amount of my DNA). The hunter example is of the reciprocal variety.

[11] Maslow, Abraham H. *The Farther Reaches of Human Nature.* New York, N.Y., U.S.A.: Arkana, 1993.

[12] Hayek, Friedrich August. *Constitution of Liberty.* London: Routledge, 2006.

[13] Norbert Wiener. *The Human Use of Human Beings: Cybernetics and Society.* Boston: Houghton Mifflin, 1954.

Chapter 3: Conspiracy of 1776

[1] Pirsig, Robert M. *Zen and the Art of Motorcycle Maintenance: an Inquiry into Values,* New York: Morrow, 1974.

[2] Wiener, Norbert. *The Human Use of Human Beings; Cybernetics and Society.* Boston: Houghton Mifflin, 1954.

[3] Hamilton, Carol V. "The Surprising Origins and Meaning of the 'Pursuit of Happiness.'" *History News Network.* 21 Jan. 2008. Web. 12 Sept. 2010. http://hnn.us/articles/46460.html.

[4] Locke, John. "An Essay concerning Human Understanding - John Locke." *Google Books.* Web. 22 Sept. 2011.

[5] Jefferson, Thomas. Letter to William Short. 31 Oct. 1819. Web. 3 June 2112. http://www.csun.edu/~hcfll004/jefflet.html.

[6] Tocqueville, Alexis De. *Democracy in America.* New York: Knopf, 1994.

[7] Putnam, Robert D. *Bowling Alone: the Collapse and Revival of American Community.* New York: Simon & Schuster, 2000.

[8] *Id.*

[9] Fromm, Erich. *Escape from Freedom.* New York: H. Holt, 1994.

[10] Putnam, Robert D. *Bowling Alone: the Collapse and Revival of American Community.* New York: Simon & Schuster, 2000.

[11] Fromm, Erich. *Escape from Freedom*. New York: H. Holt, 1994.

[12] *Id.*

[13] Ali, Syed. *Dubai: Gilded Cage*. New Haven, Conn.: Yale UP, 2010.

[14] Recent use of drones to capture suspected criminals on U.S. soil is evidence of the potential danger posed by surveillance technology to privacy.

[15] The Northern Chinese culture is more collectivist in its history than the Southern Chinese culture. The North was shaped more by the communal values of Confucius while the South was shaped more by the individualist values of Taoism and Zen. By finding our commonality, such as appreciating the need for strong communities that are built on a foundation of self-actualizing individuals, we may be able to transcend the "East-West divide."

[16] Friedman, Milton, and Rose D. Friedman. *Capitalism and Freedom*. Chicago: University of Chicago, 2002.

[17] *Id.*

[18] Leven, David C. "Curing America's Addiction to Prisons." *Fordham Urban Law Journal* 40 (1993): 641. Accord-

ing to Leven, in 1980 there were 22,600 inmates in California prisons. In 2010 the number was 167,000.

[19] Sullivan, Laura. "Embodies California's Prison Blues." *All Things Considered*. National Public Radio. 13 Aug. 2009. Radio.

[20] DiSalvo, Daniel. The Trouble with Public Sector Unions. *National Affairs*. Fall 2010.

[21] *Id.*

[22] Friedman, Milton, and Rose D. Friedman. *Capitalism and Freedom*. Chicago: University of Chicago, 2002.

[23] Murdoch's Fox News has, for example, seemingly intentionally slighting libertarian presidential hopeful Ron Paul: "Fox News Caught Running Old CPAC Footage After Ron Paul's Straw Poll Win?" *Breaking News and Opinion on The Huffington Post*. 16 Feb. 2011. Web. 28 Sept. 2011. http://www.aolnews.com/2011/02/16/fox-news-caught-running-old-cpac-footage-after-ron-pauls-straw/.

[24] "Government Launches Big Society Programme - Number 10." *Number 10 - The Official Site of the British Prime Minister's Office*. 18 May 2010. Web. 20 July 2011. http://www.number10.gov.uk/news/big-society/.

[25] Fromm, Erich. *Escape from Freedom.* New York: H. Holt, 1994.

Chapter 4: Surf or Sink

[1] Putnam, Robert D. *Bowling Alone: the Collapse and Revival of American Community.* New York: Simon & Schuster, 2000: "Over the last twenty years more than a dozen large studies ... have shown that people who are socially disconnected are between two and five times more likely to die from all causes, compared with matched individuals who have close ties with family, friends, and the community."

[2] Soros, George. *Open Society: Reforming Global Capitalism.* New York: Public Affairs, 2000. Soros explains his long-touted theory concerning the "reflex" nature of much of reality, and financial markets in particular.

[3] Lipton, Bruce H. *The Biology of Belief: Unleashing the Power of Consciousness, Matter & Miracles.* Carlsbad, CA: Hay House, 2009.

[4] "Epigenetics and Stress: A Mother's Stress While She Is Pregnant Can Have a Long-lasting Effect on Her Children's Genes." *The Economist.* 21 July 2011. Web. 1 Aug. 2011. http://www.economist.com/node/18985981.

[5] Silberman, Steve. "Placebos Are Getting More Effective. Drugmakers Are Desperate to Know Why." *Wired.com.*

24 Aug. 2009. Web. 17 May 2011. http://www.wired.com/medtech/drugs/magazine/17-09/ff_placebo_effect?currentPage=all.

[6] Goleman, Daniel. *Social Intelligence: the New Science of Human Relationships*. New York: Bantam, 2006.

[7] Sapolsky, Robert M. "A Natural History of Peace." *Foreign Affairs* (January/February 2006). Print.

Chapter 5: Attaining Happiness

[1] Freud, Sigmund, and James Strachey. *Civilization and Its Discontents*. New York: Norton, 2005.

[2] Quoted in Linden, David J. *The Compass of Pleasure: How Our Brains Make Fatty Foods, Orgasm, Exercise, Marijuana, Generosity, Vodka, Learning, and Gambling Feel so Good*. New York: Viking, 2011.

[3] Weiner, Eric. *The Geography of Bliss: One Grump's Search for the Happiest Places in the World*. New York: Twelve, 2008.

[4] Once again, Western science finds itself unwittingly pointing to ancient wisdom: Maslow's hierarchy of needs is remarkably similar to the chakras of the Yogis. The base chakras are concerned with the needs of the gross body – food, shelter, sex – the middle (heart) chakra is concerned with love and belonging, and the higher chakras are concerned with the needs of the spirit – inde-

pendence, intuition, creativity and unity with the ground of being.

[5] Maslow, Abraham H. *The Farther Reaches of Human Nature.* New York, N.Y., U.S.A.: Arkana, 1993.

[6] Frankl, Viktor E. *The Unheard Cry for Meaning: Psychotherapy and Humanism.* New York: Simon and Schuster, 1978.

[7] Maslow, Abraham H. *The Farther Reaches of Human Nature.* New York: Arkana, 1993.

[8] Frankl, Viktor E. *The Unheard Cry for Meaning: Psychotherapy and Humanism.* New York: Simon and Schuster, 1978.

[9] *Id.*

[10] *Id.*

[11] Ariely, Dan. *Predictably Irrational: the Hidden Forces That Shape Our Decisions.* New York, NY: Harper, 2008

[12] Elias, Marilyn. "Psychologists Now Know What Makes People Happy." *The New York Times.* 10 Sept. 2010. Quoting psychologist Ed Diener of the University of Illinois.

[13] Putnam, Robert D. *Bowling Alone: the Collapse and Revival of American Community.* New York: Simon & Schuster, 2000.

[14] *Id.*

[15] Pirsig, Robert M. *Zen and the Art of Motorcycle Maintenance: an Inquiry into Values*, New York: Morrow, 1974.

[16] Gospel of Matthew. 6:19-6:21.

[17] Elias, Marilyn. "Psychologists Now Know What Makes People Happy." *The New York Times*. 10 Sept. 2010.

[18] Soros, George. "The Soros Lectures at the Central European University." Central European University, Budapest, Hungary. Oct. 2009. Lecture. Soros provides an insightful view of the dangers of market fundamentalism to global economic stability.

[19] Dawkins, Richard. *The Selfish Gene*. Oxford: Oxford University Press, 2006. "Money is a formal token of delayed reciprocal altruism" that provides a means of preventing cheating.

[20] Maslow, Abraham H. *The Farther Reaches of Human Nature*. New York: Arkana, 1993.

Chapter 6: The Philosopher's Stone

[1] Jung, C. G. *Psychology and Alchemy*. [Princeton, N.J.]: Princeton University Press, 1968.

[2] *Id.*

[3] *Alchemical Dream: Rebirth of the Great Work.* Prod. Sheldon Rocklin, Maxine Rocklin, and Morgan Harris. Perf. Terence K McKenna. 2008. This film offers a fascinating look at the connection between Descartes and alchemy.

[4] Paracelsus (the quintessential alchemist) explained, "The philosophers [i.e., alchemists] should most carefully ascertain whether their designs are in harmony with Nature." *The Alchemical Catechism.* Web. 11 Sept. 2011. http://www.sacred-texts.com/alc/tschoudy.htm.

[5] William James, an otherwise enlightened psychologist and philosopher of the 19th century, advocated that instead of military conscription "the whole youthful population" be enlisted "against *Nature*" where they would do their part "in the immemorial human warfare against nature." James, William. "The Moral Equivalent of War." Ed. Harrison Ross Steeves. *Representative Essays in Modern Thought: A Basis for Composition.* Ed. Frank Humphrey Ristine. New York: American Book, 1913. 518-33. Web. 12 Sept. 2011. http://books.google.com/books?id=FbA3AVrFkTUC&pg=PA519&dq=james+moral+equivalent#v=onepage&q=james%20moral%20equivalent&f=false.

[6] Maslow, Abraham H., and John J. Honigmann. "Synergy: Some Notes of Ruth Benedict." *American Anthropologist* 72.2 (1970): 320-33.

[7] Bedau, Mark A. "Weak Emergence." *Noûs* 31 (1997): 375-99.

[8] The connection between evolution and the transmission of information may be rooted in the underlying fabric of the universe, which many physicists think may consist entirely of information. For an insightful and entertaining survey of the information theory of the universe we recommend *Decoding the Universe*. Seife, Charles. *Decoding the Universe: How the New Science of Information Is Explaining Everything in the Cosmos, from Our Brains to Black Holes*. New York: Viking, 2006.

[9] Pinker, Steven. *The Blank Slate : The Modern Denial of Human Nature*. New York: Viking, 2002.

[10] Friedman, Milton, and Rose D. Friedman. *Free to Choose: A Personal Statement*. New York: Harcourt Brace Jovanovich, 1980.

[11] Weber, Max. *The Protestant Ethic and the Spirit of Capitalism*. Mineola, NY: Dover Publications, 2003.

[12] Interestingly, the success of Gandhi and King and the movements they led can, in part, be traced to the rise of Nazism – once the British and Americans became self-identified as vanquishers of evil, it became untenable to continue following their own policies of discrimination and oppression. This is an example of the unpredictable and often counterintuitive dynamics of human systems.

Chapter 7: Metamorphosis

[1] Lao, Tzu, and Stephen Mitchell. *Tao Te Ching: A New English Version*. New York, NY: Harper Perennial, 1992.

[2] "7 Solutions | Strengthening Higher Education for Texas' Future." Texas Public Policy Foundation. Web. 21 May 2012. http://texashighered.com/7-solutions.

[3] Haurwitz, Ralph K.M. "UT Dean Criticizes Proposals by Governor, Regent, Policy Group." *American Statesman* [Austin, Texas] 6 July 2011.

[4] Halla, Martin, Mario Lackner, and Friedrich G. Schneider. "An Empirical Analysis of the Dynamics of the Welfare State: The Case of Benefit Morale." *Kyklos* 63.1 (2010): 55-74.

[5] Jon Bogle astutely described a powerful trend that is amplifying the short sightedness of business – as corporate ownership has become more diffuse over the past several decades the power base within corporate America has shifted from owners to managers. Managers are too often compensated on the basis of near-term financial performance rather than longer term sustainability, thus shortening the time horizon against which tactics and strategies are evaluated. Bogle, John C. *The Battle for the Soul of Capitalism*. New Haven: Yale University Press, 2005.

[6] Harrison, S. E. *Plutonomics: A Unified Theory of Wealth*. Los Angeles, CA: EPoet, 2006.

[7] Bogle, John C. "A Tale of Two Markets." Speech. The 17th Annual Conference on Financial Reporting. The Haas School of Business, University of California, Berkeley. 27 Oct. 2006. Web. 21 May 2012. http://johncbogle.com.

[8] Meadows, Donella H., and Diana Wright. *Thinking in Systems: A Primer*. White River Junction, VT: Chelsea Green Pub., 2008.

[9] A comprehensive survey of proposed alternatives to measuring well-being can be found in *Survey of Existing Approaches to Measuring Socio-Economic Progress*, Joint Insee-OECD document prepared for the first plenary meeting of CMEPSP by (at Insee) Cédric Afsa, Didier Blanchet, Vincent Marcus, Pierre-Alain Pionnier, Laurence Rioux, and (at OECD) Marco Mira d'Ercole, Giulia Ranuzzi, Paul Schreyer, April 2008. Web. 21 May 2012. http://www.stiglitz-sen--itoussi.fr/documents/Survey_of_Existing_Approaches_to_Measuring_Socio-Economic_Progress.pdf

Chapter 8: The Art of Steering

[1] Meadows, Donella H., and Diana Wright. *Thinking in Systems: A Primer*. White River Junction, VT: Chelsea Green Pub., 2008. (Emphasis in original.)

[2] There was a time in the U.S. not long ago when the line between for profit and nonprofit enterprises was not so bright. Until the 1950s, charitable organizations (i.e., those serving a sufficiently public purpose) were free to compete with for profit companies in any area of commerce, the only factor that determined an enterprise's right to tax exemption was the use to which its profits were put. Under these rules New York University operated a spaghetti factory throughout the late 1940s and significantly improved its facilities with the profits. In 1950, Congress passed the unrelated business income tax ("UBIT"). As the name implies, the UBIT taxes the income of tax-exempt charities to the extent income is derived from the active conduct of a business unrelated to a charity's exempt purpose. The primary reason given for the UBIT was protecting taxable businesses against unfair competition; however, the relationship between the alleged "unfairness" and the specific terms of the UBIT is quite dubious: whether a business activity is related to a charitable purpose is of questionable relevance to fairness: private hospitals have to compete with charitable hospitals, so why shouldn't conventional pasta companies have to compete with charitable pasta companies?

[3] $853 million = 769.5 billion revenue passenger miles in 2009 (U.S. Census Bureau, Statistical Abstract of the United States: 2012. http://www.census.gov/prod/2011 pubs/12statab/trans.pdf) x 40% of air travel booked online in 2012(http://www.slideshare.net/mfredactie/

Endnotes | 347

presentation-cees-bosselaar-phocus-wright) x $0.00277 per mile to purchase carbon offsets for 1 mile of air travel (based on a Flight calculated from LAX to DFW using this calculator: http://www.carbonneutralcalculator.com/flightcalculator.aspx).

[4] $946 million = $669 million in cash flow generated by Expedia for twelve months ending September 30, 2012 (i.e., $896mm in EBITDA - $227 of capital expenditures) x 58% of global air travel revenue for Expedia was US revenue during 2011 as per annual report) / 41% (i.e., divided by Expedia's estimated market share of 41% http://t2impact.blogspot.com/2011/04/us-travel-q1-2011-decline-in.html).

[5] Hotel News Resource. "Survey Shows American Travelers Turning Green." 5 Oct. 2007. Web. 21 May 2012. http://www.ecorooms.com/uploads/Survey_shows_American_Travelers_turning_Green.pdf.

[6] "Industry Statistics & Trends." *AmericanPetProducts.org*. American Pet Products Association. Web. 21 May 2012. http://www.americanpetproducts.org/press_industrytrends.asp.

[7] "A Shot in the Arm: The World's Market for Vaccines Is Being Turned Upside down." *The Economist*. 16 June 2011. Web. 21 May 2012. http://www.economist.com/node/18836582.

[8] "Reformed Church in America." *Feed One: Feed Children.* Web. 21 May 2012. https://www.rca.org/feedone.

[9] *EcologyFund.com.* Web. 21 May 2012. http://www.ecologyfund.com/.

[10] Rodriguez, Gregory. "Compassionate Consumerism: Don't Buy into It." *Los Angeles Times.* 2 May 2011. Web. 1 May 2012. http://articles.latimes.com/2011/may/02/opinion/la-oe-rodriguez-giving-20110502.

[11] Hayek, Friedrich A. Von. *The Road to Serfdom.* Chicago, IL: University of Chicago, 1944. Hayek explored the role of price as a medium of information exchange.

[12] Meadows, Donella H., and Diana Wright. *Thinking in Systems: A Primer.* White River Junction, VT: Chelsea Green Pub., 2008.

[13] Economists studying the psychological underpinnings of price have made some findings that fundamentally undermine the *homo economicus* ideal of a strictly rational human value calculator that is the bedrock of classical economic theory. Dan Airely describes an experiment, in the form of an auction, he conducted on some unsuspecting MIT undergraduates. Airely and a colleague (Drazen Prelec, a professor at MIT's Sloan School of Management) presented to Airely's class a number of items, including some choice bottles of French wine and electron-

ic gadgets. Each student was given a list of the items presented and was asked to write down the last two digits of his or her social security number at the top of the page. Then next to each item each student wrote these two digits as a price (i.e., preceded by a "$" sign); then they were asked to indicate whether they would be willing to pay that amount for each of the products (i.e., "yes" or "no"). Finally, the students were asked to bid on each item, the highest bidders won the items in the auction. When they were done and had turned in their sheets to Airely he asked whether the students thought that the preliminary exercise of writing down the last digits of their social security numbers had any effect on their bidding – they replied with a resounding "no way."

As you will have guessed by now, despite their reports to the contrary, the preliminary exercise had a significant impact on the students' final bids: students with social security numbers ending in the upper 20 percent placed bids 216 to 346 percent higher than those of students with social security numbers ending in the lowest 20 percent. This experiment demonstrates a phenomenon known as "anchoring" – once our minds create a connection between two ideas (regardless of how irrational or attenuate) they tend to stay connected even when the context has changed completely. Anchoring is a specific and fascinating instance of value rigidity that undermines the assumed rationality of *homo economicus*. Ariely, Dan. *Predictably Irrational: the Hidden Forces That Shape Our Decisions.* New York, NY: Harper, 2008.

[14] For a great description of the messiness watch Brene Brown's 2010 TEDx talk available at http://www.youtube.com/watch?v=iCvmsMzlF7o.

[15] The term "blended value" to describe companies that seek to create profit as well as social and environmental good was coined by Jed Emerson. Information on his work can be found at www.BlendedValue.org.

[16] The literature in this area often uses social *and* environmental responsibility as the two variables in addition to profit; however, we believe social responsibility includes environmental responsibility and relying too heavily on this duality distorts our perception of the interconnectedness between the two. Simply put, the interests of human beings are inextricably connected to the health of our planet.

[17] Clark, Cathrine H., and Selen Ucak. *RISE For-Profit Social Entrepreneur Report: Balancing Markets and Values.* Rep. Research Initiative on Social Entrepreneurship, Mar. 2006. Web. 3 June 2011. http://www.riseproject.org/rise-sep-report.pdf.

[18] Whether Rodrick was true to her image as a social responsibility icon, is far from clear. See e.g., http://www.jonentine.com/the-body-shop.html.

[19] Orr, Deborah. "Slave Chocolate?" *Forbes*. 24 Apr. 2006. Web. 4 June 2011. http://www.forbes.com/forbes/2006/0424/096.html.

[20] This is not to say Dow Chemical Company is not moving in the right direction, but the picture it paints of itself to the public is in direct conflict with many of its current business practices (to say nothing of its historical conduct). Indeed, recently a powerful new herbicide, aminopyralid, which is manufactured by Dow and is not approved for use in human food crops, made its way from grass growers, through the intestines of cows and horses, into compost heaps, before being sold to UK gardeners as fertilizer, resulting in contaminated vegetable gardens across the UK. Dow's response was to warn gardeners to check the provenance of their fertilizer, and Dow made no commitment to compensate for the resulting losses – not very responsible behavior and inconsistent with its stated commitment "to the development of responsible ... practices and procedures that safeguard the community, workplace and environment." (Quote from Dow's company website, accessed May 1, 2011.) Davies, Caroline. "Home-grown Veg Ruined by Toxic Herbicide." *The Observer* 28 June 2008, Main sec. Web. 2 May 2011. http://www.guardian.co.uk/environment/2008/jun/29/food.agriculture.

Chapter 9: Ripple Effects

[1] Capra, Fritjof. *The Turning Point: Science, Society, and the Rising Culture.* New York: Simon and Schuster, 1982.

[2] "More Millionaires than Australians." *The Economist (US)* 22 Jan. 2011.

[3] "I've Got You Labelled; Status Displays." *The Economist (US)* 2 Apr. 2011. Web. 2 May 2012. http://www.economist.com/node/18483423.

[4] Domhoff, G. William. "Wealth, Income, and Power." *Who Rules America.* Sept. 2005. Web. 30 June 2011. http://whorulesamerica.net/power/wealth.html.

[5] There is no simple answer to the causes of the Great Depression, but extreme wealth disequilibrium combined with erratic and ill-conceived monetary policy by the Federal Reserve (a stable and resilient money supply is absolutely critical to the metabolic process of the human organism) are prime culprits. See Friedman, Milton, and Anna Jacobson. Schwartz. *A Monetary History of the United States: 1867-1960.* Princeton: Princeton University Press, 1971.

[6] As the historians Will and Ariel Durant explained, "Nature smiles at the union of freedom and equality in our utopias. For freedom and equality are sworn and everlasting enemies, and when one prevails, the other dies. Leave men free, and their natural inequalities will multi-

ply almost geometrically, as in England and America in the nineteenth century under laissez-faire. To check the growth of inequality, liberty must be sacrificed, as in Russia after 1917. Even when repressed, inequality grows; only the man who is below the average in economic ability desires equality; those who are conscious of superior ability desire freedom, and in the end superior ability has its way." Durant, Will, and Ariel Durant. *The Lessons of History,*. New York: Simon and Schuster, 1968. One benefit of the eco-nomic model is that it starts with liberty, but ends with a more equal distribution of wealth.

[7] Laffer, Arthur B., Wayne H. Winegarden, and John Childs. *The Economic Burden Caused by Tax Code Complexity*. Rep. The Laffer Center for Supply Side Economics, May 2011. Web. 4 May 2012. http://www.laffercenter.com/wp-content/uploads/2011/06/2011-Laffer-TaxCodeComplexity.pdf.

[8] Domhoff, G. William. "Wealth, Income, and Power." *Who Rules America*. Sept. 2005. Web. 30 June 2011. http://whorulesamerica.net/power/wealth.html.

[9] Warner, Judith. "The Charitable-Giving Divide." *The New York Times* 20 Aug. 2010. Web. 4 June 2012. http://www.nytimes.com/2010/08/22/magazine/22FOB-wwln-t.html.

[10] Dynan, Karen E., and Dean M. Maki. *Does Stock Market Wealth Matter for Consumption?* Tech. no. 23-2001. Federal Reserve. Web. 4 June 2012. http://www.federalreserve.gov/pubs/feds/2001/200123/200123pap.pdf.

[11] "Difference Engine: Luddite Legacy." *The Economist (US)* 4 Nov. 2011. Web. 10 Nov. 2011. http://www.economist.com/blogs/babbage/2011/11/artificial-intelligence.

[12] Harbaugh, W. T., U. Mayr, and D. R. Burghart. "Neural Responses to Taxation and Voluntary Giving Reveal Motives for Charitable Donations." *Science* 316.5831 (2007): 1622-625.

[13] Otake, Keiko, Satoshi Shimai, Junko Tanaka-Matsumi, Kanako Otsui, and Barbara L. Fredrickson. "Happy People Become Happier through Kindness: A Counting Kindnesses Intervention." *Journal of Happiness Studies* 7.3 (2006): 361-75. Web. 2 May 2012. http://www.ncbi.nlm.nih.gov/pmc/articles/PMC1820947/.

[14] Carlson, Michael, Ventura Charlin, and Norman Miller. "Positive Mood and Helping Behavior: A Test of Six Hypotheses." *Journal of Personality and Social Psychology* 55.2 (1988): 211-29.

[15] Singh, Jitendra, and Adam Grant. "The Problem with Financial Incentives." Knowledge@Wharton, 30 Mar.

2011. Web. 04 May 2012. http://knowledge.wharton.upenn.edu/article.cfm?articleid=2741.

Chapter 10: 21st Century Dreamers

[1] Bstan-'dzin-rgya-mtsho, Dalai Lama XIV. *The Universe in a Single Atom: the Convergence of Science and Spirituality.* New York: Random House, 2005.

[2] Bstan-'dzin-rgya-mtsho, Dalai Lama XIV. *The Universe in a Single Atom: the Convergence of Science and Spirituality.* New York: Random House, 2005.

[3] Bstan-'dzin-rgya-mtsho, Dalai Lama XIV. *How to Practice: The Way to a Meaningful Life.* New York: Pocket, 2002.

[4] We benefited greatly from attending Learning as Leadership seminars in San Rafael, California (which, incidentally, Paul first encountered as part of development program required by his employer, the private equity firm of McCown De Leeuw & Co.)

[5] Siegel, Daniel J. *Mindsight: The New Science of Personal Transformation.* New York: Bantam, 2010.

[6] According to psychologist Carl Rogers, "Any experience which is inconsistent with the organization of the structure of the self may be perceived as a threat, and the more of these perceptions there are, the more rigidly the self structure is organized to maintain itself." (This is the

16th of Rogers' 19 Propositions set forth in his book, *Client-centered therapy: Its current practice, implications and theory*. London: Constable, 1951.) Thus, the more ego-identified we are with the ideas, beliefs and institutions, the more we resist change.

[7] Gates, Bill. "Making Capitalism More Creative." *Time* 31 July 2008. Web. 15 Aug. 2008. http://www.time.com/time/magazine/article/0,9171,1828417,00.html#ixzz1ShJ7g98m.

[8] Boss, Suzie. "Retailing with Heart." *Stanford Social Innovation Review*. Spring 2011. Web. 12 July 2011. http://www.ssireview.org/articles/entry/whats_next_retailing_with_heart/.

[9] Panera Cares. *Panera Bread Foundation Opens Third Panera Cares Community Cafe in Portland, OR*. PaneraBread.com. 6 Jan. 2011. Web. 12 July 2011. http://www.panerabread.com/pdf/pr-20110116.pdf.

[10] Shaich, Ron. "Panera Cares Cafe." Speech. TEDx. St. Louis Science Center, St.Louis. 17 Nov. 2010. Web. 2 May 2012. http://tedxstlouis.com/speakers/ron-shaich-panera/.

[11] Yunus, Muhammad, and Karl Weber. *Creating a World without Poverty: Social Business and the Future of Capitalism*. New York: PublicAffairs, 2009.

[12] Hart, Kim, and Megan Greenwell. "'Causes' Social Networking May Be All Talk, No Cash for Nonprofits Seeking Funds." *Washington Post*. The Washington Post, 22 Apr. 2009. Web. 22 June 2011. http://www.washingtonpost.com/wp-dyn/content/article/2009/04/21/AR2009042103786.html.

[13] Loaning money to a for-profiting-humanity enterprise at market returns (i.e., debt investments), rather than buying a portion of the enterprise (i.e., equity investments) and getting a share of the profits, is completely in alignment with maximizing beneficial systemic dynamics. Habitat for Humanity is a charitable enterprise offering investors the opportunity to put their investing dollars into housing people in need while earning up to 2% per year (see http://www.habitat.org/invest/ for details).

[14] Tasch, Woody. "Life After Fast Money and Fast Food." *Fast Company*. 21 Sept. 2011. Web. 3 May 2012. http://www.fastcompany.com/1781341/life-after-fast-money-and-fast-food.

[15] A 2006 report by the Office of Federal Housing Enterprise Oversight (OFHEO), charged with monitoring the financial health of Fannie Mae and Freddie Mac, described the arrogant and unethical culture at Fannie Mae. According to James Lockhart (OFHEO director when the report was released) they "found an environment where the ends justified the means. Senior management ma-

nipulated accounting; reaped maximum, undeserved bonuses; and prevented the rest of the world from knowing. They co-opted their internal auditors. They stonewalled OFHEO." "Eyes on the Wrong Prize: Leadership Lapses That Fueled Wall Street's Fall." *Knowledge@Wharton*. 17 Sept. 2008. Web. 3 May 2012. http://knowledge.wharton.upenn.edu/article.cfm?articleid=2048.

Made in the USA
Charleston, SC
17 February 2013